GETTYSBURG

GETTYSBURG

THE STORY OF THE BATTLE WITH MAPS

The Editors of
STACKPOLE BOOKS

STACKPOLE
BOOKS

Published by
STACKPOLE BOOKS
5067 Ritter Road
Mechanicsburg, PA 17055
www.stackpolebooks.com

Library of Congress Cataloging-in-Publication Data

Gettysburg : the story of the battle with maps / the editors of Stackpole Books.
    pages cm
  Includes bibliographical references.
  ISBN 978-0-8117-1218-7
  1. Gettysburg, Battle of, Gettysburg, Pa., 1863. 2. Gettysburg, Battle of, Gettysburg, Pa., 1863—Maps. I. Stackpole Books (Firm)
  E475.53.G424 2013
  973.7'349—dc23

                                                                    2013000965

Contents

Foreword

Our aim is to give the reader a sense of the flow of the battle.

 **LEE** and **MEADE** command two great armies, of which the first subunit is a corps (Confederate ≈ 18,000 men; Union ≈ 11,500):

... composed of divisions (Confederate ≈ 6,500; Union ≈ 3,800):

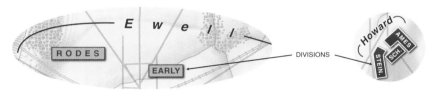

... made up of brigades (Confederate and Union ≈ 1,400–1,500, but ranging from 600 to 2,500):

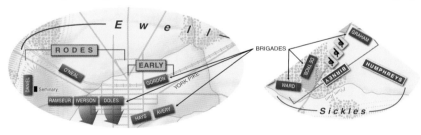

(Regiments — ■■■■◆ — are seldom divided out, in our treatment.)

Arrows — , , , , — mean movement, ✷✷ fighting or firing.

🔫 is artillery (generally and partially shown), 🐎 cavalry.

 Blue **STEIN.** is for the Union, gray **EARLY**, **HAYS** **AVERY** for the Confederacy, green ⇒ for what might have been.

THE EDITORS

To those gone before
To those yet to come

Prelude

Above the map, north of Gettysburg, ROBERT E. LEE's Army of Northern Virginia is spread across more than twenty-five miles of Pennsylvania farmland. Below the map, GEORGE MEADE's Army of the Potomac covers a similar swath of southernmost Pennsylvania and northern Maryland:

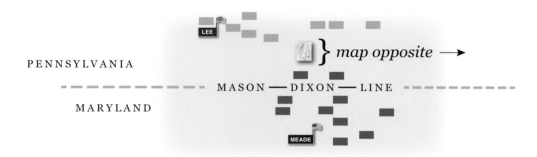

The Union army is larger and better equipped. Weighing morale, generalship, and the string of Confederate victories to date, the match is even. ROBERT LEE needs no introduction. GEORGE MEADE is new to highest command. Lincoln has been going through generals frustratedly. No one knows what the capable, splenetic MEADE will do.

Each army is unclear on the other's whereabouts. The Confederates have been in Pennsylvania, menacing Harrisburg and the Industrial North; MEADE has been keeping between them and Washington, D.C. Both feel blindly out with parties of horsemen, antennas of spies, scouts, talkative locals, skirmishers, pickets, and lookouts—the cloaking screens and early-warning-system "eyes and ears" indispensable to any great army in the field.

The day before the Battle of Gettysburg begins, Union cavalry under Buford, patrolling around Gettysburg, hear from the citizenry of a Confederate column northwest of town, up the Chambersburg Pike. Buford explores in that direction and sees some Rebels. Following a brief at-a-distance encounter, possibly without a shot fired, both sides retire amicably, part of the reconnoitering process being to probe, engage (only a little), withdraw, report—no major fighting before top command can garner sufficient info.

On the eve of Day One, Buford's 2,500-plus dismounted cavalry (brigade commanders Gamble, Devin) are in temporary camp (bivouac) west of town. Pickets (small rifle detachments) and vedettes (lookouts) are flung wide, ringing the area like sensors.

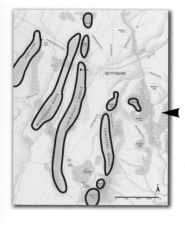

Note the key points of high ground: Oak Hill, Cemetery and Culp's Hills, Little and Big Round Top, and the ridges.

MEADE and LEE are at their respective headquarters, off the map as indicated.

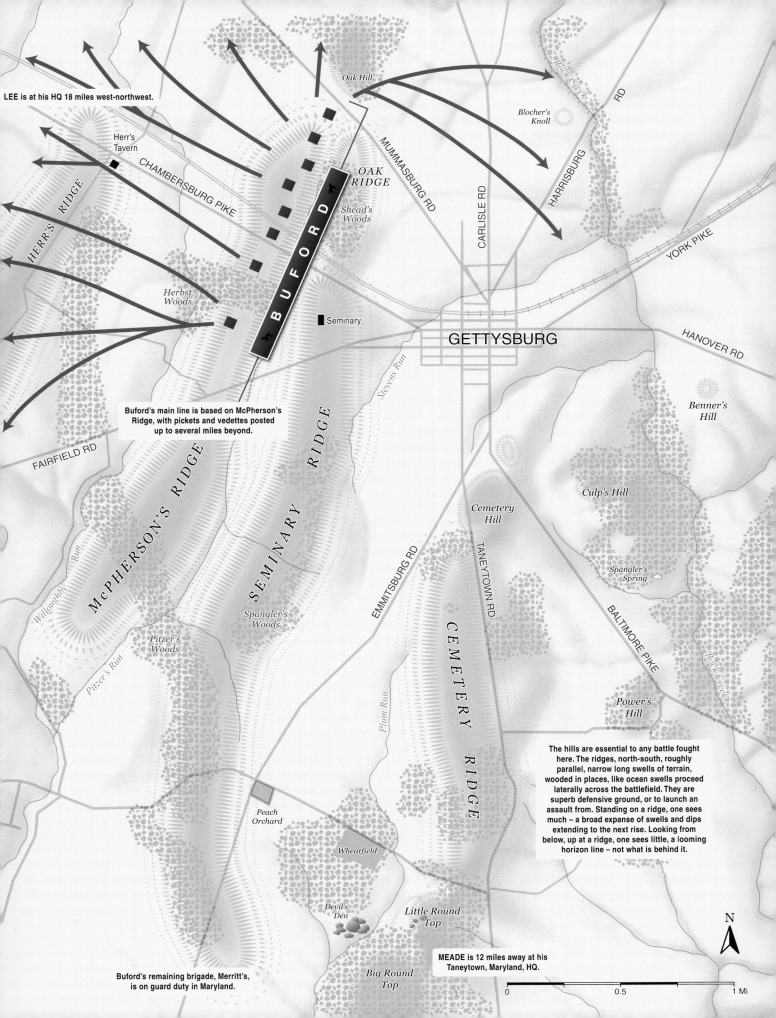

LEE is at his HQ 18 miles west-northwest.

Herr's Tavern

CHAMBERSBURG PIKE

HERR'S RIDGE

Oak Hill

MUMMASBURG RD

OAK RIDGE

Shead's Woods

Blocher's Knoll

CARLISLE RD

HARRISBURG RD

BUFORD

Herbst Woods

Seminary

Buford's main line is based on McPherson's Ridge, with pickets and vedettes posted up to several miles beyond.

YORK PIKE

GETTYSBURG

HANOVER RD

Benner's Hill

FAIRFIELD RD

McPHERSON'S RIDGE

SEMINARY RIDGE

Stevens Run

Willoughby Run

Spangler's Woods

Pitzer's Woods

Pitzer's Run

EMMITSBURG RD

TANEYTOWN RD

Culp's Hill

Cemetery Hill

Spangler's Spring

BALTIMORE PIKE

Rock Creek

Power's Hill

CEMETERY RIDGE

Plum Run

Peach Orchard

The hills are essential to any battle fought here. The ridges, north-south, roughly parallel, narrow long swells of terrain, wooded in places, like ocean swells proceed laterally across the battlefield. They are superb defensive ground, or to launch an assault from. Standing on a ridge, one sees much – a broad expanse of swells and dips extending to the next rise. Looking from below, up at a ridge, one sees little, a looming horizon line – not what is behind it.

Wheatfield

Devil's Den

Little Round Top

N

Buford's remaining brigade, Merritt's, is on guard duty in Maryland.

Big Round Top

MEADE is 12 miles away at his Taneytown, Maryland, HQ.

0   0.5   1 Mi

July 1, Early Morning

In the first hours of summer daylight, July 1, 1863, with after-rain steam rising off the farm fields, Confederates exploring in force move southeast down the Chambersburg Pike toward Gettysburg. They encounter Buford's lookout parties. Misty figures exchange shots.

These forward parties of Buford's dismounted cavalry are greatly outnumbered. They commence an hours-long, guerrilla-style delaying action, slowing and disrupting the Confederate advance. The Yankees harry and harass. The Confederate marching columns slow, are blunted, must become cautious—spread some of their number out to either side of the dirt road into adjoining fields and woods to meet the challenge, screen their marching columns from diagonal danger, try to take the fight to the harassing Yankee skirmishers who hide and fire, retreat to new cover on either side of the fenced earthen road, lay down more fire, run again, attack from yet a different angle:

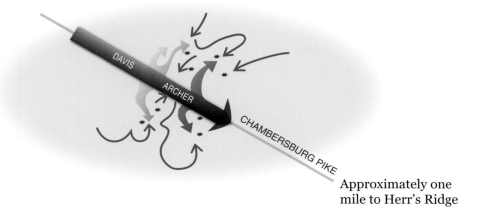

Approximately one mile to Herr's Ridge

Buford's "dismounted cavalry" fights on foot. It might be called "mounted infantry." Troopers gallop swiftly to each new position to dismount, one man in four serving as horse-holder with his and the other three's horses to rearward while the remaining three men fight as infantry. When it's time to move, all mount and ride. Speed being all-important on any battlefield, this technique multiplies infantry power.

Less romantic than the sabers-drawn mounted raids and sallies associated with, say, the renowned horsemen of Southern *beau sabreur* Jeb Stuart, Buford's method has proven deadly effective. Gruff, grizzled, methodical and practical, Buford chooses to fight his men off their horses, in the dirt.

The leading Confederate infantry brigades of Archer and Davis decelerate, coping with the welcome Buford has prepared for them.

As the sun rises toward midmorning and the air heats up, thickening with mugginess, Buford's initial pot shots turn to rapid-fire skirmishes, to real fire fights. Buford's men avail themselves of the quicker-loading carbines they've been issued (versus the Confederates' ramrod-each-shot muzzleloaders, which do however shoot longer and generally more accurately). The fighting continues to intensify.

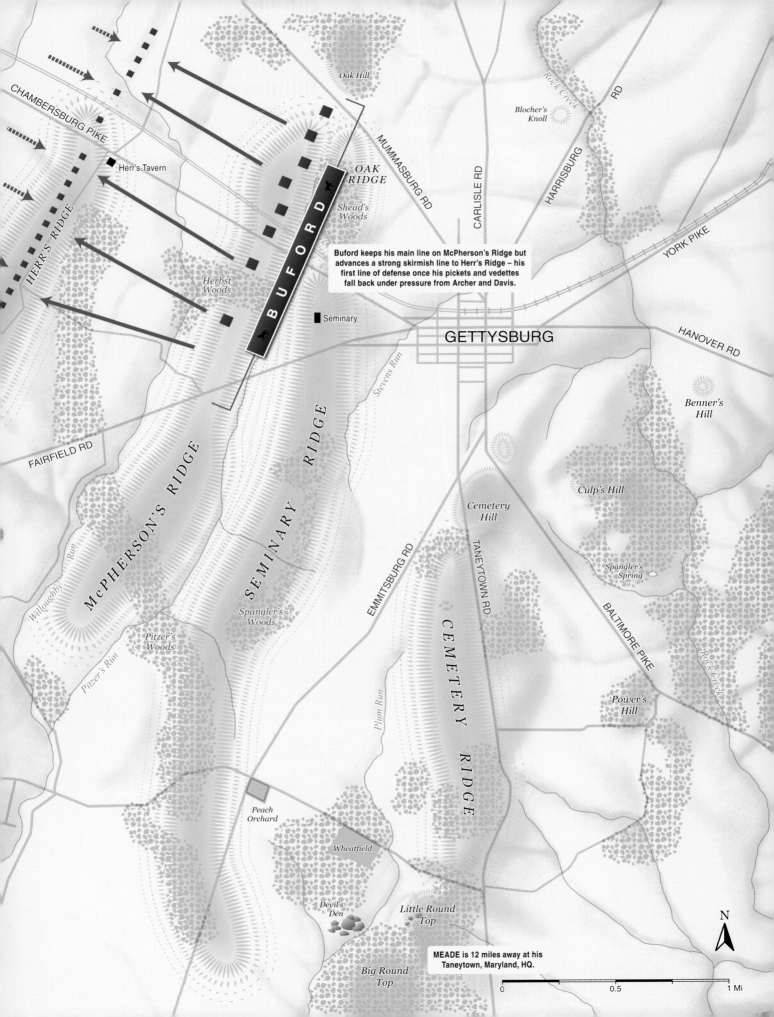

CHAMBERSBURG PIKE

Oak Hill

Rock Creek

Blocher's Knoll

MUMMASBURG RD

CARLISLE RD

HARRISBURG RD

Herr's Tavern

OAK RIDGE

Shead's Woods

YORK PIKE

HERR'S RIDGE

B U F O R D

Herbst Woods

Buford keeps his main line on McPherson's Ridge but advances a strong skirmish line to Herr's Ridge – his first line of defense once his pickets and vedettes fall back under pressure from Archer and Davis.

■ Seminary

GETTYSBURG

HANOVER RD

Stevens Run

Benner's Hill

FAIRFIELD RD

Culp's Hill

Cemetery Hill

McPHERSON'S RIDGE

SEMINARY RIDGE

Spangler's Woods

Spangler's Spring

Willoughby Run

EMMITSBURG RD

TANEYTOWN RD

BALTIMORE PIKE

Rock Creek

Pitzer's Woods

Pitzer's Run

Power's Hill

Plum Run

CEMETERY RIDGE

Peach Orchard

Wheatfield

Devil's Den

Little Round Top

MEADE is 12 miles away at his Taneytown, Maryland, HQ.

Big Round Top

N

0   0.5   1 Mi

Neither LEE nor MEADE wants a major fight—not yet. A battle is coming and both will welcome it, but only when each can know more of the other's location, disposition, strength . . . and of terrain. Actions taken by LEE's and MEADE's sub-commanders this morning, however, will make it increasingly likely that Gettysburg will prove the place where the great struggle will unfold.

The lead Confederate brigades of Archer and Davis move out of marching-column formation (narrow-deep), laterally into forward-facing battle array—

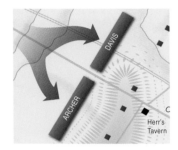

Davis advances north of the Chambersburg Pike, Archer south.

Behind them more Rebel brigades in long columns extend back into the northwest along the twenty-foot-wide dirt way, a strange Confederate reconnaissance in force. Legend has it they came to Gettysburg to look for shoes, sorely needed and rumored to be in ample supply in the town (it's not so). Four full-strength brigades plus artillery—some 7,000 men out of LEE's 75,000 total—is a lot of manpower for shoe-foraging, though. They're Yankee-hunting, of course. Their division commander, Heth, has permission—to explore only at this stage; most Rebel generals doubt much is going to happen in the Gettysburg vicinity . . . but in Buford the Confederates find what they were looking for. And they're getting in—deeper—into a real fight. Heth is committing, despite LEE's clearly expressed desire to avoid a general engagement for now, about which Heth knows or should.

With a strong line of skirmishers, Buford attempts a stand west of McPherson's Ridge. But the pressure's too great. The advancing Confederates are too numerous, their artillery superior. Buford falls his men back southeastward and up onto the good high terrain of McPherson's Ridge.

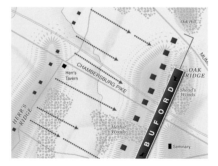

The delaying work of Buford's forward skirmishers for the past few hours has slowed the Confederate advance sufficiently to give Buford's Federals time to get into a good defensive position on the ridge.

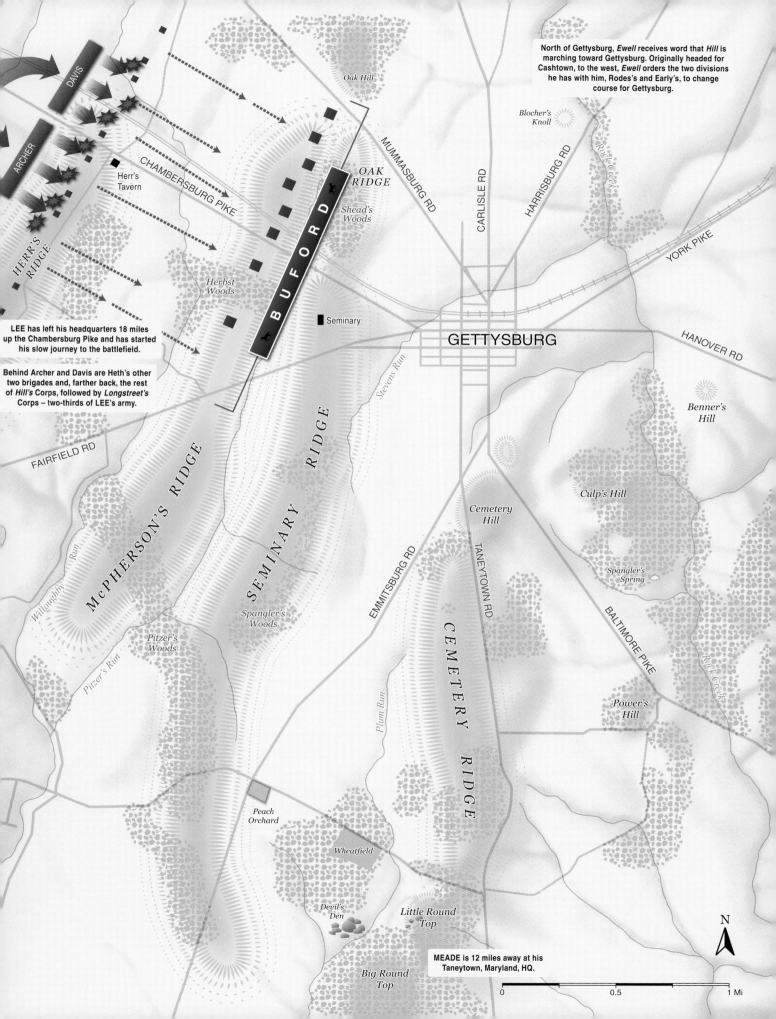

North of Gettysburg, *Ewell* receives word that *Hill* is marching toward Gettysburg. Originally headed for Cashtown, to the west, *Ewell* orders the two divisions he has with him, Rodes's and Early's, to change course for Gettysburg.

Oak Hill

Blocher's Knoll

MUMMASBURG RD

CARLISLE RD

HARRISBURG RD

Rock Creek

OAK RIDGE

Shead's Woods

YORK PIKE

DAVIS

CHAMBERSBURG PIKE

Herr's Tavern

ARCHER

HERR'S RIDGE

BUFORD

Herbst Woods

HANOVER RD

Seminary

GETTYSBURG

LEE has left his headquarters 18 miles up the Chambersburg Pike and has started his slow journey to the battlefield.

Behind Archer and Davis are Heth's other two brigades and, farther back, the rest of *Hill's* Corps, followed by *Longstreet's* Corps – two-thirds of LEE's army.

Benner's Hill

FAIRFIELD RD

Stevens Run

M c P H E R S O N ' S   R I D G E

S E M I N A R Y   R I D G E

Culp's Hill

Cemetery Hill

Spangler's Spring

Willoughby Run

Spangler's Woods

EMMITSBURG RD

TANEYTOWN RD

BALTIMORE PIKE

Rock Creek

Pitzer's Woods

Pitzer's Run

C E M E T E R Y   R I D G E

Power's Hill

Plum Run

Peach Orchard

Wheatfield

Devil's Den

Little Round Top

MEADE is 12 miles away at his Taneytown, Maryland, HQ.

Big Round Top

N

0   0.5   1 Mi

It isn't a question of whether Buford can hold. He can't . . .

But can he hold long enough? Impede the oncoming Confederates sufficiently to give help, in the form of the Union brigades of Cutler and Meredith (the Iron Brigade), time to arrive?

If Archer's and Davis's superior forces and the other Confederate brigades on their heels roll over Buford before any Union reinforcements can get up, there will be nothing to stop the Rebels from streaming down through town, pouring out the other side and south, seizing and fortifying decisive ground—Culp's and Cemetery Hills, Cemetery Ridge . . .

Holding the high ground in any battle gives great advantage due to—among other things—visibility, morale, the force of gravity, the ability of elevated firepower to rain destruction—artillery especially—on distant enemy actions and positions at a range the foe can't fire back from.

Confederate artillery unlimbers (disconnects from its traveling apparati), setting up astride the pike on the high ground of Herr's Ridge.

Opening fire, the Confederate guns compound the challenge facing Buford, whose small two brigades are supported by only a single battery of horse artillery (mobile, light).

Spread thin over the extended frontage of McPherson's Ridge and facing the wrath of superior Confederate numbers and cannon, Buford has his hands full. Doggedly, his men hold on.

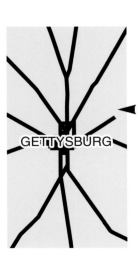

Hours away on the web of roads centering on Gettysburg, columns of Yanks and Rebs march toward the action. Picture four-abreast, miles-long brigades of sunburned, dusted, sweat-filmed faces, wagons drawn by teams, wayside stragglers prostrate from exhaustion or sick, orderlies, messengers, officers and guards agallop up and back the horizon-long lines. There are songs sometimes, a band strikes up. Always steady is the trudge of ten-thousand shoes against rutted dirt . . . stir and moan of driven cattle, trundled ammunition, towed artillery, ambulances, kitchens . . . seas of swinging arms . . . clusters of staff on horses . . . the colors unfurled if a destination is approaching . . .

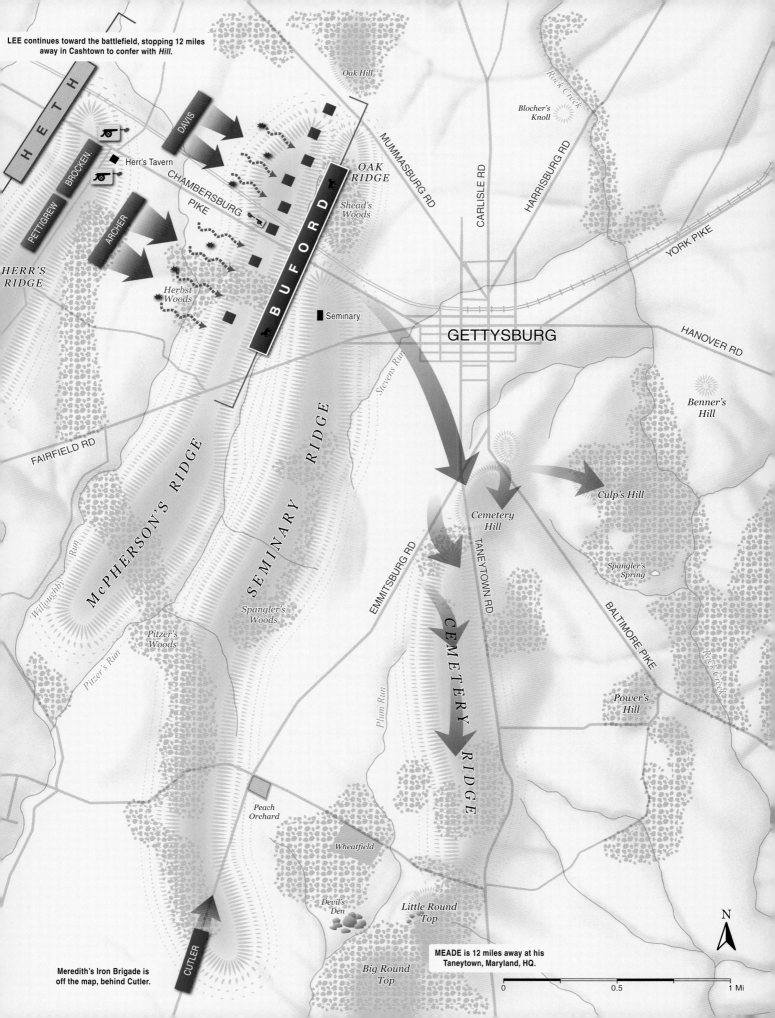

LEE continues toward the battlefield, stopping 12 miles away in Cashtown to confer with *Hill*.

HETH

DAVIS

PETTIGREW | BROCKEN. | ARCHER

Herr's Tavern

CHAMBERSBURG PIKE

HERR'S RIDGE

Herbst Woods

BUFORD

Oak Hill

OAK RIDGE

Shead's Woods

Seminary

MUMMASBURG RD

CARLISLE RD

HARRISBURG RD

Blocher's Knoll

Rock Creek

YORK PIKE

GETTYSBURG

HANOVER RD

Benner's Hill

Culp's Hill

Cemetery Hill

Spangler's Spring

TANEYTOWN RD

BALTIMORE PIKE

Power's Hill

Rock Creek

FAIRFIELD RD

McPHERSON'S RIDGE

SEMINARY RIDGE

Willoughby Run

Pitzer's Run

Pitzer's Woods

Spangler's Woods

EMMITSBURG RD

Stevens Run

Plum Run

CEMETERY RIDGE

Peach Orchard

Wheatfield

Devil's Den

Little Round Top

MEADE is 12 miles away at his Taneytown, Maryland, HQ.

Big Round Top

CUTLER

Meredith's Iron Brigade is off the map, behind Cutler.

N

0   0.5   1 Mi

July 1, Midmorning

...LEE knows little. He has no Buford out and about to scope out enemy activity. Jeb Stuart's elite Confederate cavalry, LEE's "eyes and ears" in every run-up to battle, has flown the coop. Plaintively, LEE keeps asking after Stuart's whereabouts.

(LEE does have cavalry other than Stuart, but it is scattered to the four winds or else deemed untrustworthy for the delicate intelligence work of palpating the enemy.)

LEE knows a general fight is coming. He wants it. But not blind. He knows he must focus his forces lest he be surprised piecemeal, yet he cannot be sure where to aim. At his orders his army is gradually, increasingly gravitating toward the Gettysburg area ... above all LEE wants no general engagement yet. He feels he has made this clear.

MEADE, at his headquarters to the south, craves information. He wants his options kept open. He has orders to protect Washington and Baltimore. He has ordered a circumspect advance toward Gettysburg: LEE may be there. The coming clash may happen there. MEADE doesn't know. He has sent one of his most trusted generals, *John Reynolds*, north to Gettysburg to see, assess, and report, in addition designating *Reynolds* "wing" commander of nearly half the Union army (three of MEADE's seven infantry corps).

MEADE's brain is an engineer's. He is not flamboyant. MEADE does not skip steps. He is solid, smart, and processes information coolly. New to highest command, he is getting a feel for his army. Warily preparing for one option (a clash at Gettysburg) of several, MEADE has also sketched out and circulated a plan possibly to withdraw south to ideal defensive terrain in Maryland, where, should *that* option eventuate, MEADE would like nothing better than to make LEE attack a strong Union defense.

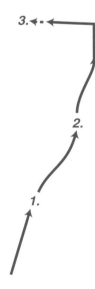

Reynolds rides north with his escort and staff. Well south of town [1], he receives a message from Buford: Confederates are coming down the Chambersburg Pike in force. A forward-leaning man (despite the fact that once, after a battle, he fell asleep and was taken prisoner of war—or perhaps because of this), *Reynolds* is unfamiliar with the verb "to hesitate." He immediately sends word back down the line of marching columns south of him to tighten up ranks and march at speed.

Reynolds hastens north. Almost to town [2], he learns from a distraught civilian that Buford is in a real fight to the northwest. An accomplished horseman, *Reynolds* spurs his mount through town at a clip, stopping only to ask directions, and, heading on out of town to the west, finds Buford at the Seminary. Together they go out to McPherson's Ridge [3].

Buford explains the situation. *Reynolds* can see it. He appreciates Buford's valor, as well as the danger to the whole Union cause.

Cutler's and Meredith's (the renowned Iron) brigades are on the way.

Reynolds asks Buford if he can hold. Buford "reckons" he can.

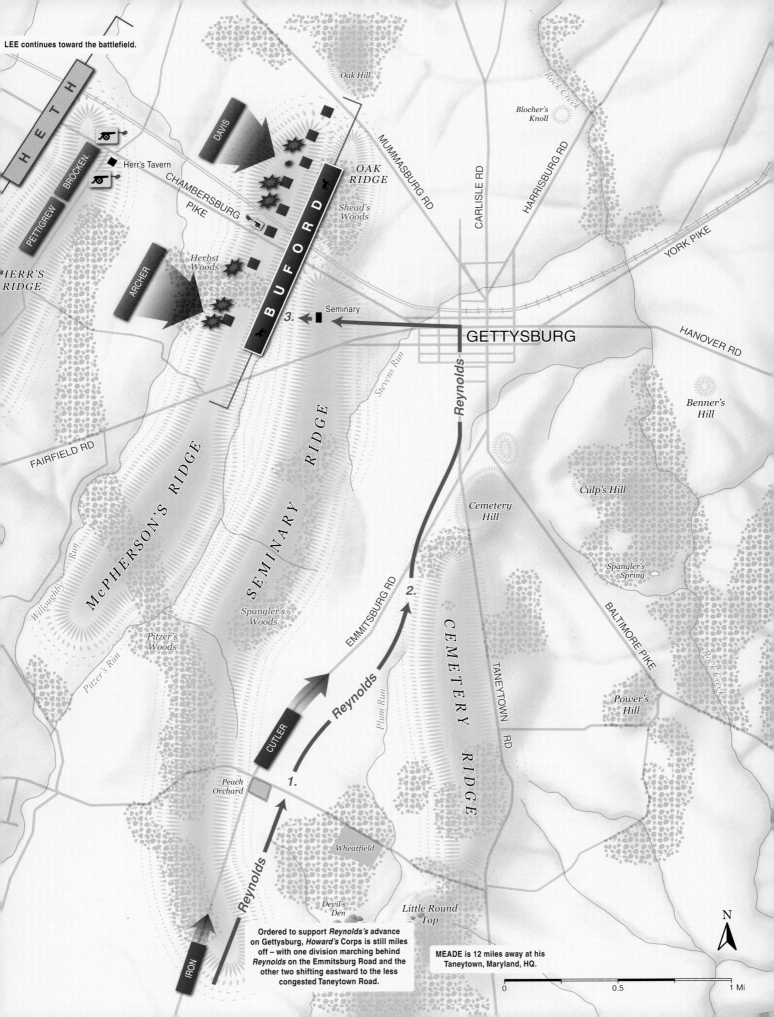

LEE continues toward the battlefield.

HETH

DAVIS

PETTIGREW BROCKEN

■ Herr's Tavern

HERR'S RIDGE

CHAMBERSBURG PIKE

ARCHER

Herbst Woods

BUFORD

Oak Hill

OAK RIDGE

Shead's Woods

MUMMASBURG RD

CARLISLE RD

HARRISBURG RD

Rock Creek

Blocher's Knoll

3. ■ Seminary

Reynolds

GETTYSBURG

YORK PIKE

HANOVER RD

Benner's Hill

FAIRFIELD RD

McPHERSON'S RIDGE

Willoughby Run

SEMINARY RIDGE

Spangler's Woods

Stevens Run

EMMITSBURG RD

Reynolds

2.

Culp's Hill

Cemetery Hill

Spangler's Spring

BALTIMORE PIKE

Rock Creek

Pitzer's Woods

Pitzer's Run

Plum Run

CEMETERY RIDGE

TANEYTOWN RD

Power's Hill

Peach Orchard

CUTLER

Reynolds

1.

Wheatfield

Devil's Den

Little Round Top

Reynolds

IRON

Ordered to support *Reynolds*'s advance on Gettysburg, *Howard's* Corps is still miles off – with one division marching behind *Reynolds* on the Emmitsburg Road and the other two shifting eastward to the less congested Taneytown Road.

MEADE is 12 miles away at his Taneytown, Maryland, HQ.

N

0   0.5   1 Mi

July 1, Midmorning

4.

5.

6.

5.

Galloping back the way he came, through town and out again to the south **[4–5]**, *Reynolds* orders the men with him and any others he can lay hands on to proceed up through the fields diagonally to the northwest **[5–6]**. He commands them to tear big gaps in all the fences there, making a short-cut for the arriving Union infantry. (Otherwise Cutler and those behind him would have to go north, through the cramped streets of the town, then at right angles back out again to the west.) Fast as they arrive, Cutler's desper-ately needed troops start up the short way *Reynolds* has made for them, toward the sound of the guns with the famous Iron Brigade on their heels.

Buford's stand against the Confederate advance is starting to crumble.

Reynolds messages MEADE that the situation is grave. Confederates are heavily concentrated coming down the Chambersburg Pike ... we're fighting. The prize high ground south of town is at risk ... I intend to fight street by barricaded street if necessary, whether reinforced or no.

Reynolds messages *Howard*: get here as fast as possible.

The arriving infantry of Cutler, followed by Meredith's Iron Brigade, are hurried up toward Buford's disintegrating position by way of the diagonal shortcut *Reynolds* had made.

Reynolds gallops back up toward the action **[5–6]**, spurring on Cutler's quick-timing men as he passes them.

Strung out on McPherson's Ridge, outnumbered, deprived of the mobility-advantage of being cavalry by the fact that they are defending essentially in place and therefore are without the option to maneuver, Buford's men can't hold ...

But they have held long enough. The first units of Cutler's infantry pour up onto the ridge, relieving Buford and allowing his units to slide left and right (north/south) out of the battle line to rest from their hours of killing labor (and eventually to regroup).

Riding about the field of battle through air alive with bullets, *Reynolds* cheers his Yankees on, directing and positioning each troop unit as it comes up, showing utter disregard for his own safety.

He places what artillery is available to him (Hall's six-gun battery) by the pike, where its fire can draw the Confederate artillery's attention off the all-important deployment of Cutler's arriving regiments. Mutually to protect Hall's guns and their crews in this key but risky forward position (as well as to face oncoming Archer and Davis), *Reynolds* spreads most of Cutler's infantry by either side of Hall, whose fire soon succeeds in distracting the Confederate artillerists, even forcing a couple Rebel cannon to go silent, by way of being forced to take cover.

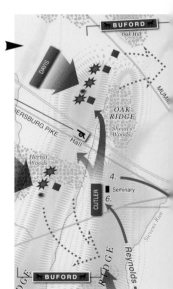

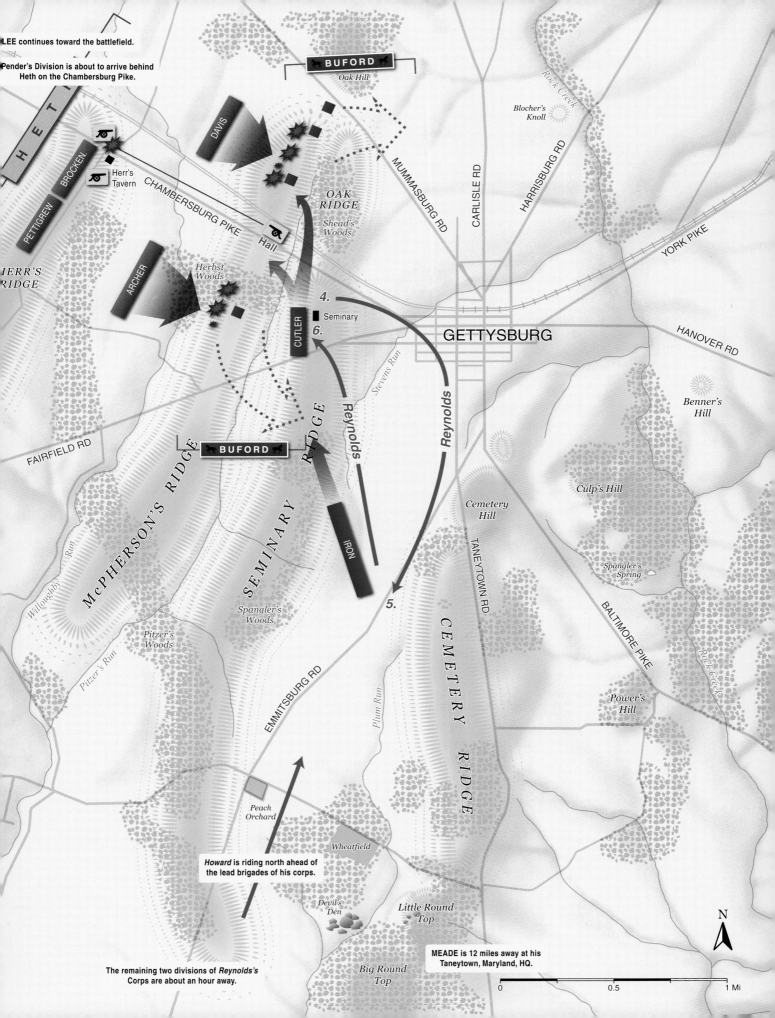

LEE continues toward the battlefield.

Pender's Division is about to arrive behind Heth on the Chambersburg Pike.

BUFORD

Oak Hill

Blocher's Knoll

HET

DAVIS

Herr's Tavern

BROCKEN.

PETTIGREW

HERR'S RIDGE

ARCHER

CHAMBERSBURG PIKE

Hall

OAK RIDGE

Shead's Woods

MUMMASBURG RD

CARLISLE RD

HARRISBURG RD

YORK PIKE

Herbst Woods

4.

Seminary

6.

CUTLER

Reynolds

Reynolds

GETTYSBURG

HANOVER RD

Stevens Run

Benner's Hill

McPHERSON'S RIDGE

FAIRFIELD RD

Willoughby Run

SEMINARY RIDGE

BUFORD

IRON

5.

Cemetery Hill

Culp's Hill

Spangler's Spring

TANEYTOWN RD

BALTIMORE PIKE

Rock Creek

Spangler's Woods

Pitzer's Woods

Pitzer's Run

Plum Run

EMMITSBURG RD

CEMETERY RIDGE

Power's Hill

Peach Orchard

Wheatfield

Howard is riding north ahead of the lead brigades of his corps.

Devil's Den

Little Round Top

N

The remaining two divisions of *Reynolds's* Corps are about an hour away.

Big Round Top

MEADE is 12 miles away at his Taneytown, Maryland, HQ.

0   0.5   1 Mi

Scarcely have Cutler's regiments gotten into position north of the pike, facing west, when Davis's bigger force hits them head-on as well as on their right.

Cutler is hurled back.

(Brig. Gen. Joseph R. Davis personifies the foisting of certain commanders and unit configurations on LEE by the president of the Confederacy, Jefferson Davis, against LEE's preferences. Blatant nepotism, the acceleration of the inexperienced Davis, Jefferson Davis's nephew, to brigade command, will have its consequences.)

Meanwhile, south of the pike, through the bare lower trunks of Herbst Woods can be glimpsed Confederate foot soldiers ascending the incline. It's Archer's Brigade, and their advance will be virtually unopposed! This, combined with Davis's repulse of Cutler on the other side of the pike, threatens to get the Rebels in around and behind Cutler, on his left. The advantage is suddenly very much with the Confederates.

No opposition but a thin, exhausted shred of Buford

Reynolds is a whirlwind. He has sent word south to *Howard* to spur his corps' lead elements north as fast as possible. *Reynolds* rides to where the 2nd Wisconsin—lead regiment of the Iron Brigade—is beginning to arrive; the Badgers are rushed forward (westward) up onto the ridge on *Reynolds's* order. There's no time. On his warhorse *Reynolds* orders the 2nd forward: "Forward for God's sake . . . drive those fellows out of the woods."

The Iron men rush forward, meeting Archer's advance, charging into a hail of withering Rebel fire. The 2nd takes terrific casualties, yet persists . . . in their iconic brimmed large black hats (of which many a foe has learned not to make fun), the Wisconsins send their own return volleys into the wall of fire being laid down by Archer's surprised Confederates. The 2nd Wisconsin charges. Seeing the hats, one Reb is heard excitedly to shout: "Hell that ain't no milishy, that's the Army of the Potomac!"

More Iron Brigade regiments come up and join the fray.

Archer's advance is halted in its tracks.

It is reversed, and finally the soldiers in blue are driving Archer's troops back on their heels and on back into the west. The advantage seems the Union's.

✝ Turning in his saddle, looking over his shoulder to see how close more reinforcements might be, *Reynolds* takes a bullet in the neck at the spine. His hat flies off. He crumples, toppling, dead as he lands.

The Iron men press their advantage, hotly pursuing Archer's men, who wade wildly back through the currents of Willoughby Run and beyond into the west seeking cover. The victorious Yanks take prisoners, including General Archer himself, whom an enterprising Union enlisted man spotted standing with his staff. Archer, fatigued to the point of disorientation, is conducted behind the Union lines, where he encounters his old friend General *Doubleday*, now in command of the Union forces following *Reynolds's* death.

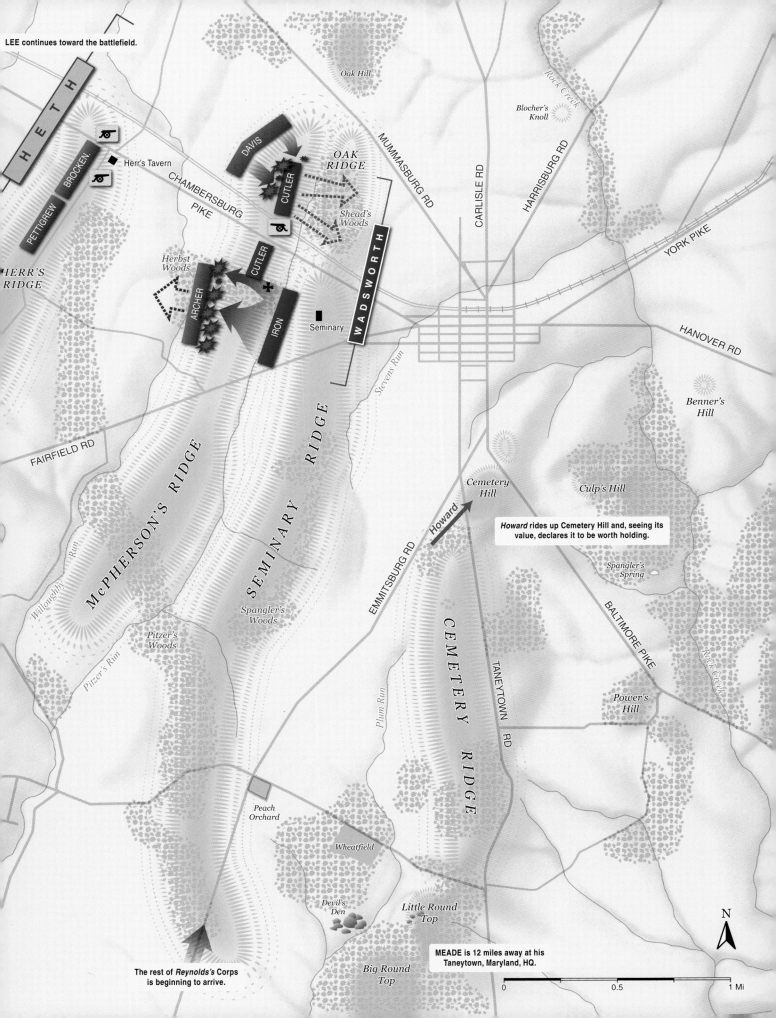

LEE continues toward the battlefield.

HETH

Herr's Tavern

PETTIGREW   BROCKEN.

HERR'S RIDGE

CHAMBERSBURG PIKE

Oak Hill

Blocher's Knoll

MUMMASBURG RD

CARLISLE RD

HARRISBURG RD

DAVIS

OAK RIDGE

CUTLER

Shead's Woods

Herbst Woods

CUTLER

ARCHER

IRON

WADSWORTH

Seminary

YORK PIKE

HANOVER RD

Benner's Hill

McPHERSON'S RIDGE

Willoughby Run

FAIRFIELD RD

SEMINARY RIDGE

Stevens Run

Spangler's Woods

Cemetery Hill

Culp's Hill

Howard

Howard rides up Cemetery Hill and, seeing its value, declares it to be worth holding.

Spangler's Spring

Pitzer's Woods

Pitzer's Run

EMMITSBURG RD

CEMETERY RIDGE

BALTIMORE PIKE

Rock Creek

Power's Hill

Peach Orchard

Plum Run

TANEYTOWN RD

Wheatfield

Devil's Den

Little Round Top

MEADE is 12 miles away at his Taneytown, Maryland, HQ.

The rest of *Reynolds's* Corps is beginning to arrive.

Big Round Top

N

0   0.5   1 Mi

Doubleday offers to shake hands, saying he's glad to see Archer, who grumbles, "I'm not glad to see you by a damn sight."

The sun will soon be at noon. North of the pike, Davis has pushed Cutler's regiments there back a quarter of a mile. As a result of Cutler's retreat, the small Federal artillery battery (Hall)—riskily and with success placed by *Reynolds* to draw fire—loses, on its right, the infantry protection *Reynolds* gave it. Still in place, forgotten and unprotected with his right vulnerable to Davis, Hall is forced angrily to retreat on his own. Hall has words with the commander who ordered the infantry retreat (Wadsworth), neglecting to inform Hall. Hall makes his displeasure clear.

South of Cutler, the Iron Brigade drives Archer farther back to westward even as Davis, north of the pike, has pushed Cutler east: a mirror-opposite flow of advantage.

Despite the Iron Brigade's repulse of Archer, Davis's battering of Cutler puts Davis in position to smash the Union right flank and drive on down across the pike, get in behind Cutler's regiments that remain south of the pike (where the late *Reynolds* placed them to protect Hall's artillery) . . . and then Davis could get in behind the Iron Brigade possibly, confounding and folding up the entire Federal position, with little to prevent a Confederate swoop down through town and out onto the precious high-ground real estate to the south.

Seeing this, *Doubleday* sends word to the 6th Wisconsin, a regiment which he has wisely kept in reserve in the vicinity of the Seminary during the hammering of Archer by the rest of the Iron Brigade.

Doubleday's command is plain: turn north toward the pike and rush there, help Cutler: "Go like hell."

The Badgers of the 6th do not need to hear it twice. Pivoting right into line, they quick-time north to the pike by a difficult but well-executed maneuver, deploy, assume prone position, steady their weapons on the bottom rail of the pike's south fence, and open fire at a deadly angle on Davis's advancing Confederates:

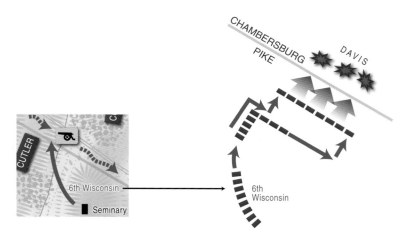

The 6th Wisconsin's Approach to the Pike

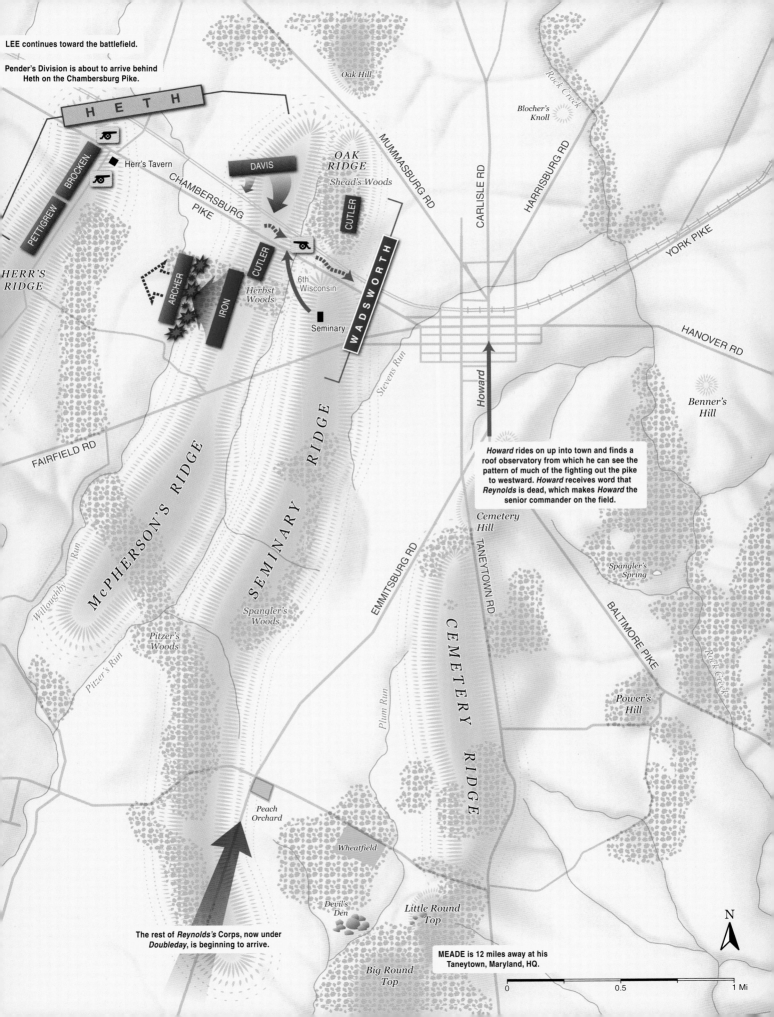

LEE continues toward the battlefield.

Pender's Division is about to arrive behind Heth on the Chambersburg Pike.

HETH

Herr's Tavern

PETTIGREW

BROCKEN

DAVIS

HERR'S RIDGE

CHAMBERSBURG PIKE

OAK RIDGE

Shead's Woods

CUTLER

CUTLER

WADSWORTH

ARCHER

IRON

Herbst Woods

6th Wisconsin

Seminary

Oak Hill

Blocher's Knoll

Rock Creek

MUMMASBURG RD

CARLISLE RD

HARRISBURG RD

YORK PIKE

HANOVER RD

Howard

Stevens Run

Howard rides on up into town and finds a roof observatory from which he can see the pattern of much of the fighting out the pike to westward. *Howard* receives word that *Reynolds* is dead, which makes *Howard* the senior commander on the field.

Benner's Hill

Cemetery Hill

Spangler's Spring

FAIRFIELD RD

McPHERSON'S RIDGE

Willoughby Run

SEMINARY RIDGE

EMMITSBURG RD

TANEYTOWN RD

CEMETERY RIDGE

BALTIMORE PIKE

Rock Creek

Power's Hill

Pitzer's Woods

Pitzer's Run

Spangler's Woods

Plum Run

Peach Orchard

Wheatfield

Devil's Den

Little Round Top

The rest of *Reynolds's* Corps, now under *Doubleday*, is beginning to arrive.

Big Round Top

MEADE is 12 miles away at his Taneytown, Maryland, HQ.

N

0   0.5   1 Mi

Joining the 6th, Cutler's regiments that remain south of the pike turn north also, ordered to wheel up to the pike by their commander, who, having observed the successful charges of Davis, rightly fears an attack from that direction.

This two-regiment maneuver by the Yankees, added to *Doubleday's* diverting of the 6th Wisconsin up to the pike, results in a fortuitously coordinated, tight alignment of three Union regiments abreast in attack on Davis's advance, as if it had been planned.

Raining a hail of fire on the Rebels ...

... the Union regiments ... watch in astonishment ... as Davis's Confederate infantry ... *disappears!*

In fact, the Rebels have taken refuge by dropping out of sight into an unfinished railroad cut. This level, dead-straight, trench-like road bed, where track has yet to be laid, runs through the swells and dips of the farm country approximately parallel to the pike, immediately north of it.

The Confederates are aware of the cut. Earlier in the fight when Davis made his initial attack on Cutler's regiments just as they were arriving in position north of the pike, one of Davis's attacking Confederate regiments utilized the cut for cover and concealment, advancing straight down it at Cutler's left flank to spring out of nowhere on Cutler's surprised Yankees. Now, not three quarters of an hour later, Davis's men again avail themselves of the cover afforded by the cut's high banks where the road bed runs below the gentle countryside rises:

It's a logical move ... and a great mistake.

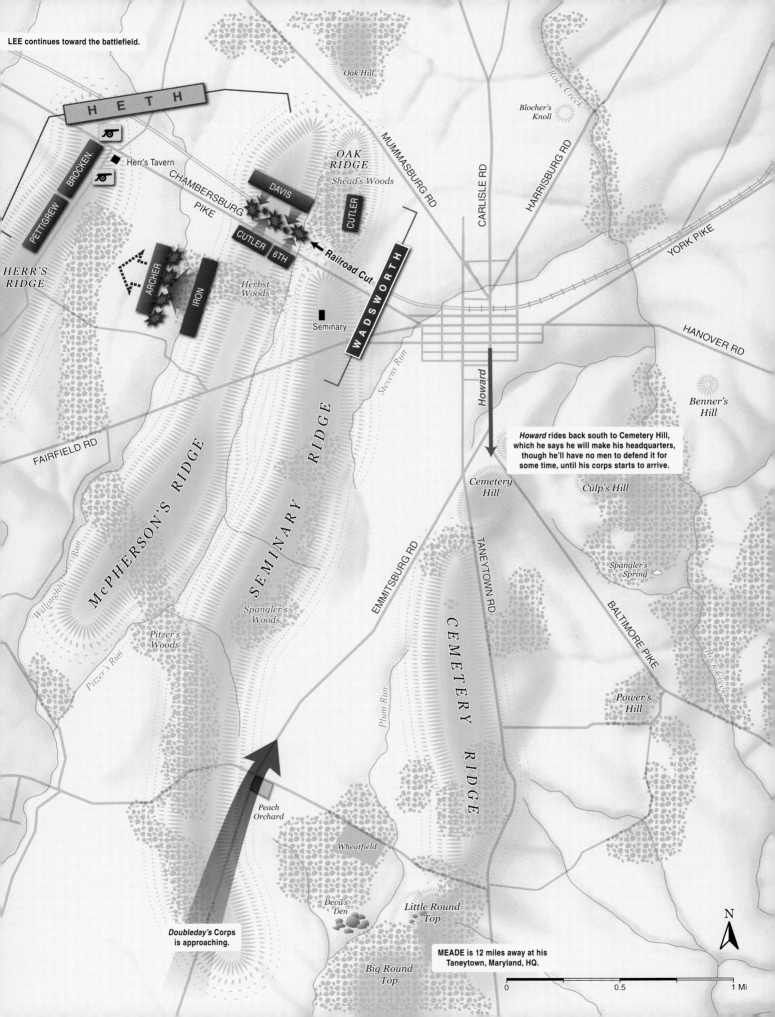

LEE continues toward the battlefield.

HETH

Herr's Tavern

PETTIGREW **BROCKEN.**

CHAMBERSBURG PIKE

DAVIS

Oak Hill

OAK RIDGE

Shead's Woods

CUTLER

MUMMASBURG RD

Blocher's Knoll

Rock Creek

CARLISLE RD

HARRISBURG RD

CUTLER **6TH**

Railroad Cut

WADSWORTH

YORK PIKE

HERR'S RIDGE

ARCHER **IRON**

Herbst Woods

Seminary

Stevens Run

HANOVER RD

Howard

Howard rides back south to Cemetery Hill, which he says he will make his headquarters, though he'll have no men to defend it for some time, until his corps starts to arrive.

Benner's Hill

Cemetery Hill

Culp's Hill

FAIRFIELD RD

McPHERSON'S RIDGE

SEMINARY RIDGE

Spangler's Woods

Willoughby Run

EMMITSBURG RD

TANEYTOWN RD

Spangler's Spring

Pitzer's Woods

Pitzer's Run

Plum Run

CEMETERY RIDGE

BALTIMORE PIKE

Power's Hill

Rock Creek

Peach Orchard

Wheatfield

Devil's Den

Little Round Top

Doubleday's Corps is approaching.

MEADE is 12 miles away at his Taneytown, Maryland, HQ.

Big Round Top

N

0   0.5   1 Mi

Side view of the cut

The cut does give the Confederates excellent cover to fire from. When the 6th Wisconsin bravely charges, having to halt, under heavy fire, to climb over the two fences that run along either side of the pike, the loss of life is tremendous. But the Badgers will not be denied, even at a death rate half their number . . . soon Yanks, the 6th as well as Cutler's soldiers, stand atop the cut's earthen embankments. Below, disordered and disorganized by having to crowd together pell-mell in the narrow trench (which is deeper than they had thought), and unable to go forward or back or to flee down it (when the Federals close off the trench lengthwise), with their enemy literally over them and able to deliver point-blank fire down into the milling Rebel masses, Davis's men surrender.

Enlisted men throw down their arms. Confederate officers not a quarter-hour ago ready to fold up and defeat the entire Federal position hand over their swords. The rest of Davis's force is withdrawing.

The morning's hard fight is over: advantage Union. A lull comes over the battlefield. From about noon 'til about two, things will be quiet. The two armies rest, reconstitute, reposition, and fresh troops stream onto the grid, arriving down the web of roads to be placed where their generals think best.

MEADE: A courier has galloped south to MEADE's Maryland headquarters to deliver *Reynolds's* midmorning message apprising MEADE of the gravity of the encounter northwest of town, the concentration of Rebel units jostling down the pike, the potential availability, to the Confederates, of the priceless ridges and hills south of town, and of his—*Reynolds's*—determination to contest the Confederate advance street by barricaded street if need be, whether reinforced or no.

Unable to know that *Reynolds* is dead (due to messages' twelve-mile travel time), MEADE is heartened by his valued lieutenant's characteristic resolve. At the same time, MEADE is dismayed not to know more. *Is* it LEE's main army at Gettysburg? What can be known of terrain detail? What does *Reynolds* think of Gettysburg as a place to fight? What *exactly* are *Reynolds's* intentions? What *in detail* does he face? Has *Reynolds* received MEADE's circular laying out the option of withdrawing south to defend in Maryland? *Reynolds* has not, MEADE discovers, and the Army of the Potomac headquarters clerks feel the sting of MEADE's famous temper.

LEE's exact location and doings this noontime period are not clear to history. He has moved east toward town and is somewhere about the Chambersburg Pike with no immediate plan except to learn more and above all avoid a major engagement for the present.

In point of fact, LEE has been drifting toward Gettysburg this day, by hours moving down the Chambersburg Pike toward the action he knows to be developing. He starts, stops—has visited with *Hill*, corps commander of the divisions of Heth, Pender, and (still en route) Anderson. *Hill*, new to corps command and needing managing, is somewhat antithetical to such aggressive, take-charge MEADE proxies as *Hancock* and the late *John Reynolds*.

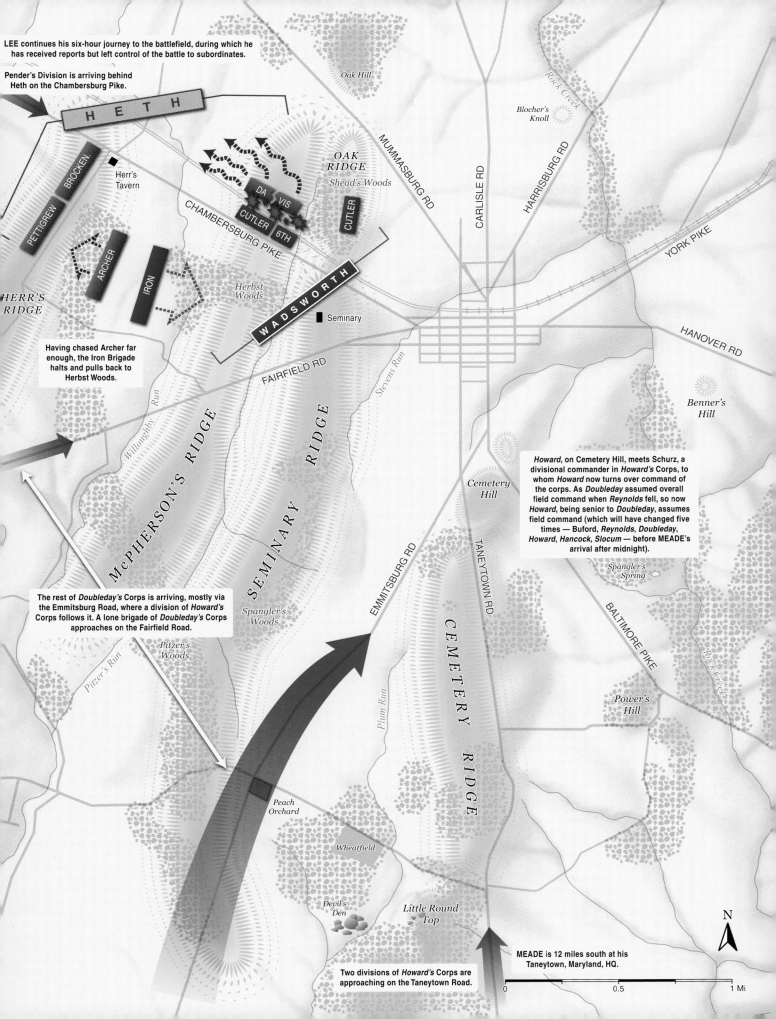

LEE continues his six-hour journey to the battlefield, during which he has received reports but left control of the battle to subordinates.

Pender's Division is arriving behind Heth on the Chambersburg Pike.

HETH

Oak Hill

Blocher's Knoll

Rock Creek

BROCKEN

PETTIGREW

Herr's Tavern

OAK RIDGE

Shead's Woods

DA VIS

CUTLER 6TH

CUTLER

ARCHER

IRON

MUMMASBURG RD

CARLISLE RD

HARRISBURG RD

YORK PIKE

CHAMBERSBURG PIKE

HERR'S RIDGE

Herbst Woods

WADSWORTH

Seminary

Having chased Archer far enough, the Iron Brigade halts and pulls back to Herbst Woods.

FAIRFIELD RD

Stevens Run

HANOVER RD

Willoughby Run

Benner's Hill

McPHERSON'S RIDGE

SEMINARY RIDGE

EMMITSBURG RD

Cemetery Hill

TANEYTOWN RD

Howard, on Cemetery Hill, meets Schurz, a divisional commander in Howard's Corps, to whom Howard now turns over command of the corps. As Doubleday assumed overall field command when Reynolds fell, so now Howard, being senior to Doubleday, assumes field command (which will have changed five times — Buford, Reynolds, Doubleday, Howard, Hancock, Slocum — before MEADE's arrival after midnight).

Spangler's Spring

The rest of Doubleday's Corps is arriving, mostly via the Emmitsburg Road, where a division of Howard's Corps follows it. A lone brigade of Doubleday's Corps approaches on the Fairfield Road.

Pitzer's Run

Spangler's Woods

Pitzer's Woods

BALTIMORE PIKE

Rock Creek

Power's Hill

CEMETERY RIDGE

Plum Run

Peach Orchard

Wheatfield

Devil's Den

Little Round Top

MEADE is 12 miles south at his Taneytown, Maryland, HQ.

Two divisions of Howard's Corps are approaching on the Taneytown Road.

N

0   0.5   1 Mi

During the lull, see the weight of each side building, units pouring onto the grid, the likelihood of a major encounter hardening to inevitability. Don't try to fix every position, each name—some will prove less important to the afternoon's drama . . .

North of town, Schimmelfennig's Division (Amsberg's Brigade, Krzyzanow-ski's Brigade) and Barlow's Division (Ames, Gilsa) face, to their northwest, the right flank of Rodes's huge Rebel division (Daniel, Iverson, O'Neal, Doles, and—about to arrive—Ramseur), and, to their northeast, the Harrisburg Road, down which fire-eating Jubal Early's Southerners are on the march.

At Cemetery Hill, *Howard* makes good his commitment to that valuable high ground by placing the two brigades of Steinwehr's Division there—a move for which the U. S. Congress will later formally thank him. West of town, the Union has Wadsworth's Division (Cutler, the Iron), whom we followed through the morning fight, and midday arrivals Rowley (Biddle, Stone) and Robinson (Paul, Baxter).

The Confederate division of Heth (Heth started things in the morning by getting into it with Buford up on the pike) faces Rowley, Robinson, Wadsworth (*Doubleday's* Corps [formerly *Reynolds's*]).

Heth's brigades are Davis and Archer, who have fought today, and Petti-grew and Brockenbrough, who haven't. Behind Heth is Pender's Division (Per-rin, Lane, Thomas, Scales), which has yet to see combat at Gettysburg.

(Note: The average Confederate division has more brigades—thus manpower—than its Union counterpart.)

Rodes's and Early's Divisions are in the Confederate corps of *Ewell*. Heth and Pender are commanded by *Hill*.

In *Schurz's* Union corps are the divisions of Steinwehr, Schimmelfennig, Barlow. *Schurz* has assumed acting corps command because *Howard*, due to seniority, on arrival replaces *Doubleday* as chief Union field commander (until the arrival of *Hancock*), just as *Doubleday* earlier replaced the fallen *Reynolds*.

All can't be kept straight. A sense of the battle's flow can't include the myriad command changes, the myriad changes back again as acting com-manders are relieved and return to their original command, the many gener-als and colonels with the same last name, the corps and division numerals, each division's artillery brigade, the hundreds of cannon positions over the three days, the blurred reporting lines of who, at given moments, is in com-mand of whom. With this map detail must get—and stay—broader.

Note: The Southern forces converging down out of the north (Rodes) and from the northeast (Early) have not been particularly held up. But in the northwest, up along the Chambersburg Pike, down which route the prepon-derance of LEE's army must come, there's a traffic jam. This delay—brigades stacked up—caused in no small measure by the doughty energies of Buford, *Reynolds*, *Doubleday*, Hall, Cutler, and the Iron Brigade in the morning, merits emphasis. It is a huge timing beat in favor of the Yankees and to the detriment of Rebel momentum, and its effect can be seen rippling forward throughout the rest of the battle.

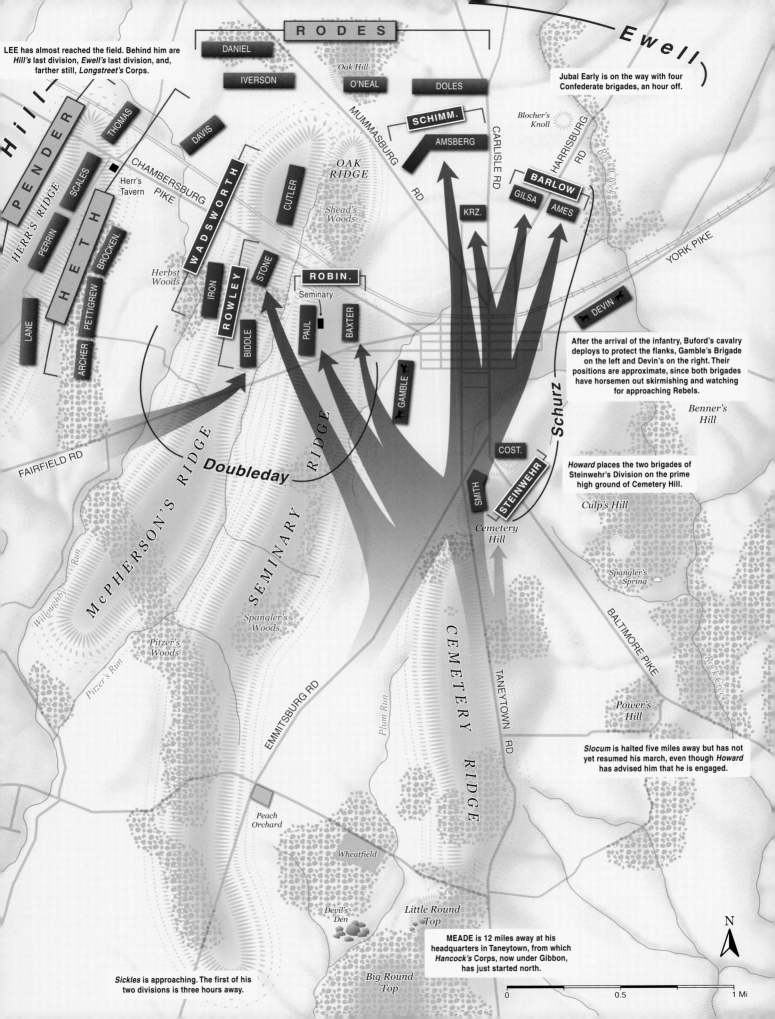

LEE has almost reached the field. Behind him are *Hill's* **last division,** *Ewell's* **last division, and, farther still,** *Longstreet's* **Corps.**

RODES

DANIEL

IVERSON

O'NEAL

DOLES

Oak Hill

E w e l l

Jubal Early is on the way with four Confederate brigades, an hour off.

Blocher's Knoll

Harrisburg

SCHIMM.

AMSBERG

CARLISLE RD

MUMMASBURG RD

BARLOW

GILSA   AMES

Hill

PENDER

THOMAS

DAVIS

CHAMBERSBURG PIKE

Herr's Tavern

WADSWORTH

CUTLER

OAK RIDGE

Shead's Woods

KRZ.

HARRISBURG RD

Rock Creek

YORK PIKE

DEVIN

After the arrival of the infantry, Buford's cavalry deploys to protect the flanks, Gamble's Brigade on the left and Devin's on the right. Their positions are approximate, since both brigades have horsemen out skirmishing and watching for approaching Rebels.

HERR'S RIDGE

SCALES

PERRIN

BROCKEN

HETH

STONE

Herbst Woods

IRON

ROWLEY

Seminary

ROBIN.

PAUL   BAXTER

LANE

PETTIGREW

ARCHER

BIDDLE

GAMBLE

Benner's Hill

FAIRFIELD RD

McPHERSON'S RIDGE

Doubleday

SEMINARY RIDGE

COST.

SMITH

STEINWEHR

Schurz

Cemetery Hill

Howard places the two brigades of Steinwehr's Division on the prime high ground of Cemetery Hill.

Culp's Hill

Spangler's Spring

Willoughby Run

Spangler's Woods

Pitzer's Woods

Pitzer's Run

CEMETERY RIDGE

EMMITSBURG RD

Plum Run

TANEYTOWN RD

BALTIMORE PIKE

Power's Hill

Rock Creek

Slocum is halted five miles away but has not yet resumed his march, even though *Howard* **has advised him that he is engaged.**

Peach Orchard

Wheatfield

Devil's Den

Little Round Top

MEADE is 12 miles away at his headquarters in Taneytown, from which *Hancock's* **Corps, now under Gibbon, has just started north.**

Big Round Top

Sickles is approaching. The first of his two divisions is three hours away.

N

0   0.5   1 Mi

July 1, Afternoon

At his headquarters to the south, MEADE learns of *Reynolds's* death. He orders another of his finest, most trusted generals, *Hancock*, to Gettysburg to take battlefield command.

LEE has come onto the field. On Herr's Ridge the Southern Commander in Chief tries to get a sense of the condition and position of things.

Toward the end of the lull, Rodes, at the head of his five Rebel brigades, in consultation with his boss, Confederate corps commander *"Baldy" Ewell*, sits his horse on Oak Hill with *Ewell* beside him strapped securely into *his* saddle, lacking, as he does, a leg.

Oak Hill commands a rare view of the Confederate and Union lines stretching to the generals' south. The Union forces look vulnerable to attack from the side, i.e., from the Oak Hill area. *Ewell* orders it.

First the Confederate artillery on the height shells the Union positions. This relinquishes the element of surprise as well as confirming to the Yankees that the important high ground of Oak Hill is in Confederate hands. It also drives Cutler back into the woods. In anticipation of an attack on his right, *Doubleday* shifts Baxter north to meet it:

Rodes, after some delay in getting his units ready, launches a badly coordinated assault. His brigades advance out of sync, piecemeal, at times downright foolishly.

O'Neal's Brigade, by itself and at less than two-thirds full strength due to muddy orders, attacks too soon. They run into withering fire from Baxter and, on Baxter's right, the westernmost elements of Amsberg.

Having ordered the attack, O'Neal remains to the rear during it!

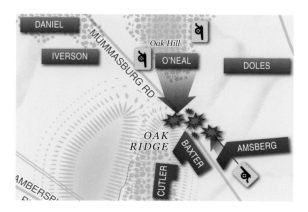

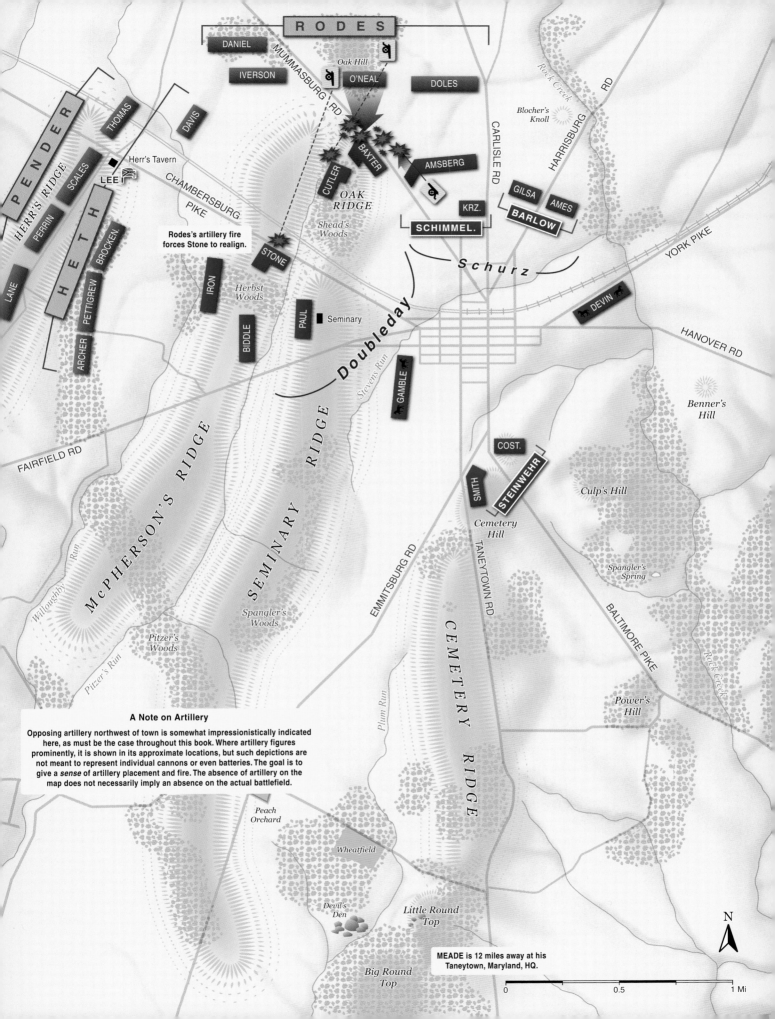

RODES

DANIEL

IVERSON

O'NEAL

DOLES

Oak Hill

Blocher's
Knoll

Rock Creek

HARRISBURG RD

MUMMASBURG RD

CARLISLE RD

PENDER

THOMAS

DAVIS

SCALES

Herr's Tavern

LEE

CHAMBERSBURG PIKE

HETH

PERRIN

BROCKEN.

LANE

PETTIGREW

ARCHER

BAXTER

CUTLER

OAK RIDGE

AMSBERG

KRZ.

SCHIMMEL.

GILSA

AMES

BARLOW

Schurz

YORK PIKE

Rodes's artillery fire
forces Stone to realign.

STONE

Shead's
Woods

IRON

Herbst
Woods

BIDDLE

PAUL

Seminary

Doubleday

Stevens Run

GAMBLE

DEVIN

HANOVER RD

Benner's
Hill

McPHERSON'S RIDGE

SEMINARY RIDGE

COST.

SMITH

STEINWEHR

Cemetery
Hill

Culp's Hill

Spangler's
Spring

Willoughby Run

FAIRFIELD RD

Spangler's
Woods

Pitzer's
Woods

Pitzer's Run

EMMITSBURG RD

TANEYTOWN RD

CEMETERY RIDGE

BALTIMORE PIKE

Rock Creek

Power's
Hill

A Note on Artillery

Opposing artillery northwest of town is somewhat impressionistically indicated
here, as must be the case throughout this book. Where artillery figures
prominently, it is shown in its approximate locations, but such depictions are
not meant to represent individual cannons or even batteries. The goal is to
give a *sense* of artillery placement and fire. The absence of artillery on the
map does not necessarily imply an absence on the actual battlefield.

Plum Run

Peach
Orchard

Wheatfield

Devil's
Den

Little Round
Top

MEADE is 12 miles away at his
Taneytown, Maryland, HQ.

Big Round
Top

N

0   0.5   1 Mi

O'Neal's Brigade is brushed back by a wall of fire from Baxter's and Amsberg's men and a Union artillery battery, which fires canister (cylindrical metal cans that burst when cannon-fired, splattering the shot tight-packed in them).

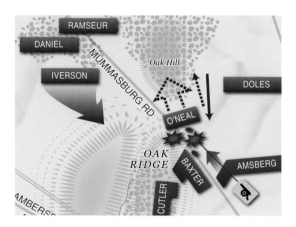

Rodes's five-brigade division, Lee's largest, attacks in spasms, disjointed, in separated parts, discontinuously.

To help O'Neal's Brigade, one of his regiments, held back due to confused orders, is ordered by an annoyed Rodes to advance, but approaching the action, under heavy fire and with O'Neal's attack in retreat, it can do nothing. (As for O'Neal remaining to the rear, he will later give as a reason, and accurately so, that he couldn't find a horse!)

Rodes's last brigade (Ramseur) arrives. Iverson's Brigade has begun an advance. Early's a mile off.

Paul has been ordered north to help Baxter.

The afternoon's fight is on. A hot contest it will be, involving four corps, ten divisions, and countless brigades representing more than a quarter of LEE's and MEADE's armies.

Both LEE and MEADE have indicated to their subordinates a desire not to get into a major engagement before being able to know more and better prepare. Yet both have been acting, often, as if a general engagement at Gettysburg were desired.

MEADE put *Reynolds's* entire corps in motion north toward the town—some 12,000 men—on top of that directing *Howard* to follow *Reynolds*—another 9,000 men—with instructions to back *Reynolds* up if need be. And all this MEADE ordered last night!

LEE permitted—or allowed a corps commander, *Hill*, to permit—Heth to sally down the Chambersburg Pike toward Gettysburg with a full division of 7,000 men before knowing much about terrain, enemy intent, or whereabouts. Pender's Division and 6,000 more men followed right behind Heth. LEE repeatedly cautions his commanders to avoid a general engagement. Likewise MEADE has repeated he wants his options left open, even to the extent of having circulated a plan—some might say a directive—to withdraw south to ideal defensive terrain picked out in Maryland. This plan circulated *after* ordering *Reynolds/Howard* north. But actions speak.

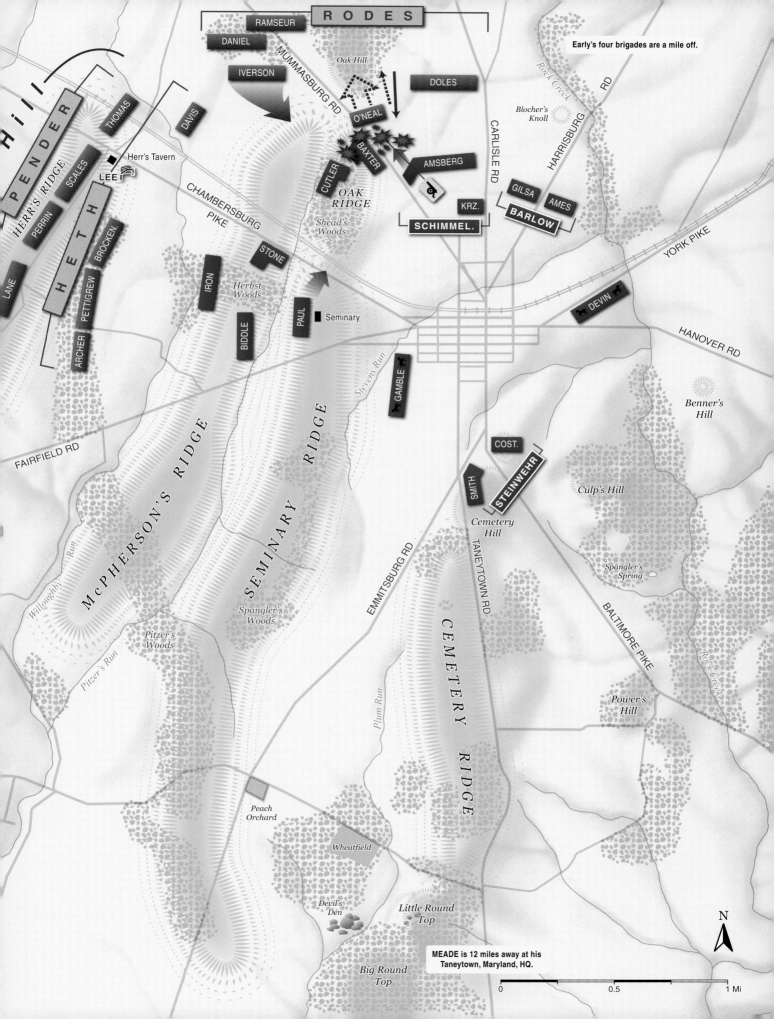

RODES

RAMSEUR

DANIEL

IVERSON

Oak Hill

O'NEAL

DOLES

Early's four brigades are a mile off.

Rock Creek

Blocher's Knoll

CARLISLE RD

HARRISBURG RD

HILL

PENDER

THOMAS

DAVIS

MUMMASBURG RD

BAXTER

AMSBERG

SCALES

HERR'S RIDGE

Herr's Tavern

LEE

CUTLER

OAK RIDGE

KRZ.

GILSA   AMES

BARLOW

PERRIN

HETH

BROCKEN.

CHAMBERSBURG PIKE

Shead's Woods

SCHIMMEL.

LANE

PETTIGREW

STONE

Herbst Woods

IRON

YORK PIKE

ARCHER

BIDDLE

PAUL

Seminary

DEVIN

HANOVER RD

FAIRFIELD RD

Stevens Run

GAMBLE

Benner's Hill

McPHERSON'S RIDGE

SEMINARY RIDGE

COST.

SMITH

STEINWEHR

Culp's Hill

Willoughby Run

Cemetery Hill

Spangler's Spring

EMMITSBURG RD

TANEYTOWN RD

Pitzer's Woods

Spangler's Woods

Pitzer's Run

Power's Hill

BALTIMORE PIKE

Rock Creek

CEMETERY RIDGE

Plum Run

Peach Orchard

Wheatfield

Devil's Den

Little Round Top

MEADE is 12 miles away at his Taneytown, Maryland, HQ.

N

Big Round Top

0   0.5   1 Mi

Soldiers are trained to fight. They also train to reconnoiter—all caution. But fighting's their thing. For the best especially. Many of whom have marched to Gettysburg. LEE and MEADE, for all their words of caution, have set in motion great masses of fighters centering on each other. It's like aiming hordes of arsonists toward a well filled with gasoline and reminding them, however, not to toss a lit match.

Iverson's Brigade attacks, is bloodied catastrophically. Baxter, after throwing back O'Neal, shifted his brigade formation neatly, facing it in the direction of the attack Baxter correctly expected next—and here it comes . . . over open terrain without cover in impeccable parade ranks, Iverson's men march toward Baxter's waiting Union line. Unbelievably, Iverson, like O'Neal, has stayed behind, not accompanying the attack he sets in motion. In full view of the enemy and unscreened by skirmishers, Iverson's troops arrive at a stone wall. Behind it Baxter's Federals crouch with cocked weapons: they spring up: sheets of flame. Two-thirds of Iverson's brigade lost.

Iverson, believing a swath of his men to be surrendering because in the distance he can make them out "lying down," is in fact looking at his dead and wounded. Iverson will write later that he attempted "to make a charge with my remaining regiment and the 3rd Alabama, but in the noise and excitement I presume my voice could not be heard."

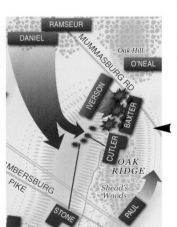

Daniel advances to try to help Iverson, but he can do little: Iverson is already breaking and Cutler on Oak Ridge and Stone along the pike are creating a deadly crossfire. Daniel heads for Stone (lower arrow).

Below Baxter, Paul's Brigade continues northward as ordered, to bolster the Union position. In the northeast Early's Division is minutes away.

All day the Confederates have been fighting disjointedly, bad mistakes compounding and compounded by a dearth of coordination. This has not been for lack of brave fighters—the Rebs are the best—but rather due to command confusion or, worse, rank ineptitude.

Barlow, taking his assigned position along the Harrisburg Road along Rock Creek, likes the look of Blocher's Knoll, a gentle breast isolated in open fields to the north. Without permission Barlow decides to advance his two Union brigades to there as shown (driving off a smattering of Confederate skirmishers). It's high ground after all. Stretching his units to do so and leaving air in the Union line behind him, Barlow, by moving forward to occupy the knoll, effectively makes his division, astride and atop the knoll, the extreme Union right. The isolated northernmost extremity of the entire Federal line. With a third of a mile of empty space to Barlow's rear (i.e., to the nearest possible "help" of Krzyzanowski):

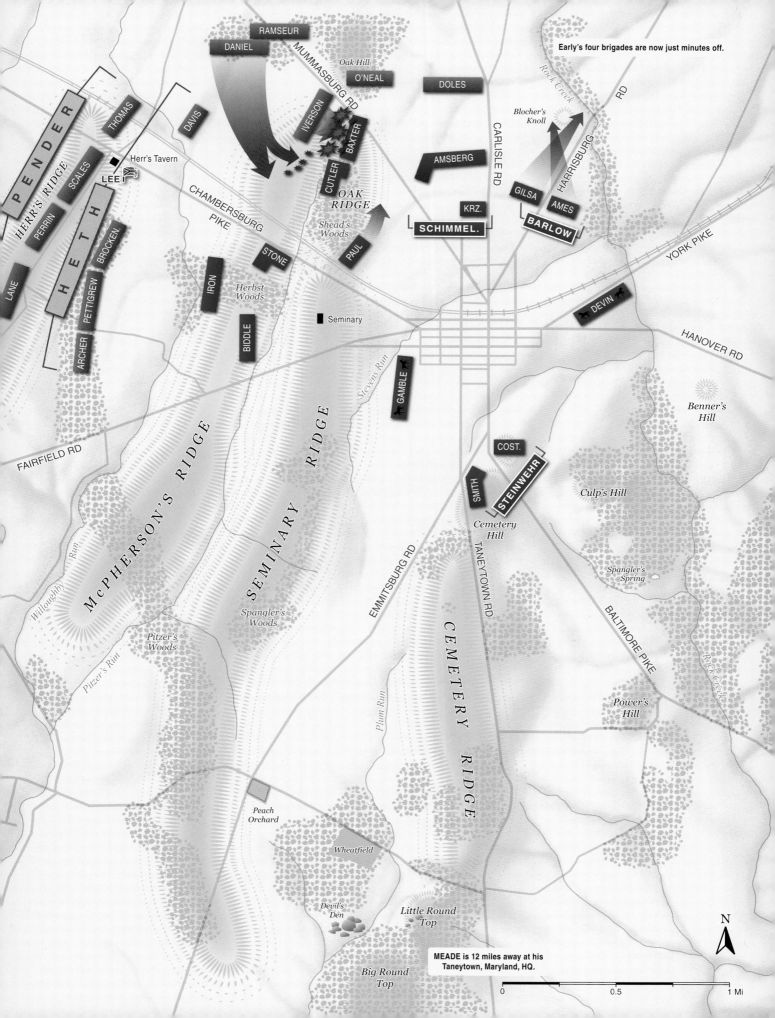

Early's four brigades are now just minutes off.

PENDER

HERR'S RIDGE

HETH

THOMAS

SCALES

PERRIN

BROCKEN

PETTIGREW

ARCHER

LANE

DAVIS

Herr's Tavern

LEE

CHAMBERSBURG PIKE

STONE

IRON

BIDDLE

Herbst Woods

Seminary

RAMSEUR

DANIEL

MUMMASBURG RD

Oak Hill

O'NEAL

DOLES

IVERSON

BAXTER

CUTLER

OAK RIDGE

Shead's Woods

PAUL

AMSBERG

KRZ.

SCHIMMEL.

CARLISLE RD

Blocher's Knoll

Rock Creek

GILSA

AMES

HARRISBURG RD

BARLOW

YORK PIKE

DEVIN

HANOVER RD

GAMBLE

Stevens Run

McPHERSON'S RIDGE

Willoughby Run

Pitzer's Run

FAIRFIELD RD

SEMINARY RIDGE

Spangler's Woods

Pitzer's Woods

Peach Orchard

Wheatfield

Devil's Den

EMMITSBURG RD

Plum Run

COST.

SMITH

STEINWEHR

Cemetery Hill

TANEYTOWN RD

Benner's Hill

Culp's Hill

Spangler's Spring

CEMETERY RIDGE

BALTIMORE PIKE

Power's Hill

Rock Creek

Little Round Top

Big Round Top

MEADE is 12 miles away at his Taneytown, Maryland, HQ.

N

0   0.5   1 Mi

Iverson's destroyed, finished off in a charge by Baxter. Daniel's in a fight, persevering, leaving the Yankees on Oak Ridge alone, advancing against Stone. Stone's Pennsylvanians repulse Daniel before learning, like so many others, the perils inside the railroad cut.

Paul has arrived on Oak Ridge to relieve Baxter and Cutler, who are almost out of ammunition.

Slashing out of the northeast, Jubal Early throws the men of Gordon's Georgia brigade into battle, gashing the Union brigades—Ames, Gilsa—of Barlow's Division atop Blocher's Knoll. Falling on Barlow like a scimitar, Early's men tear into the lonely Union forward position.

As if synchronized, an advance by Doles, who did not fail to notice Barlow sticking his neck out in the advance to the knoll, hits Barlow's left, multiplying the impact of Early's assault.

The knoll's high ground affords Barlow's Federals little leverage due to the Gordon/Doles momentum, manpower and firepower . . . and Early's ferocity.

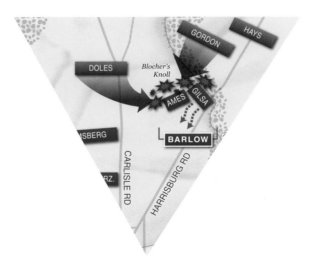

The knoll is geographically lonely. Unconnected to a ridge or other high ground, in addition to being unprotected by any natural barrier, it does not prove real estate prudent to have pushed out to. (A stream lies to the northeast, two to three feet deep. Its banks present an imposing but brief obstacle for Early's adrenaline-charged Rebels to clamber up.)

Barlow's advance out well beyond his assigned position means no Union help for him is near, as Early seizes the advantage, and, soon, though the Federals put up a gallant fight, the Union position is broken.

Gilsa and Ames are knocked off the knoll into a retreat southward toward town that will snowball.

Moral: take the high ground . . . but never without the boss's permission.

West of town, facing each other, the two sides aren't fighting, only skirmishing and artillery-firing. South of the Chambersburg Pike, Biddle and the Iron face an overwhelmingly superior Confederate array. Heth asks LEE if he may attack. LEE: No. I still want to avoid a major engagement if possible.

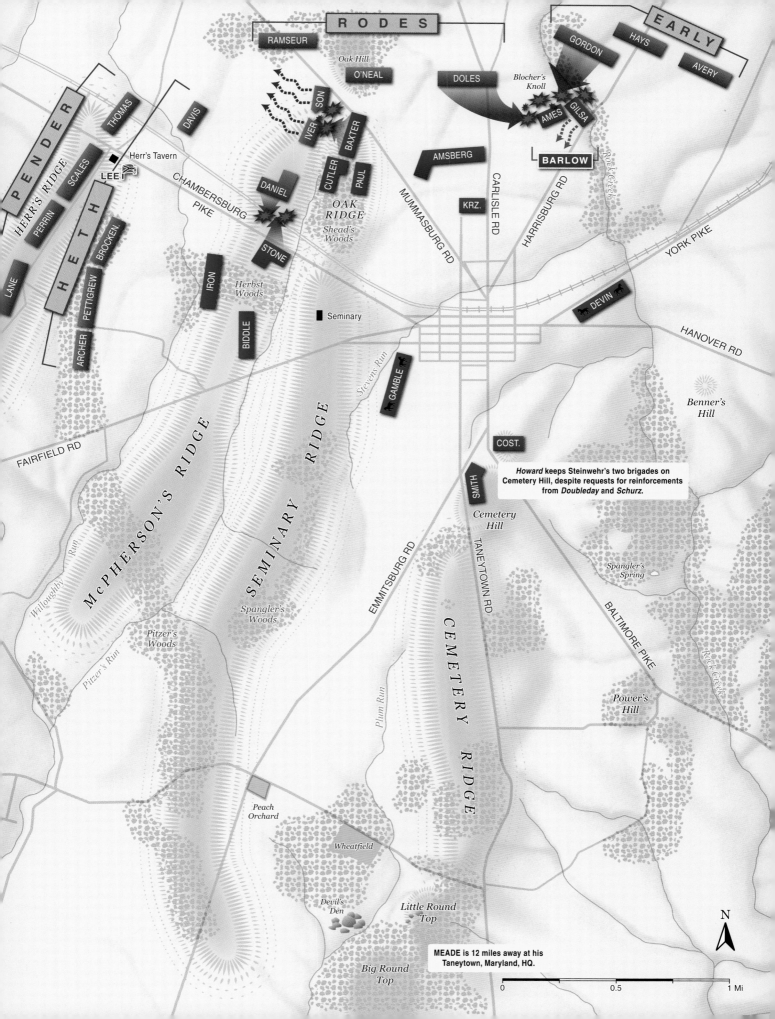

RODES

RAMSEUR

Oak Hill

O'NEAL

DOLES

Blocher's Knoll

EARLY

GORDON   HAYS

AVERY

DAVIS

THOMAS

PENDER

SCALES

Herr's Tavern

LEE

HERR'S RIDGE

PERRIN

BROCKEN

HETH

ARCHER

PETTIGREW

LANE

DANIEL

IVER-SON

BAXTER

CUTLER

PAUL

STONE

CHAMBERSBURG PIKE

OAK RIDGE

Shead's Woods

AMSBERG

BARLOW

AMES   GILSA

KRZ.

MUMMASBURG RD

CARLISLE RD

HARRISBURG RD

Rock Creek

YORK PIKE

DEVIN

HANOVER RD

IRON

Herbst Woods

BIDDLE

■ Seminary

Stevens Run

GAMBLE

M c P H E R S O N ' S   R I D G E

FAIRFIELD RD

Willoughby Run

S E M I N A R Y   R I D G E

Spangler's Woods

Pitzer's Woods

Pitzer's Run

COST.

SMITH

Howard keeps Steinwehr's two brigades on Cemetery Hill, despite requests for reinforcements from *Doubleday* and *Schurz*.

Benner's Hill

Cemetery Hill

EMMITSBURG RD

TANEYTOWN RD

C E M E T E R Y   R I D G E

Spangler's Spring

BALTIMORE PIKE

Rock Creek

Power's Hill

Plum Run

Peach Orchard

Wheatfield

Devil's Den

Little Round Top

MEADE is 12 miles away at his Taneytown, Maryland, HQ.

Big Round Top

N

0   0.5   1 Mi

With Early's arrival the Confederates begin, gradually at first, then like a machine, attacking in concert. On all fronts. In formations with little or no "holes" between them for enemy to pry into. And with more men now than the Union. Timing and angle of strike nearly always to Confederate advantage, as if LEE himself, at his best, were working the tactical controls hands-on (he's not).

MEADE continues working at his Maryland headquarters.

In the northeast (O'Neal and Iverson having met their ruin), Daniel hits Stone a second time—

—failing in back-and-forth heavy fighting. Perseverant, Daniel has re-tried essentially the same attack as his first, calling it off when he sees it won't work. (His bravely attacking troops got, among other things, tangled up in the railroad cut!)

Northeast of town, Gordon and Doles are driving Barlow's Division off Blocher's Knoll as we've seen.

West of town, LEE has given Heth permission to advance his brigades on the Union positions there. Having seen elements of Stone shifting north to meet Daniel, Heth has asked a second time if he may attack the thus-diluted Union line facing him. LEE assents. Heth's fresh brigades (Pettigrew/Brockenbrough), arrayed tightly against an outnumbered Union line and supported on their right by Archer's fought-out brigade, advance on Biddle's Brigade and, north of Biddle, on the Iron, which is imperfectly deployed and tired from its gallant charges of the morning. Heth commences a slow, steady, relentless, often bloody push-back of the valiantly resisting Yankees—

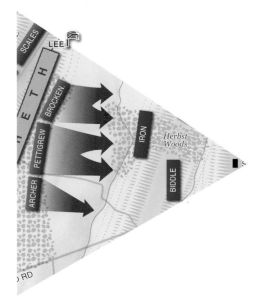

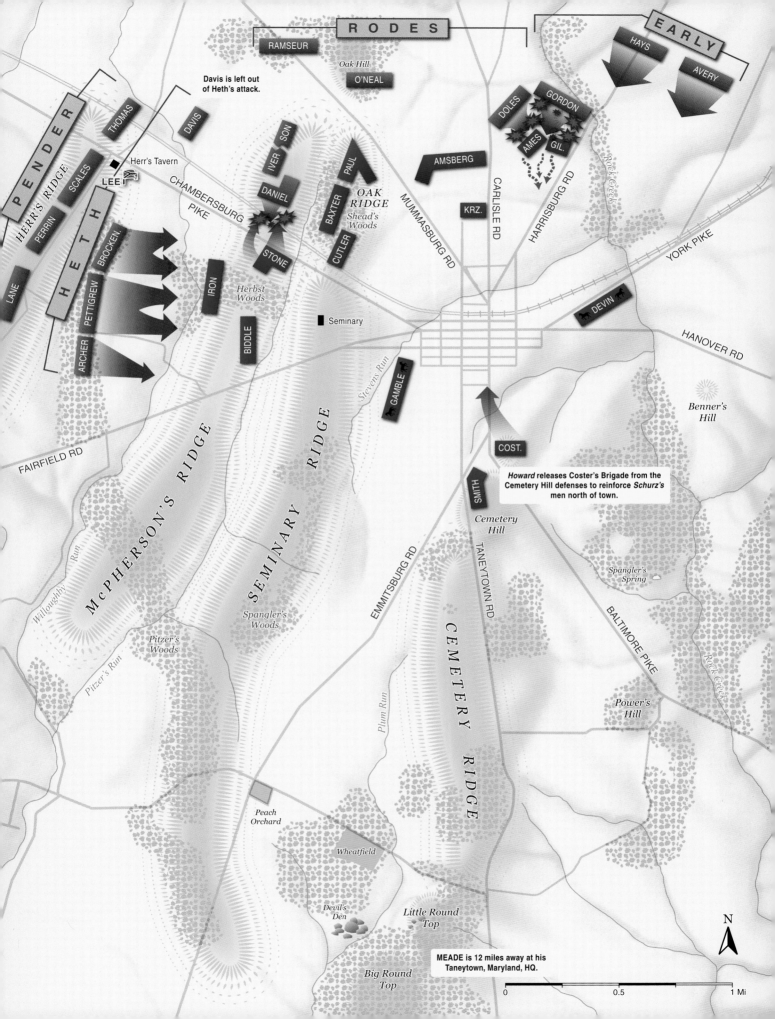

RODES

EARLY

RAMSEUR

Oak Hill

O'NEAL

Davis is left out of Heth's attack.

HAYS

AVERY

DAVIS

THOMAS

DOLES

GORDON

Herr's Tavern

IVER SON

PENDER

SCALES

LEE

DANIEL

AMES

GIL.

PERRIN

HERR's RIDGE

BAXTER

PAUL

AMSBERG

CARLISLE RD

HARRISBURG RD

Rock Creek

HETH

BROCKEN

CHAMBERSBURG PIKE

DANIEL

STONE

OAK RIDGE

Shead's Woods

MUMMASBURG RD

KRZ.

YORK PIKE

LANE

PETTIGREW

CUTLER

IRON

DEVIN

ARCHER

BIDDLE

Herbst Woods

Seminary

HANOVER RD

Stevens Run

GAMBLE

Benner's Hill

McPHERSON'S RIDGE

SEMINARY RIDGE

COST.

Howard releases Coster's Brigade from the Cemetery Hill defenses to reinforce Schurz's men north of town.

FAIRFIELD RD

Willoughby Run

SMITH

Cemetery Hill

Spangler's Spring

Pitzer's Woods

Spangler's Woods

EMMITSBURG RD

TANEYTOWN RD

Power's Hill

BALTIMORE PIKE

Rock Creek

Pitzer's Run

CEMETERY RIDGE

Plum Run

Peach Orchard

Wheatfield

Devil's Den

Little Round Top

MEADE is 12 miles away at his Taneytown, Maryland, HQ.

Big Round Top

N

0   0.5   1 Mi

Daniel won't give up. He regroups and prepares for yet a third effort. Daniel commands in the thick of things, blessed with a stentorian authority voice fabled to be understandable at a third of a mile. He's a capable tactician. He can see that the prize is the high ground of Oak Ridge to his east. But so long as Stone can cause trouble from the pike [1], west of Oak Ridge, i.e., menacing the southern flank of any Confederate attack [2] on Oak Ridge, taking Oak Ridge will be problematical.

But Daniel has been unable, so far, to break Stone. He needs help—and sees it coming from his southwest. Brockenbrough, with his northernmost brigade of Heth's west-of-town advance, will soon be putting heavy pressure [3] on Stone's left and rear, thus eroding Stone's threat to the flank of an attack on Oak Ridge.

To the north, Daniel's fellow brigade commander, Ramseur, is moving down to attack the ridge. Daniel intends to join in with most of his North Carolinians . . . if Stone can be taken out of the equation.

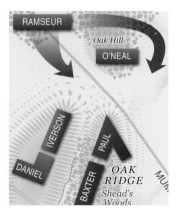

Daniel orders a portion of his command to attack Stone a third time.

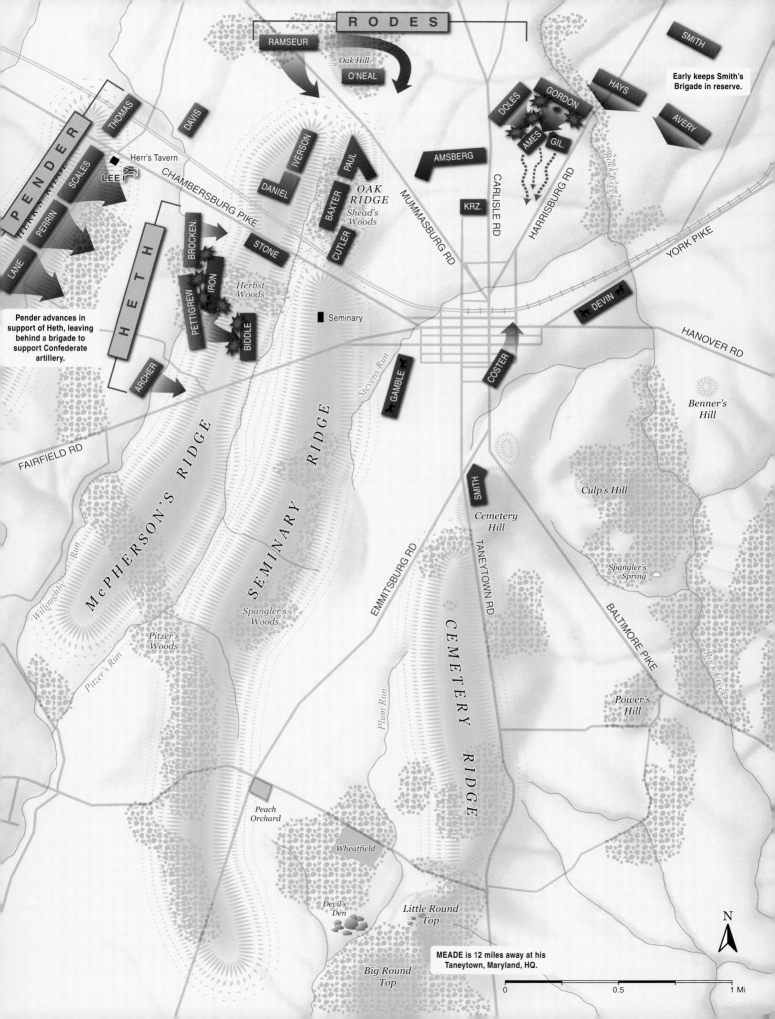

RODES

RAMSEUR

SMITH

Oak Hill

O'NEAL

Early keeps Smith's Brigade in reserve.

HAYS

GORDON

DOLES

AVERY

AMSBERG

AMES

GIL.

THOMAS

DAVIS

PENDER

HERR'S RIDGE

Herr's Tavern

LEE

SCALES

CHAMBERSBURG PIKE

IVERSON

DANIEL

PAUL

BAXTER

OAK RIDGE

Shead's Woods

PERRIN

MUMMASBURG RD

CARLISLE RD

KRZ.

HARRISBURG RD

Rock Creek

LANE

STONE

BROCKEN.

CUTLER

YORK PIKE

Pender advances in support of Heth, leaving behind a brigade to support Confederate artillery.

HETH

PETTIGREW

IRON

Herbst Woods

Seminary

DEVIN

HANOVER RD

BIDDLE

Stevens Run

ARCHER

GAMBLE

COSTER

Benner's Hill

FAIRFIELD RD

McPHERSON'S RIDGE

SEMINARY RIDGE

SMITH

Culp's Hill

Cemetery Hill

Willoughby Run

Pitzer's Run

Spangler's Woods

EMMITSBURG RD

TANEYTOWN RD

Spangler's Spring

BALTIMORE PIKE

Rock Creek

Pitzer's Woods

CEMETERY RIDGE

Power's Hill

Plum Run

Peach Orchard

Wheatfield

Devil's Den

Little Round Top

MEADE is 12 miles away at his Taneytown, Maryland, HQ.

Big Round Top

N

0   0.5   1 Mi

July 1, Afternoon

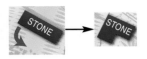

Stone's realignment.

This time around, Daniel attacks less head-on, and the railroad cut is left out of things. It's a tough assignment for fewer men than Daniel allocated for his previous attacks on Stone, who has realigned to face the dual threat of Brockenbrough/Daniel.

With the elements of his brigade not dedicated to his attack on Stone, Daniel joins Ramseur in a move on the Union Oak Ridge position. Even troops from the earlier-battered, since-regrouped brigades of O'Neal and Iverson get in on the act.

Stone is neutralized, just as Daniel had hoped. Stone is rendered unable to interfere from the side (from the south) with the Rebel attack on Oak Ridge. Stone is forced to retire east, back down the pike toward town, while on Oak Ridge the concerted, gapless effort by Daniel/Ramseur/Iverson/O'Neal dismantles the Union position of Baxter/Cutler/Paul.

All this Confederate success happens notably in connection with, and hinged seamlessly to, Brockenbrough, on the left flank of Heth's attack on the Union brigades of *Doubleday's* divisions west of town. To Daniel's south, Brockenbrough and especially Pettigrew begin to drive back Biddle and the Iron.

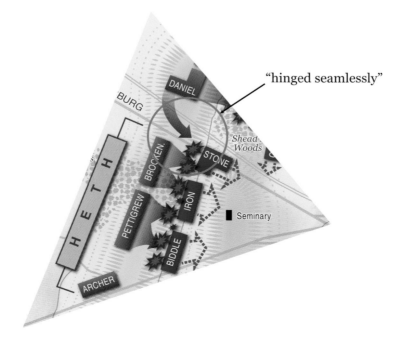

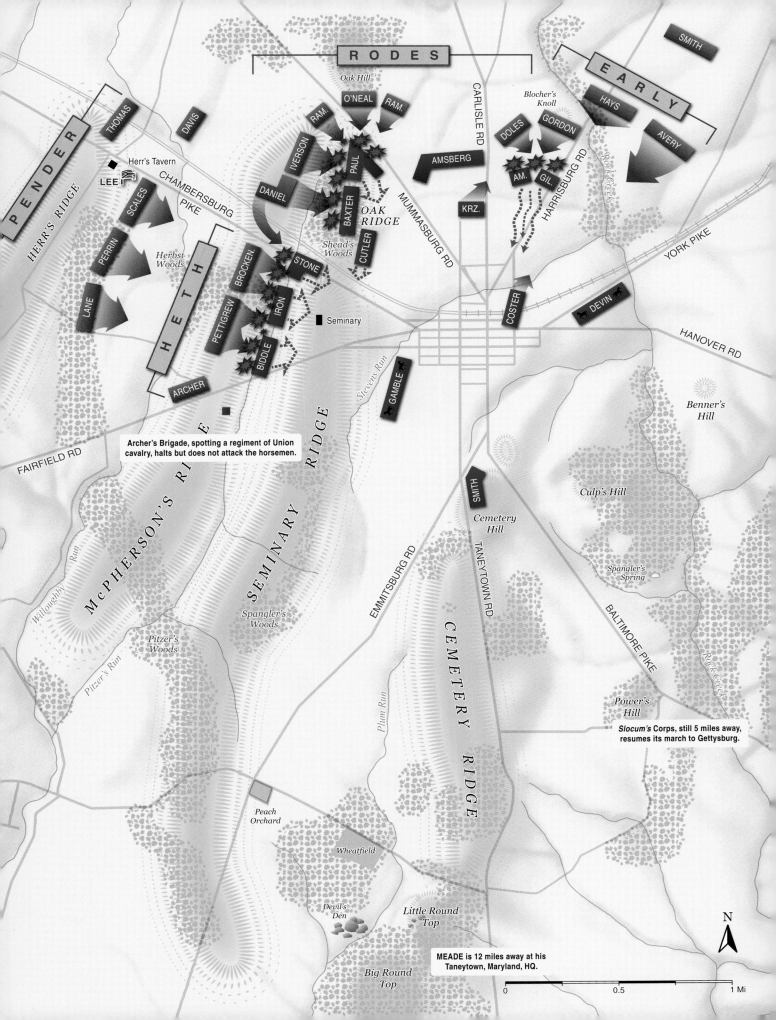

RODES

Oak Hill

O'NEAL
RAM.
RAM.

SMITH

EARLY

Blocher's Knoll

HAYS

DOLES
GORDON

AVERY

AMSBERG

AM.
GIL.

KRZ.

CARLISLE RD

MUMMASBURG RD

HARRISBURG RD

Rock Creek

YORK PIKE

PENDER

THOMAS

DAVIS

Herr's Tavern

LEE

CHAMBERSBURG PIKE

SCALES

PERRIN

Herbst Woods

LANE

HETH

BROCKEN.

PETTIGREW

IRON

BIDDLE

ARCHER

IVERSON

DANIEL

RAM.

PAUL

BAXTER

STONE

OAK RIDGE

Shead's Woods

CUTLER

Seminary

■

COSTER

DEVIN

HANOVER RD

GAMBLE

Stevens Run

Archer's Brigade, spotting a regiment of Union cavalry, halts but does not attack the horsemen.

Benner's Hill

FAIRFIELD RD

McPHERSON'S RIDGE

Willoughby Run

SEMINARY RIDGE

Spangler's Woods

Pitzer's Woods

Pitzer's Run

SMITH

Cemetery Hill

Culp's Hill

Spangler's Spring

EMMITSBURG RD

TANEYTOWN RD

CEMETERY RIDGE

Plum Run

BALTIMORE PIKE

Power's Hill

Rock Creek

Slocum's Corps, still 5 miles away, resumes its march to Gettysburg.

Peach Orchard

Wheatfield

Devil's Den

Little Round Top

MEADE is 12 miles away at his Taneytown, Maryland, HQ.

Big Round Top

N

0   0.5   1 Mi

Heth, at great cost of life and limb to his Rebel infantrymen, pushes the Union defense off McPherson's Ridge, driving the Federals yet farther back toward town. Union forces take heavy casualties too in their game contesting of every victorious step of the cheering, firing, oncoming, long-walking, quick-gaited Rebel ranks. Casualties in many units are greater than 30 percent on both sides. What is essentially a slow-motion retreat against superior numbers of hard-fighting Confederates continues . . .

Early, in the northeast, having bested Ames and Gilsa, whose shattered formations are long since off Blocher's Knoll and in disarray pouring south through the streets of town, now strikes Krzyzanowski. Krzyzanowski's Union brigade tries to stand in Early's way, but they can't stanch the slashing offensive by Gordon's Brigade. Confronted with Doles as well, Krzyzanowski's men are forced to choose retreat over destruction.

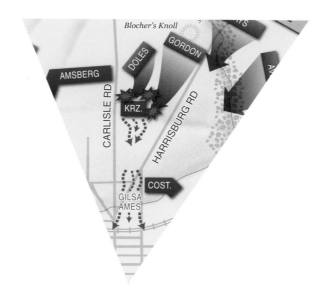

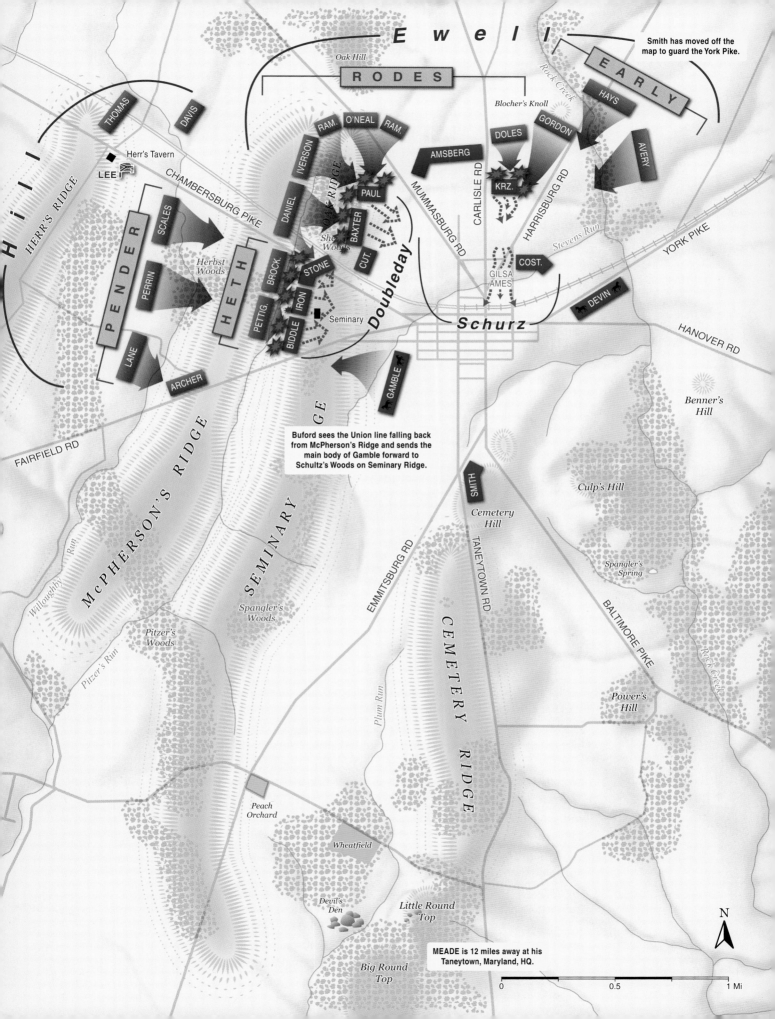

Ewell

Smith has moved off the map to guard the York Pike.

Oak Hill

RODES

EARLY

HAYS

Blocher's Knoll

Rock Creek

H i l l

THOMAS

DAVIS

Herr's Tavern

LEE

CHAMBERSBURG PIKE

HERR'S RIDGE

RAM. O'NEAL RAM.

IVERSON

DANIEL

OAK RIDGE

PAUL

AMSBERG

DOLES

GORDON

AVERY

CARLISLE RD

KRZ.

HARRISBURG RD

Stevens Run

YORK PIKE

PENDER

SCALES

PERRIN

Herbst Woods

HETH

BROCK.

STONE

BAXTER

Shea's Woods

CUT.

MUMMASBURG RD

Doubleday

COST.

GILSA AMES

DEVIN

LANE

PETTIG.

IRON

BIDDLE

Seminary

Schurz

HANOVER RD

ARCHER

Benner's Hill

GAMBLE

Buford sees the Union line falling back from McPherson's Ridge and sends the main body of Gamble forward to Schultz's Woods on Seminary Ridge.

SMITH

Culp's Hill

Cemetery Hill

FAIRFIELD RD

McPHERSON'S RIDGE

Willoughby Run

SEMINARY RIDGE

Spangler's Woods

Pitzer's Woods

Pitzer's Run

EMMITSBURG RD

TANEYTOWN RD

Spangler's Spring

BALTIMORE PIKE

Rock Creek

Power's Hill

CEMETERY RIDGE

Plum Run

Peach Orchard

Wheatfield

Devil's Den

Little Round Top

MEADE is 12 miles away at his Taneytown, Maryland, HQ.

Big Round Top

N

0   0.5   1 Mi

July 1, Late Afternoon

West of town, after completing their desperate chore of driving the Federals off McPherson's Ridge, Heth's brigades are no longer fresh. The brigades of Pender's Division, fresh indeed and spoiling for a fight, spell Heth's units, passing from behind Heth, whom they've been following, through and out ahead of Heth's exhausted ranks, to the fighting front. They confront a Union line barricaded on the next and last ridge (Seminary) available to the Yankees before town.

Arrayed along the ridge, the Union brigades (north to south) of Stone, the Iron, Biddle, and Gamble (of Buford's dismounted cavalry) are depleted. They have no fresh division such as Pender's to come up and help meet the greater, rested Rebel numbers moving on them. The Federals have well-positioned artillery. (Our look at the battle shows artillery sporadically perforce. But here, without the Union batteries which the map gives a sense of, the inevitable would have happened to *Doubleday's* Yankees even quicker.)

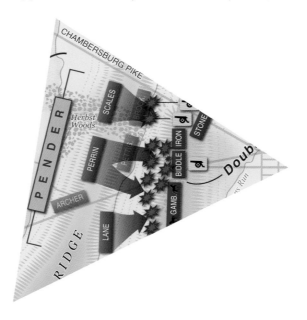

North of town, Coster's Union brigade makes a valiant but forlorn last stand against Early. Sent north earlier from Steinwehr's reserves on Cemetery Hill, when Barlow's distress on the knoll became evident, Coster has hastened his men up through town against a countervailing tide of fleeing comrades. And now, dug in at a brickyard on the northern outskirts of Gettysburg, Coster's Federals suffer the wrath of Early's brigades of Avery and Hays (Gordon deservedly resting from having helped destroy a third of a Union corps). Set upon from three sides and outnumbered two-to-one, Coster hasn't a prayer.

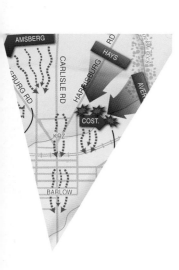

Amsberg can't do anything. He's not had much of a threat facing him—just some sharpshooters filling the gap between Doles and the rest of Rodes's Division. But to Amsberg's right and left, Confederate forces are pouring into the vacuum left by the increasingly general Union retreat: he must follow suit. Coster, whose men have stood firm in the brickyard for as long as humanly possible, and Amsberg, suffering huge casualties must join the chaotic tatters of *Schurz* (*Howard's* Corps) in full retreat or be ignominiously taken prisoner.

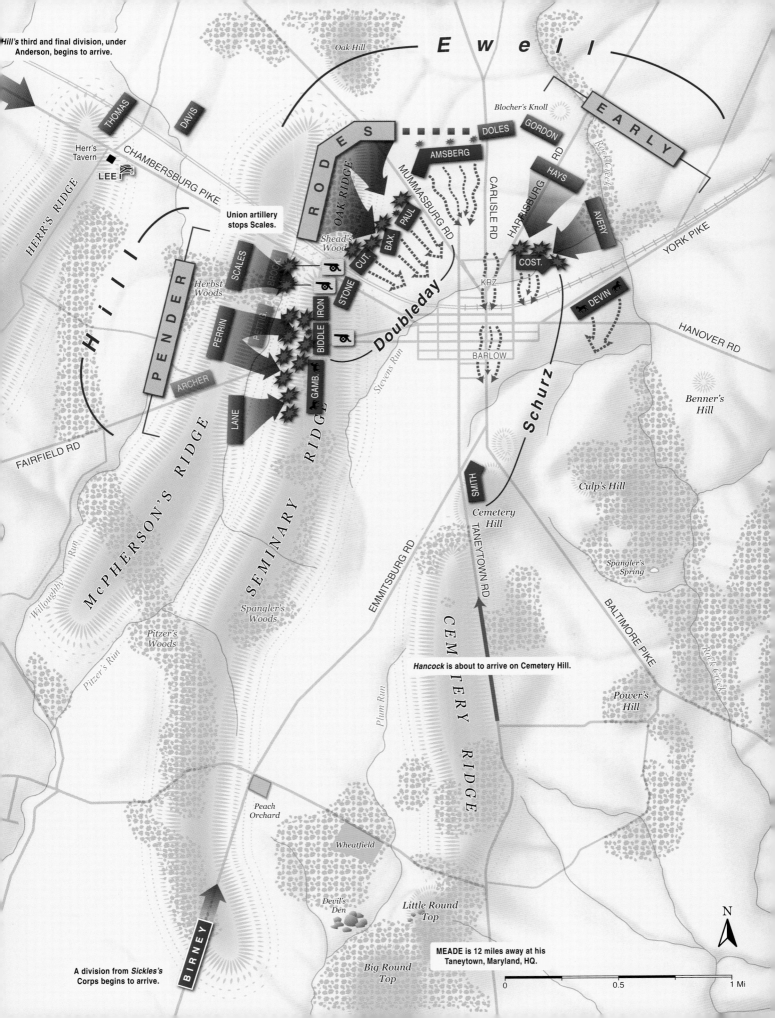

Hill's third and final division, under Anderson, begins to arrive.

E w e l l

Oak Hill

Blocher's Knoll

EARLY

RODES

DOLES

GORDON

AMSBERG

Rock Creek

HAYS

HARRISBURG RD

OAK RIDGE

MUMMASBURG RD

CARLISLE RD

AVERY

PAUL

Herr's Tavern

LEE

CHAMBERSBURG PIKE

THOMAS

DAVIS

BAX.

Shead's Wood

COST.

YORK PIKE

Union artillery stops Scales.

SCALES

CUT.

BROCK

STONE

KRZ.

DEVIN

HANOVER RD

Herbst Woods

PENDER

PERRIN

IRON

BIDDLE

Doubleday

Schurz

Doubleday

HERR'S RIDGE

HILL

ARCHER

LANE

GAMB.

BARLOW

Stevens Run

Benner's Hill

SEMINARY RIDGE

Culp's Hill

SMITH

Cemetery Hill

Spangler's Spring

Spangler's Woods

McPHERSON'S RIDGE

FAIRFIELD RD

Willoughby Run

Pitzer's Run

Pitzer's Woods

EMMITSBURG RD

TANEYTOWN RD

Hancock is about to arrive on Cemetery Hill.

C E M E T E R Y   R I D G E

BALTIMORE PIKE

Rock Creek

Power's Hill

Plum Run

Peach Orchard

Wheatfield

N

Devil's Den

Little Round Top

MEADE is 12 miles away at his Taneytown, Maryland, HQ.

BIRNEY

Big Round Top

A division from *Sickles's* Corps begins to arrive.

0   0.5   1 Mi

July 1, Late Afternoon

Collapse.

The Rebels strike the Union left north of the Fairfield Road west of town and the Union Seminary Ridge defense crumbles regiment by regiment.

For almost two hours lines of soldiers have been falling like mown wheat to the sharp discharge of sunlit steel and iron barrels in ranks, artillery hails of metal, foot soldiers advancing into it leaning forward with lowered chins as if into a stiff breeze. Color bearers crumple one after another—obvious targets. Other brave hearts spring to hold aloft again the giant battle flags that guide and inspire . . .

The Confederates drive the Yankees, lapping like rising floodwater to left and right in around the corners of the doomed Union resistance. Among many gallant holding actions by the Federals, Gamble's Brigade, of Buford's dismounted cavalry, makes a stand in Schultz's Woods that arguably delays the rout to come long enough to preserve some semblance of order in retreat. As has been emphasized, such delays (another being Coster's doomed stand at the brickyard) ripple forward in time in their impact on the three days of fighting. The first, of course, and greatly significant, being Buford's skirmishes against the Confederate vanguard massing down the Chambersburg Pike in the first-light hours.

The names of the valiant—7th Wisconsin, 24th Michigan, 26th North Carolina, 121st Pennsylvania, 151st Pennsylvania, 14th South Carolina—with their horrendous losses are, in our time, quiet . . . gratitude chiseled in granite . . .

Doubleday sees at his back the chaos of *Howard's* Corps (*Schurz* in temporary command)—Barlow's brigades followed by Krzyzanowski, Coster, Amsberg crowding frantically through the narrow streets and blind alleys of town. Doles is about to close in around *Doubleday's* rear even as from the west Pender is upon him. No choice: *Doubleday* retreats to Cemetery Hill, a retrograde movement (retreating while under attack), tactically extremely difficult, which his units carry off in relatively orderly fashion . . . orderly certainly compared to *Howard's/Schurz's* dismembered remnants lost in the tortuous jammed ways of Gettysburg, straggling, hiding, running, being scooped up as prisoners by the exultant Rebs: a chaos of scattered firing, bollixed units, careening carriages and wagons, aimless drays, and the stretcher-borne wounded . . .

The Union flight stops at Cemetery Hill, retrenching there. We saw *Howard* (nickname "Old Prayer Book") earlier decide to headquarter himself—and place Steinwehr's fresh division and artillery—on Cemetery Hill.

Hancock, just arrived, by dint of a noble command presence, clean-cut confidence, and hyperactive—yet collected—exercise of authority, attentively sorts out and directs the disordered human traffic of the Union rout, reinjecting assurance in the broken Yankee ranks.

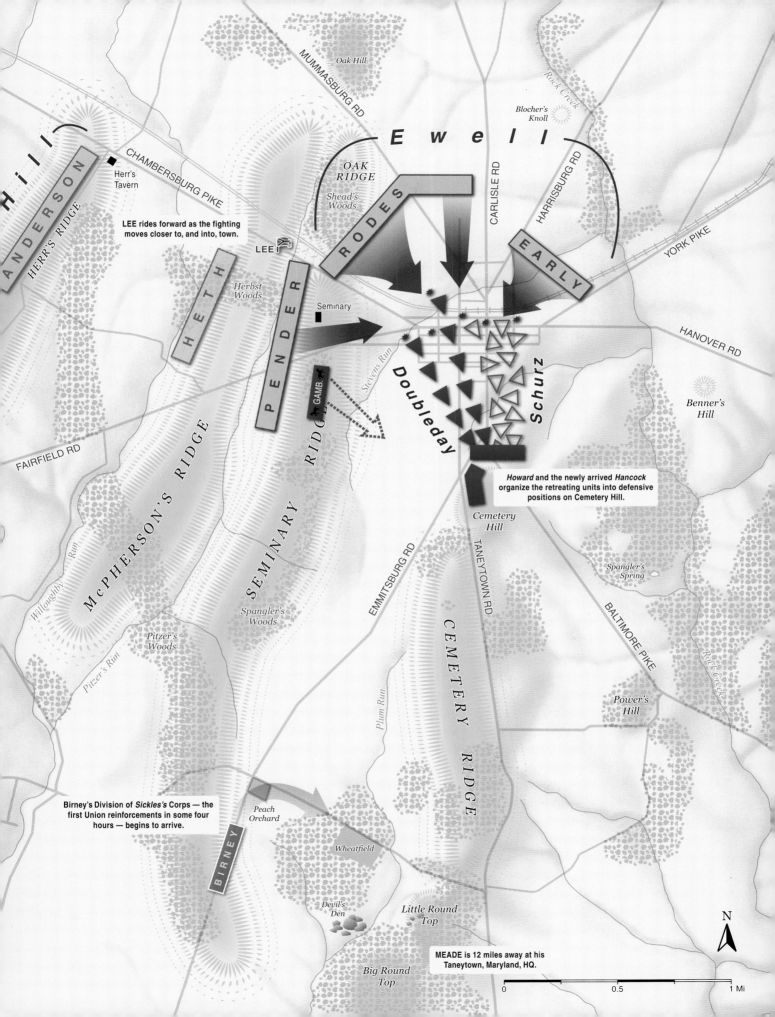

Hill

ANDERSON

HERR'S RIDGE

Herr's Tavern

CHAMBERSBURG PIKE

Ewell

MUMMASBURG RD

Oak Hill

Rock Rd

Blocher's Knoll

OAK RIDGE

RODES

Shead's Woods

CARLISLE RD

HARRISBURG RD

LEE rides forward as the fighting moves closer to, and into, town.

LEE

HETH

Herbst Woods

PENDER

Seminary

EARLY

YORK PIKE

HANOVER RD

Schurz

Doubleday

GAMB.

Stevens Run

Benner's Hill

McPHERSON'S RIDGE

Willoughby Run

FAIRFIELD RD

SEMINARY RIDGE

Howard and the newly arrived *Hancock* organize the retreating units into defensive positions on Cemetery Hill.

Cemetery Hill

Pitzer's Woods

Pitzer's Run

Spangler's Woods

EMMITSBURG RD

TANEYTOWN RD

Spangler's Spring

BALTIMORE PIKE

Rock Creek

Plum Run

CEMETERY RIDGE

Power's Hill

Birney's Division of *Sickles's* Corps — the first Union reinforcements in some four hours — begins to arrive.

Peach Orchard

Wheatfield

BIRNEY

Devil's Den

Little Round Top

MEADE is 12 miles away at his Taneytown, Maryland, HQ.

Big Round Top

N

0   0.5   1 Mi

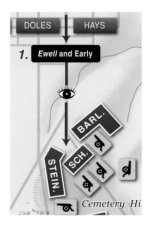

The afternoon's fight has ended in a clear Confederate victory.

The last hours of summer light see a key development, a negative one: the Rebels fail to take Cemetery Hill. They fail to take Culp's. *Ewell* and Early **[1]** ride south through the confusion of town. They observe the Yankee troops and artillery rallying on the steep heights of Cemetery Hill. *Ewell*, hot and pained by his infected stump, tells Early and Rodes to ready their divisions for an attack on the hill. Early has only Hays's and Avery's Brigades, spent and victorious, having allowed his other two fresh brigades to go northeast where a huge Union advance is rumored to be looming. (The rumor's false, and Early will later say he was skeptical—begging a question.) He tells *Ewell* that to attack, he—Early—and Rodes will need support from *Hill*. *Ewell* messages LEE: I want to attack, but to do so I will need support from *Hill*. At practically the same moment a message arrives from LEE telling *Ewell* to take Cemetery Hill "if practicable" but "avoid a general engagement."

LEE, on Seminary Ridge with *Longstreet* **[2]**, whose corps is hours away up the traffic-snarled pike, receives *Ewell's* message indicating an inclination to attack Cemetery Hill but needing help from *Hill* to do so. LEE has "help" on tap, a fresh Pender brigade plus an entire unused division, Anderson's, halted along Herr's Ridge. LEE has well-placed artillery. But *Longstreet's* pressing to maneuver southward—get in around and behind the Union left, plant ourselves between the Yankees and Washington, D.C. Make them attack *us*. LEE says no, he wants to attack, if the Federals are "there" (pointing to Cemetery Hill) "tomorrow." *Longstreet* allows that if they're there tomorrow, it'll be because they want us to attack. Unconvinced, LEE messages *Ewell*: *Attack if you think you can—you'll get no help from* Hill—*and don't get into a major fight.*

Ewell's mind changes about attacking Cemetery Hill. It's visibly well fortified. To carry it would be extremely difficult. Early's men are tired and two of his brigades elsewhere. Rodes's men are understandably exhausted. *Ewell's* third division (Johnson) is an hour off. It's hard to tell what LEE wants. Eying Culp's Hill—higher than Cemetery and dominant—*Ewell* thinks it empty. A party's sent to see. They report back: unoccupied. They're wrong: remnants of the Iron are in the trees on Culp's, bone tired. *Ewell* would like Early's available brigades to take Culp's. Early says no, we've been fighting all afternoon, send Johnson when he gets here. LEE meets with *Ewell*, Rodes, and Early at *Ewell's* HQ **[3]**. LEE wants an attack first thing in the morning. Early strenuously resists. All right, then could *Ewell* at least move his corps west to Seminary Ridge, i.e., align with the main Confederate position? No. With one voice LEE's generals protest. Too much post-battle work to be done. And it would kill morale to abandon ground so hard-won. LEE, baffled, acquiesces.

Toward sundown, when Johnson arrives, *Ewell* directs him to take Culp's Hill. This is news to Johnson, who gets into a profane dispute with Early.

Contrast this imprecision of decision and command—LEE and his generals in snappish dispute while the minutes tick away—with the behavior of *Reynolds*, *Hancock*, Buford, *Doubleday*—men MEADE, one way or another, entrusted to the scene. LEE carried this day, and a dramatic victory it was. Will he follow it up?

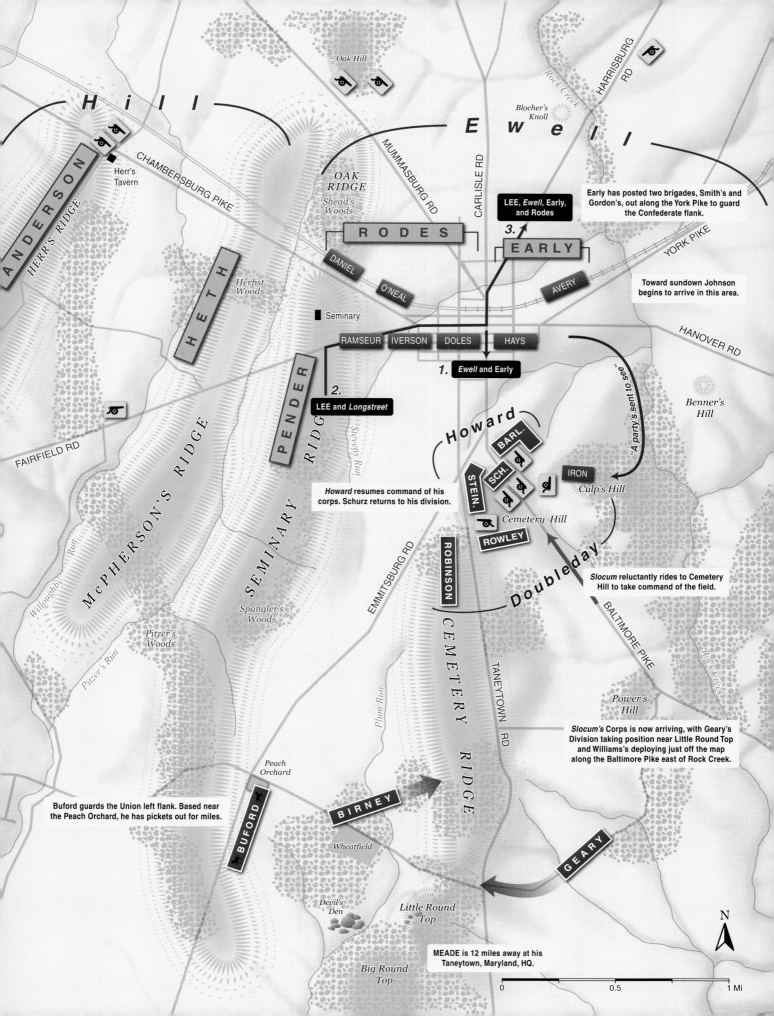

Hill

ANDERSON

HERR'S RIDGE

Herr's Tavern

CHAMBERSBURG PIKE

Oak Hill

Blocher's Knoll

Rock Creek

HARRISBURG RD

Ewell

Early has posted two brigades, Smith's and Gordon's, out along the York Pike to guard the Confederate flank.

OAK RIDGE

Shead's Woods

MUMMASBURG RD

CARLISLE RD

LEE, *Ewell*, Early, and Rodes

3.

RODES

EARLY

DANIEL

O'NEAL

AVERY

YORK PIKE

Toward sundown Johnson begins to arrive in this area.

HETH

Herbst Woods

■ Seminary

RAMSEUR   IVERSON   DOLES   HAYS

HANOVER RD

1. *Ewell* and Early

PENDER

2.

LEE and *Longstreet*

Benner's Hill

Stevens Run

"A party's sent to see"

Howard

BARL.

SCH.

IRON

STEIN.

Culp's Hill

Howard resumes command of his corps. Schurz returns to his division.

Cemetery Hill

ROWLEY

FAIRFIELD RD

McPHERSON'S RIDGE

Willoughby Run

SEMINARY RIDGE

Spangler's Woods

EMMITSBURG RD

ROBINSON

Doubleday

Slocum reluctantly rides to Cemetery Hill to take command of the field.

BALTIMORE PIKE

Rock Creek

Pitzer's Woods

Pitzer's Run

Power's Hill

CEMETERY RIDGE

TANEYTOWN RD

Slocum's Corps is now arriving, with Geary's Division taking position near Little Round Top and Williams's deploying just off the map along the Baltimore Pike east of Rock Creek.

Peach Orchard

Plum Run

BUFORD

BIRNEY

Buford guards the Union left flank. Based near the Peach Orchard, he has pickets out for miles.

Wheatfield

GEARY

Devil's Den

Little Round Top

MEADE is 12 miles away at his Taneytown, Maryland, HQ.

Big Round Top

N

0   0.5   1 Mi

Night. The thousands of campfires. Glittering, spatting with grease of fresh meat if you're lucky. There's coffee, talk, mending, letters get written, tales swapped, weapons are cleaned attentively . . . tinny music, a homesick tenor, a quiet horn . . . a tear . . . priceless sleep . . . tent streets of blocks are cities for the tens of thousands. Tethered horses in the dark are as exhausted as their masters . . . grain wagons stand. Orderlies scurry about. Troops flow in illumined shadow arriving and being fed into position. South of town the Union units begin to assume the form of an upside-down J. In and around Gettysburg, the Confederates face south.

Abroad in the shadows the grim work of the field hospitals continues. Across the farmland and littered among the trunks of the inky copses and groves the fallen bloat, explored by night's four-footed scavengers. The Union town of Gettysburg is gloom. Moans of the wounded fill church, home, schoolhouse, storage shed . . .

LEE at his headquarters near the Seminary wishes he had Stuart's cavalry to see with. His maps can't show LEE what he seeks to know. He has no *Stonewall Jackson*, killed at the height of the victory he created at Chancellorsville. *Jackson*, Aggression made flesh, if told to take Cemetery Hill "if practicable" would have been marching before the sentence ended. In a sense LEE has no *Longstreet* either. Say half a *Longstreet*, who wants nothing but to defend. LEE changes his mind about *Ewell's* position. A LEE messenger orders *Ewell* to move his corps west, to Seminary Ridge. Livid, *Ewell* orders himself hoisted and tied fast to his saddle and rides in the night through town to LEE, colorfully to demur. *Ewell* tells LEE that the enemy hasn't yet occupied Culp's Hill, which Johnson has seized or is about to, and from that height we can drive the Union men off Cemetery Hill. LEE gives in. It seems to have been left, between them, that come morning *Ewell* will wait until hearing Longstreet's guns in the attack on the Union left that LEE hopes for, then begin his own attack.

But Johnson doesn't take Culp's Hill. In the dark a party of Johnson's men advanced under a rising moon . . . but the hill holds the 7th Indiana now in addition to the Iron. Fired on, Johnson's men have retired.

MEADE arrives. He holds a wee-hours war council. He agrees with his generals who want to defend, emplaced, as they will be, securely on the high ground south of town that Buford, *Reynolds, Howard,* and *Hancock* saw the value of (and that *Longstreet* would love to hold). MEADE and his commanders are sure a Rebel assault will erupt come morning. It's what LEE does. MEADE saddles up. He takes a moonlit tour of his position, overseeing and monitoring the placement of guns and troops. His headquarters will be on Cemetery Ridge.

MEADE has taken his time coming to the battlefield, arguably, but, a good executive, he has been more often than not well represented by his delegated deputies. Still, the Army of the Potomac lost today, and momentum would seem on balance not to be with them, if LEE can pounce.

In the area are many fewer vultures than will be the case in forty-eight hours' time.

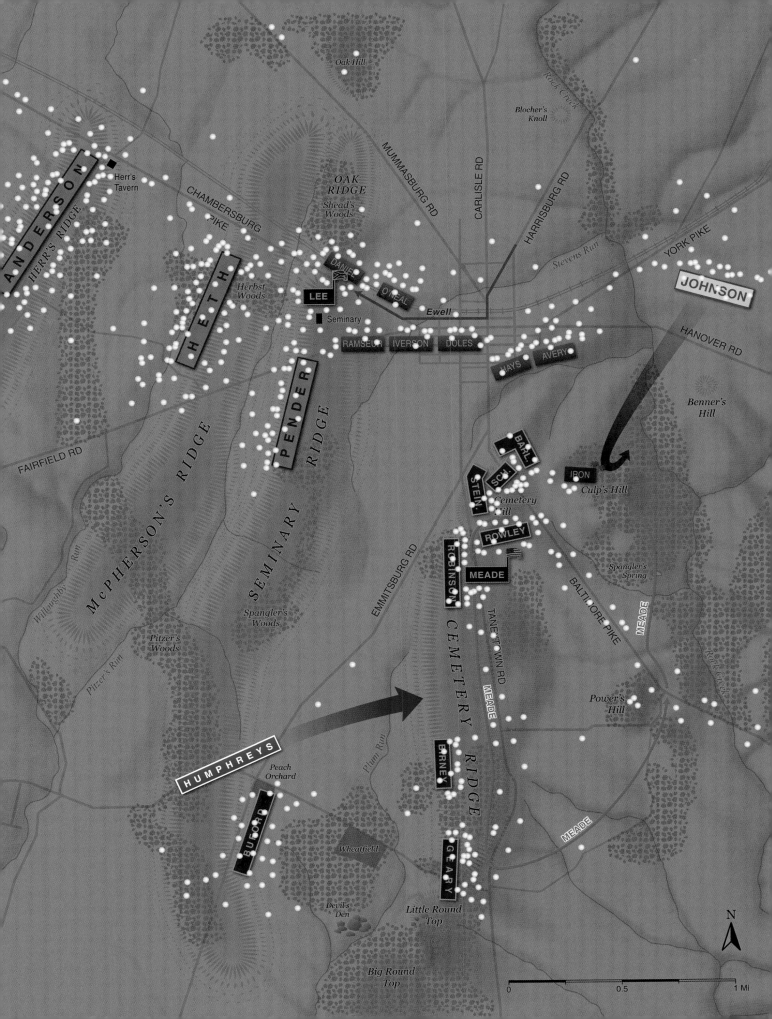

ANDERSON

HERR'S RIDGE

Herr's Tavern

CHAMBERSBURG PIKE

OAK RIDGE

Shead's Woods

MUMMASBURG RD

Oak Hill

Blocher's Knoll

Rock Creek

CARLISLE RD

HARRISBURG RD

Stevens Run

YORK PIKE

HETH

Herbst Woods

DANIEL

LEE

O'NEAL

Ewell

Seminary

RAMSEUR   IVERSON   DOLES

HAYS   AVERY

JOHNSON

HANOVER RD

PENDER RIDGE

SEMINARY RIDGE

McPHERSON'S RIDGE

FAIRFIELD RD

Willoughby Run

Pitzer's Woods

Pitzer's Run

Spangler's Woods

EMMITTSBURG RD

BARL.

SCH.

STEIN.

Cemetery Hill

ROWLEY

ROBINSON

MEADE

TANEYTOWN RD

MEADE

CEMETERY RIDGE

Benner's Hill

IRON

Culp's Hill

Spangler's Spring

BALTIMORE PIKE

MEADE

Power's Hill

Rock Creek

MEADE

HUMPHREYS

Peach Orchard

BUFORD

Wheatfield

BARNEY

Plum Run

GEARY

Devil's Den

Little Round Top

Big Round Top

N

0   0.5   1 Mi

ROBERT E. LEE is a Virginia aristocrat, God-fearing in his belief that once you've done your best, the outcome rests with Him. Soft-spoken, unfazed by shedding blood in service to the Cause, LEE gives orders suggestively and at times without definitiveness or follow-through ("avoid a general engagement"). This tendency will serve him ill at Gettysburg, where he's restless, occasionally to the point of seeming not to know what to do. A brilliant leader who employs the best and gives them their head, LEE pulled off his recent coup at Chancellorsville against overwhelming Union odds greatly with the help of Jeb Stuart's piercing "eyes and ears" and *Stonewall Jackson's* lion-hearted daring. Here, in the dark at Gettysburg with the sun rising on Day Two, LEE has no *Jackson*, no Jeb Stuart, and a *Longstreet* willfully refusing to accept LEE's attack philosophy.

LEE strangely doesn't push. But then, at Chancellorsville and elsewhere in his long victory-string, the gentle chief has not pushed exactly, rather giving his finest battle-lieutenants overall direction and letting them execute their ambitious best. It has worked. But his finest aren't with him. And LEE has crossed the Mason-Dixon Line. He's not defending soil of the South. *He's* the invader. Is God's will different in antislavery country?

The map opposite approximates the positions of the two great armies around sunrise, July 2, 1863.

LEE is in the town, east of it, west of it. His giant corps are under *Hill, Ewell.* *Hill* has the divisions of Anderson, Heth, Pender. East of *Hill, Ewell* commands Rodes, Early, Johnson. Confederate divisions are shown with their brigades. Note that two of Early's four brigades—Smith and Gordon—continue hanging out on their wild-goose watch for the phantom Union advance down the York Pike that will never come.

To the south MEADE's more numerous—each considerably smaller—corps are indicated: *Howard, Newton, Sickles, Slocum,* with those of their divisions present. *Hancock's* Corps is just beginning to arrive. (Union brigades would be too numerous, and placed into too small an area, to catalog here.)

Note also: Doubleday, whom *Howard* falsely accused to MEADE of having broken first yesterday, and whom MEADE has never liked, has been busted back to division command by MEADE. *Newton* replaces him.

Throughout the day still more units will be arriving, both sides.

After Day One's fight, losses are about even as a proportion of total manpower: some 7,000 men killed, wounded, or taken prisoner for LEE's smaller Army of Northern Virginia, some 9,000 for MEADE's Army of the Potomac. Subtracting these losses, MEADE has more than 35,000 men on the field, this dawn, and LEE in the neighborhood of 30,000. Over the three days of fighting, MEADE will have brought 95,000 men to the battle, LEE 75,000-odd.

MEADE continues to run his army methodically—not slowly—engineering the placement of his forces in all proper detail in their coiled

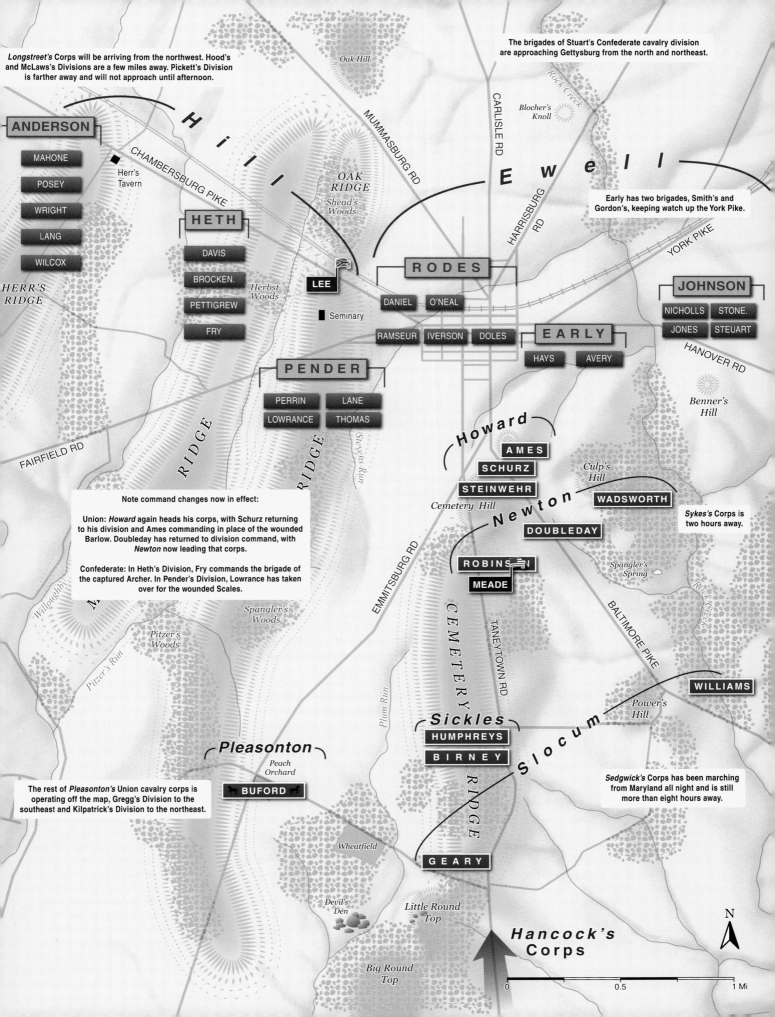

Longstreet's Corps will be arriving from the northwest. Hood's and McLaws's Divisions are a few miles away. Pickett's Division is farther away and will not approach until afternoon.

The brigades of Stuart's Confederate cavalry division are approaching Gettysburg from the north and northeast.

Oak Hill

Blocher's Knoll

Rock Creek

CARLISLE RD

MUMMASBURG RD

HARRISBURG RD

H i l l

E w e l l

CHAMBERSBURG PIKE

Herr's Tavern

OAK RIDGE

Shead's Woods

Early has two brigades, Smith's and Gordon's, keeping watch up the York Pike.

ANDERSON

MAHONE

POSEY

WRIGHT

LANG

WILCOX

HETH

DAVIS

BROCKEN.

PETTIGREW

FRY

Herbst Woods

HERR'S RIDGE

YORK PIKE

RODES

LEE

■ Seminary

DANIEL   O'NEAL

RAMSEUR   IVERSON   DOLES

EARLY

HAYS   AVERY

JOHNSON

NICHOLLS   STONE.

JONES   STEUART

HANOVER RD

Benner's Hill

PENDER

PERRIN   LANE

LOWRANCE   THOMAS

Stevens's Run

R I D G E

R I D G E

FAIRFIELD RD

Note command changes now in effect:

Union: *Howard* again heads his corps, with Schurz returning to his division and Ames commanding in place of the wounded Barlow. Doubleday has returned to division command, with *Newton* now leading that corps.

Confederate: In Heth's Division, Fry commands the brigade of the captured Archer. In Pender's Division, Lowrance has taken over for the wounded Scales.

Willoughby

Pitzer's Woods

Spangler's Woods

Pitzer's Run

EMMITTSBURG RD

Howard

AMES

SCHURZ

STEINWEHR

Cemetery Hill

Newton

DOUBLEDAY

ROBINSON

MEADE

Culp's Hill

WADSWORTH

Sykes's Corps is two hours away.

Spangler's Spring

Rock Creek

BALTIMORE PIKE

C E M E T E R Y

TANEYTOWN RD

WILLIAMS

Power's Hill

Slocum

Sedgwick's Corps has been marching from Maryland all night and is still more than eight hours away.

Pleasonton

Peach Orchard

🐎 **BUFORD** 🐎

The rest of *Pleasonton's* Union cavalry corps is operating off the map, Gregg's Division to the southeast and Kilpatrick's Division to the northeast.

R I D G E

Sickles

HUMPHREYS

BIRNEY

Plum Run

Wheatfield

GEARY

Devil's Den

Little Round Top

Hancock's Corps

Big Round Top

N

0   0.5   1 Mi

defense curve on the excellent high ground of Culp's and Cemetery Hills and on Cemetery Ridge in connected and balanced array, backed by reserves as practicable. MEADE has considered an offensive—but why do that? Always constructively worrying, he no doubt worries less as the morning unfolds without the attack he and his commanders had anticipated as characteristic of LEE. (Before today's action starts, however, MEADE will be forced to address one major pain in the neck.)

At dawn LEE sends out an experienced reconnoiterer, Captain Johnston, to try to locate the Union left flank down to LEE's southeast.

Longstreet arrives at LEE's headquarters. They confer with *Hill*, Heth, and Hood, who is out in front of his divison (not quite on the field) of *Longstreet's* Corps. LEE wants an assault on the Union left (southern) flank as soon as possible. *Hill* agrees so long as it can happen soon, before MEADE's defense can get any readier than it no doubt already is. *Longstreet* doesn't agree and says so. Get into a good defensive position, he repeats; get in around on MEADE's left: defend! This is old ground. LEE overrules *Longstreet*. *Longstreet* becomes apathetic, which is not like him.

MEADE continues his defensive preparations by—among other chores—sending an aide, his son George, a captain, down to where *Sickles's* Union corps, having arrived in the night, is supposedly assuming responsibility for terrain north-south on Cemetery Ridge.

Captain Meade finds that *Sickles* is not where MEADE wants him, namely extending from *Hancock* (Caldwell's Division) all the way down to the Little Round Top area.

Sickles has done nothing; his divisions are massed essentially where they arrived last night. *Sickles* is resting in his tent. He doesn't come out. Through an aide, he says he doesn't know where to go. This Captain Meade reports back to his dad, who sends him south again with clarification certain. This time young Meade finds *Sickles's* Corps abuzz with activity and actually speaks to *Sickles*, who he thinks "gets it." Certainly the corps is on the move. Young Meade reports back to his dad. Things seem ok. They aren't. *Sickles*, not without some justification, has been eying the higher ground out to his west along the Emmitsburg Road and in the Peach Orchard, where he would much prefer emplacing his troops—versus being attacked *from*.

Johnston returns from his first-light reconnaissance. He tells LEE he saw no Federals near the Round Tops. (Johnston's route—still debated—is approximated on the map.) This is intelligence LEE's eager for, desiring as he does to fix the location of the Union left flank in order that the *Longstreet* attack LEE intends can take informed aim. In reality there *are* Federals down there. Johnston should have seen—but missed in the misty early light, or from the vantage of some hill he mistook for the Round Tops, or by bad timing—Buford's cavalry, *Hancock's* Corps as it arrived, possibly Geary's Division (it may have left for Culp's), and Birney's Division, all within a mile of the Round Tops.

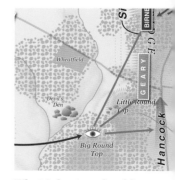

What Johnston should have seen.

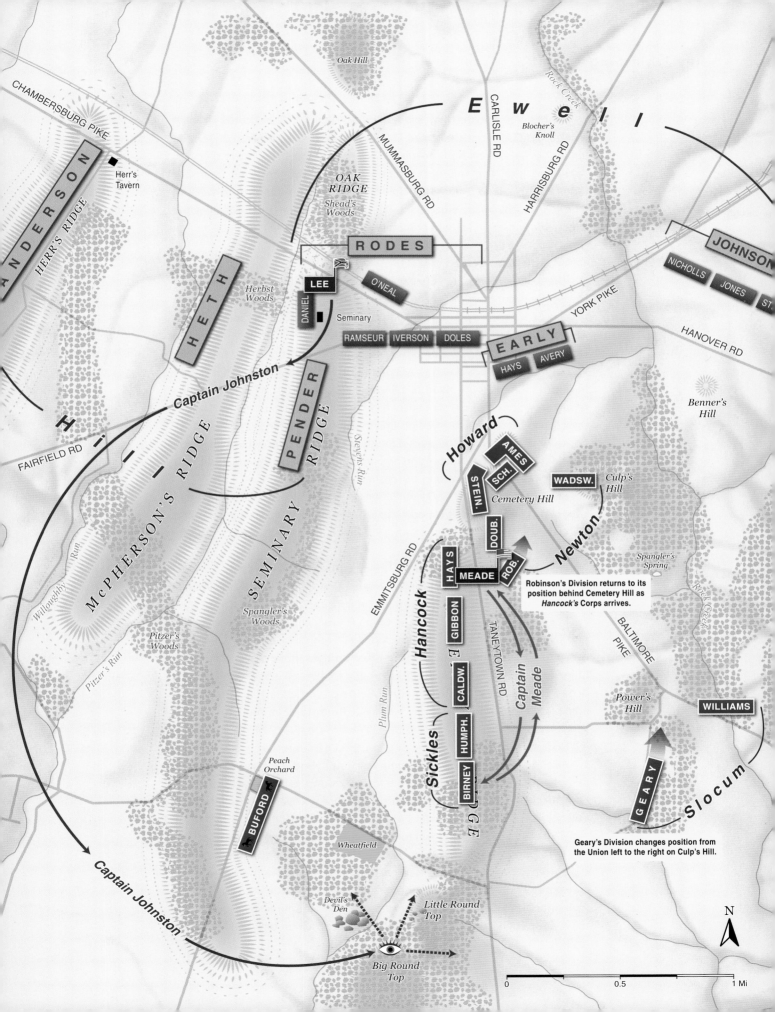

CHAMBERSBURG PIKE

Herr's Tavern

ANDERSON

HERR'S RIDGE

Oak Hill

OAK RIDGE

Shead's Woods

MUMMASBURG RD

E w e l l

CARLISLE RD

Blocher's Knoll

HARRISBURG RD

RODES

LEE

O'NEAL

DANIEL

HETH

Herbst Woods

Seminary

RAMSEUR   IVERSON   DOLES

EARLY

HAYS   AVERY

JOHNSON

NICHOLLS   JONES   ST.

YORK PIKE

HANOVER RD

Benner's Hill

HII

HETH

Captain Johnston

FAIRFIELD RD

PENDER RIDGE

Stevens Run

Howard

AMES

STEIN.

SCH.

WADSW.

Culp's Hill

Cemetery Hill

McPHERSON'S RIDGE

SEMINARY RIDGE

Spangler's Woods

Willoughby Run

Pitzer's Woods

Pitzer's Run

DOUB.

Newton

Spangler's Spring

Rock Creek

HAYS

MEADE

ROB.

Robinson's Division returns to its position behind Cemetery Hill as *Hancock's* Corps arrives.

Hancock

GIBBON

EMMITSBURG RD

CALDW.

TANEYTOWN RD

Captain Meade

BALTIMORE PIKE

Power's Hill

WILLIAMS

Sickles

HUMPH.

BIRNEY

Plum Run

RIDGE

Peach Orchard

BUFORD

Wheatfield

GEARY

Slocum

Geary's Division changes position from the Union left to the right on Culp's Hill.

Devil's Den

Little Round Top

Big Round Top

Captain Johnston

N

0   0.5   1 Mi

Johnston is a trusted staff officer, and his report to LEE accords with the picture of MEADE's position that LEE has developed from his own (terrain-limited) observations from northern Seminary Ridge. LEE doesn't question Johnston's intel. The failure to discover the blue units on lower Cemetery Ridge causes LEE to assume the Union left to be considerably northwest of where it actually *will* be when the Confederate attack starts. LEE will think the Union left ends *here* [1], when in reality, because of *Sickles*, it will be well to the south, *here* [2].

(MEADE wants *Sickles here* [3].)

The first elements of *Longstreet's* Corps begin to arrive, the brigades of Hood's Division, then McLaws's. In advance of his troops, McLaws rides to where LEE remains on Seminary Ridge, gathered with his staff and generals near his HQ. LEE ignores *Longstreet*, McLaws's direct superior, informing McLaws, and showing him on a map, right in front of *Longstreet*, where LEE wishes McLaws to position his division for the envisioned attack. That is, aiming up the Emmitsburg Road to blindside the Union left where Johnston's report has caused LEE erroneously to imagine it will be. *Longstreet* comes over and in front of LEE contradicts LEE, telling poor McLaws no, you will position your division ninety degrees differently. LEE says no, go where I said you should go. LEE has been accepting *no*'s right and left since yesterday, but here he insultingly stands his ground. *Longstreet's* mood is not good.

Longstreet tells McLaws to attack this way.

Peach Orchard

LEE tells McLaws to attack this way.

LEE tells *Hill* he wants Anderson's Division placed on Pender's right, so that *Longstreet's* two divisions (Hood/McLaws) will come in on Anderson's right once they've been marched south. LEE envisions Anderson, supported by Pender, hitting the Union center.

LEE rides through town to his other corps commander, *Ewell*, whose orders of last night gave him the impression that he was to attack early this morning in conjunction with *Longstreet's* main attack.

LEE knows the Yankees occupy Culp's Hill, which *Ewell* last evening led him to believe would be seized by Johnson—a big reason why LEE acquiesced to *Ewell's* keeping his corps in place on the left. So the enemy holds Culp's, and LEE has now surveyed the ground for himself and gauged the difficulty of making an assault on either Culp's or Cemetery Hill . . . will *Ewell* agree, at last, to move his corps west and south to LEE's right to support *Longstreet's* attack?

No.

All right then, LEE tells *Ewell*, you wait until you hear *Longstreet's* guns open in the south, then demonstrate (move around *as if* to attack), to divert MEADE's attention. Should "an opportunity" arise, go over to a real attack on Culp's.

LEE rides back through town to meet again with his other generals on the northern part of Seminary Ridge. He explains *Ewell's* role to them. LEE tells *Longstreet* to get his corps started on their march southward (and no small march it will be), without letting the Yankees see them, to get into position for their attack on MEADE's left. *Longstreet* wants to wait until he has at least two full divisions of his three, Law's Brigade of Hood's Division being still en route.

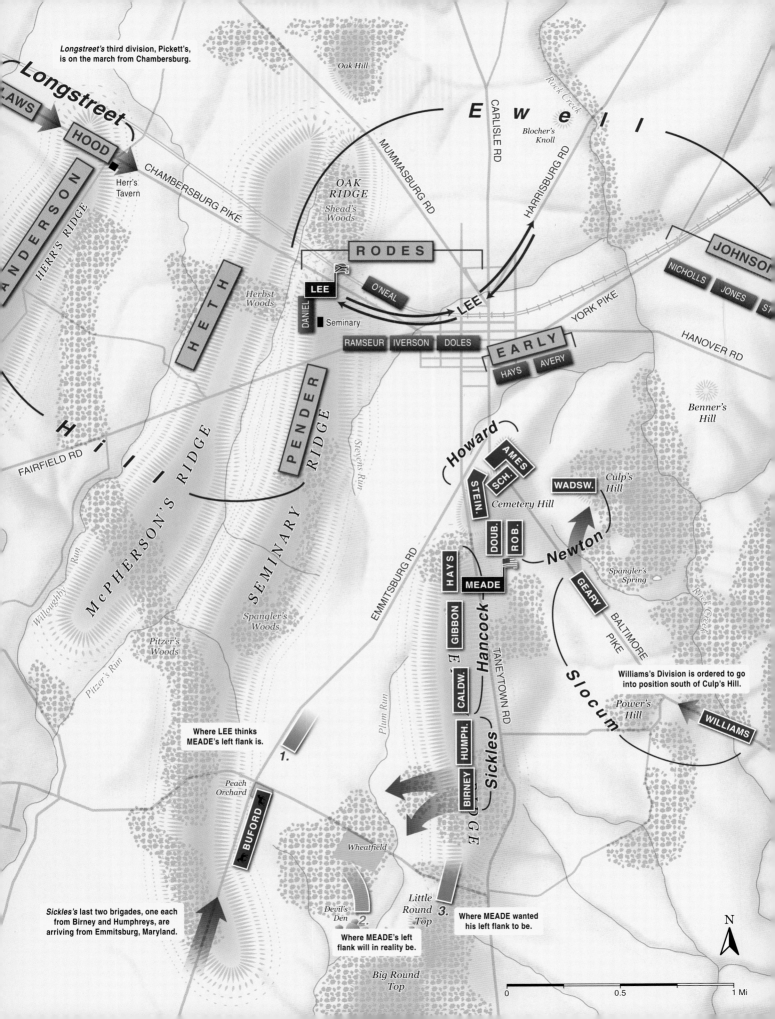

Longstreet's third division, Pickett's, is on the march from Chambersburg.

Longstreet

LAWS

HOOD

Herr's Tavern

CHAMBERSBURG PIKE

ANDERSON

Herr's Ridge

HETH

Herbst Woods

McPHERSON'S RIDGE

FAIRFIELD RD

Willoughby Run

Pitzer's Run

Pitzer's Woods

Peach Orchard

BUFORD

Devil's Den

Wheatfield

2.

Where MEADE's left flank will in reality be.

Sickles's last two brigades, one each from Birney and Humphreys, are arriving from Emmitsburg, Maryland.

Oak Hill

OAK RIDGE

Shead's Woods

MUMMASBURG RD

RODES

LEE

O'NEAL

DANIEL

Seminary

RAMSEUR   IVERSON   DOLES

SEMINARY RIDGE

PENDER

Stevens Run

Spangler's Woods

EMMITSBURG RD

Where LEE thinks MEADE's left flank is.

1.

Plum Run

Little Round Top

3.

Where MEADE wanted his left flank to be.

Big Round Top

E w e **l l**

Blocher's Knoll

Rock Creek

CARLISLE RD

HARRISBURG RD

LEE

YORK PIKE

EARLY

HAYS   AVERY

JOHNSON

NICHOLLS   JONES   ST

HANOVER RD

Benner's Hill

Howard

AMES

SCH.

STEIN.

Cemetery Hill

DOUB.   ROB.

Newton

WADSW.

Culp's Hill

Spangler's Spring

GEARY

BALTIMORE PIKE

Rock Creek

Slocum

Williams's Division is ordered to go into position south of Culp's Hill.

Power's Hill

WILLIAMS

HAYS

MEADE

GIBBON

Hancock

CALDW.

HUMPH.

BIRNEY

Sickles

TANEYTOWN RD

R I D G E

N

0   0.5   1 Mi

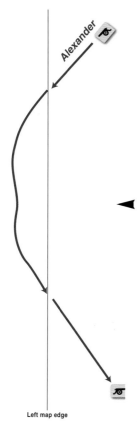

Left map edge

This further delay LEE approves, overtly or tacitly. *Longstreet* is foot-dragging. Even if LEE had in fact failed to make specifics of an attack plan clear to *Longstreet* before this (as *Longstreet* will later claim, surely mistakenly), still, as a seasoned campaigner *Longstreet* should have anticipated his corps would be needed, leaving aside for what, as soon as possible this crucial day. He should have been better attending to the expedition of its arrival. Yet even now, squirming sidelong from under a virtual direct order, *Longstreet*, in waiting for Law's Brigade to show, could easily also at the same time be starting the at-hand majority of his infantry south in the direction LEE wants. *Longstreet* does not. He does start his artillery, directing Col. Porter Alexander, at the head of the largest gun battalion in LEE's army, south on a scouting-out mission to ascertain and utilize advantageous routes and positions, pre-attack.

Per LEE's plan, Anderson swings down to face MEADE's center, with Heth in reserve. Geary's Federals are in place on Culp's Hill.

MEADE meanwhile at his headquarters receives *Sickles*, who professes to remain uncertain where MEADE wants his divisions; MEADE makes it clear yet again: I want your right beside *Hancock*; I want your left where Geary was earlier (see pp. 50–51). On his map MEADE indicates the hill called today "Little Round Top." Some accounts have MEADE taking *Sickles* outside the little headquarters building and pointing south at the visible hilltop.

It seems to MEADE that *Sickles* has understood. So, when *Sickles* asks if, within the confines of what MEADE has just ordered, he may place his men as he sees fit, MEADE agrees. This should go without saying. But it's a lawyer's question—*Sickles* is an attorney in civilian life and, given his extreme uneasiness with the position MEADE has assigned him, is leaving himself wiggle room.

Sickles rides south to his corps. He greatly dislikes the ground where MEADE wants him, i.e., along the high ground of Cemetery Ridge north-south from *Hancock* down to Little Round Top. If *Sickles* thus distributes his units, then, to his west, facing him, will be *higher* ground, where Confederate artillery for example could constitute a mortal threat. All morning long *Sickles* has not made a serious effort to occupy the Cemetery Ridge position MEADE desires. Some accounts indicate Sickles had parties out to his west in the morning taking down fences, something he never would've countenanced had he not contemplated venturing in that direction, which, in fact, he, despite the clearest possible instructions from MEADE, has Birney do in force, as shown.

Around noon, *Longstreet* at last gets started. McLaws's four brigades go first, marching in column, followed by Hood's four. *Longstreet*'s attack force will follow in Alexander's tracks, initially, snaking off the map in search of a route not visible to Union eyes. Miles long, the march is not led by *Longstreet*, LEE having assigned Captain Johnston (of the early-hours reconnaissance of the Round Tops) to guide and advise. Though clearly LEE did not intend Johnston to command the march, *Longstreet* spends

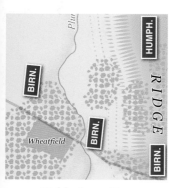

Sickles's position

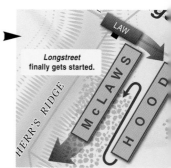

Longstreet finally gets started.

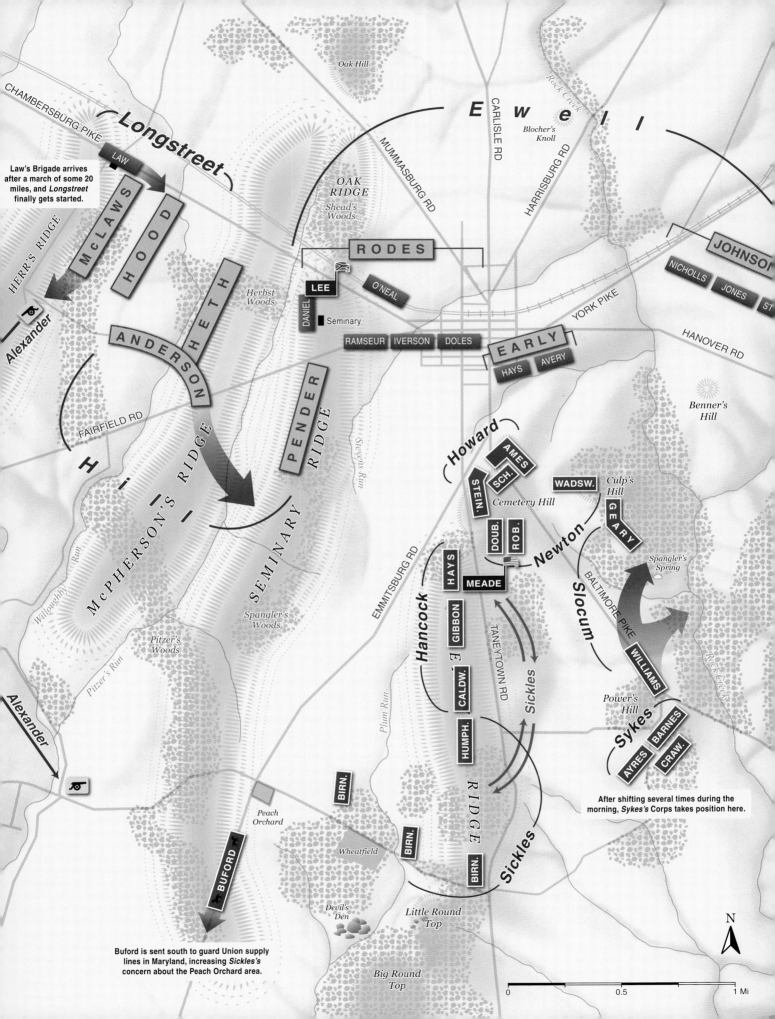

CHAMBERSBURG PIKE

Longstreet

LAW

Law's Brigade arrives after a march of some 20 miles, and *Longstreet* finally gets started.

McLAWS

HOOD

Alexander

HERR'S RIDGE

HETH

ANDERSON

FAIRFIELD RD

H i l l

McPHERSON'S RIDGE

Willoughby Run

Pitzer's Woods

Pitzer's Run

Alexander

Buford is sent south to guard Union supply lines in Maryland, increasing *Sickles's* concern about the Peach Orchard area.

Oak Hill

OAK RIDGE

Shead's Woods

Herbst Woods

DANIEL

LEE

Seminary

RAMSEUR   IVERSON   DOLES

PENDER

RIDGE

SEMINARY

Stevens Run

Spangler's Woods

EMMITSBURG RD

Peach Orchard

BIRN.

Wheatfield

BIRN.

BIRN.

Devil's Den

Little Round Top

Big Round Top

MUMMASBURG RD

E w e l l

CARLISLE RD

Blocher's Knoll

HARRISBURG RD

RODES

O'NEAL

EARLY

HAYS   AVERY

YORK PIKE

HANOVER RD

JOHNSON

NICHOLLS   JONES   ST

Benner's Hill

Rock Creek

Howard

AMES

SCH.

STEIN.

Cemetery Hill

DOUB.   ROB.

HAYS

MEADE

Hancock

GIBBON

CALDW.

HUMPH.

R I D G E

WADSW.

Culp's Hill

GEARY

Spangler's Spring

Newton

Slocum

BALTIMORE PIKE

WILLIAMS

Power's Hill

Sykes

AYRES   BARNES   CRAW.

TANEYTOWN RD

Sickles

Sickles

Plum Run

After shifting several times during the morning, *Sykes's* Corps takes position here.

BUFORD

0   0.5   1 Mi

N

the first half of it riding at the rear with Hood's Division, as opposed to being at the front of his columns where we have seen virtually all corps commanders heretofore, *Longstreet* included. In a later account *Longstreet* will say that LEE wanted Johnston, a captain, to lead (as opposed to guiding and advising). Even if this were so, still, by spending the first half of his march toward its rear, *Longstreet* is manifestly endeavoring to expedite nothing.

In the north, Stuart arrives at last with his prodigal cavalry. At LEE's headquarters, Stuart receives a greeting from his boss that leaves no doubt as to LEE's extreme displeasure. LEE icily posts Stuart's Division of horsemen near *Ewell*, whose corps is still in its—to LEE—worrisomely out-of-touch position northeast of where LEE is setting up his main line.

Sickles ventures out even farther west, even farther away from where MEADE wants him. Birney occupies the Peach Orchard area and a line running to the southeast. Humphreys leaves Cemetery Ridge. There's some logic to *Sickles* wanting to hold, rather than face head-on, this higher ground. But what he is doing is in willful contravention of MEADE's express wishes. It gravely upsets the balance of the defensive line MEADE is carefully constructing, creating, as it does, holes of open opportunity for the enemy to punch in through (green arrows at left).

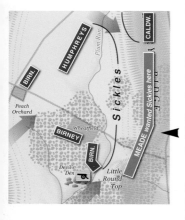

Note, by contrast, the Federal positions north of *Sickles*. Not perfect, shaped by terrain (good for defense in some places, less so in others) and based on guesswork about where LEE is most likely to attack, they nevertheless exemplify compact solidity. And—this is important—where there are holes or weak spots, reserves generally stand or are being positioned ready to plug or strengthen MEADE's line as necessary (Doubleday and Robinson near Cemetery Hill, for example).

Off our map to the left, *Longstreet's* march, shielded by many ridges from Federal view, reaches an approximate halfway mark, where, McLaws at the head of his division realizes, and Captain Johnston acting as guide realizes, they can now be seen from Little Round Top. (They don't think Little Round Top is occupied per se, but individual signalers and lookouts surely are observing from its height.) So, to avoid the massive advance behind them being seen, now they must find a more concealed way to proceed. *Longstreet* arrives. It's decided to countermarch (return the way they came) and take a more circuitous, less visible route. McLaws says he knows of one. But Porter Alexander's artillery passed this way earlier. And at that time Alexander pointed out—to someone—it's unclear whom—a route, less time-consuming but sufficiently concealed, that he, Alexander, found. For some reason this route is not taken. *Longstreet's* march will coil back on itself and proceed a far-longer-than-necessary way. Meanwhile, Hood in his well-known enthusiasm has marched his division into the rear of the halted McLaws. The air turns blue. The jammed-up line extends all the way back northward to Law's Brigade at the origin point. LEE's plan to get the jump on MEADE with an early-morning attack never had a chance.

To go back the way they've come, it would make sense for Hood, in

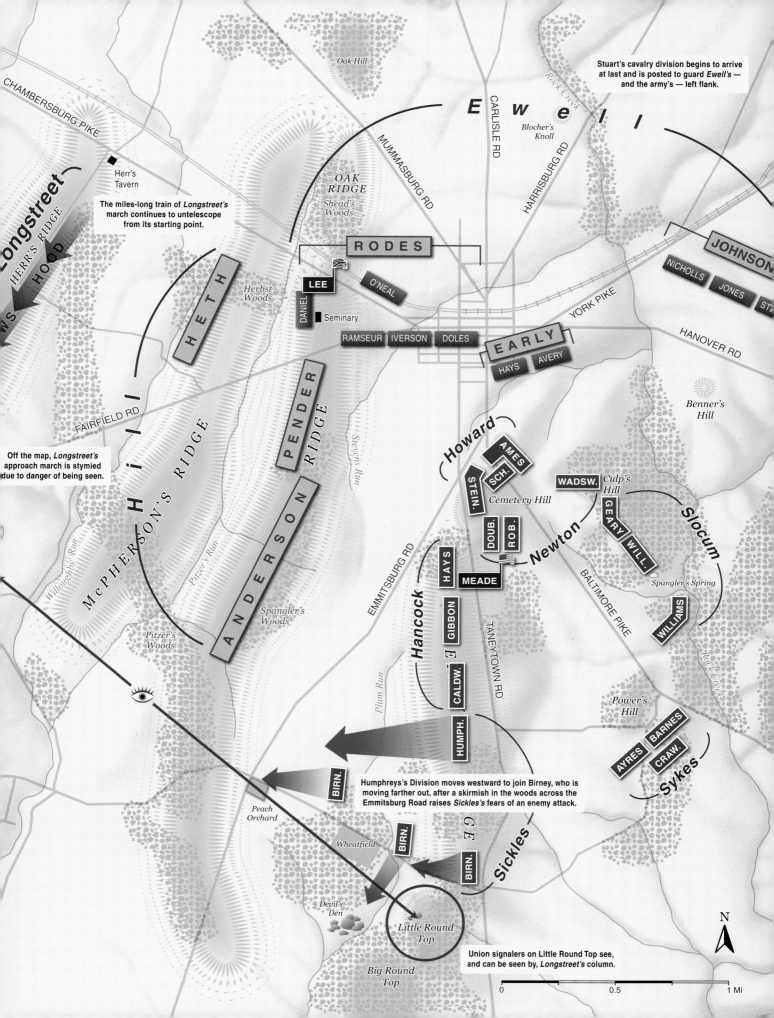

CHAMBERSBURG PIKE

Herr's Tavern

Longstreet
HERR'S RIDGE
HOOD

The miles-long train of *Longstreet's*
march continues to untelescope
from its starting point.

Oak Hill

E   w   e   l   l

Stuart's cavalry division begins to arrive
at last and is posted to guard *Ewell's* —
and the army's — left flank.

Rock Creek

CARLISLE RD

Blocher's
Knoll

HARRISBURG RD

MUMMASBURG RD

OAK
RIDGE

Shead's
Woods

RODES

JOHNSON

NICHOLLS   JONES   ST.

HETH

Herbst
Woods

LEE

O'NEAL

DANIEL   ■ Seminary

RAMSEUR   IVERSON   DOLES

YORK PIKE

EARLY

HAYS   AVERY

HANOVER RD

Benner's
Hill

Off the map, *Longstreet's*
approach march is stymied
due to danger of being seen.

McPHERSON'S RIDGE

PENDER RIDGE

ANDERSON RIDGE

FAIRFIELD RD

Stevens Run

Willoughby Run

Pitzer's Run

Spangler's
Woods

Pitzer's
Woods

Howard

AMES
SCH.
STEIN.

Cemetery Hill

WADSW.

Culp's
Hill

GEARY   WILL.

Slocum

Newton

DOUB.   ROB.

MEADE

Spangler's Spring

Hancock

HAYS

BALTIMORE PIKE

WILLIAMS

Rock Creek

EMMITSBURG RD

GIBBON

CALDW.

TANEYTOWN RD

Power's
Hill

Plum Run

HUMPH.

AYRES   BARNES

CRAW.

Sykes

Humphreys's Division moves westward to join Birney, who is
moving farther out, after a skirmish in the woods across the
Emmitsburg Road raises *Sickles's* fears of an enemy attack.

BIRN.

Peach
Orchard

Wheatfield

BIRN.

G   E

BIRN.

Sickles

Devil's
Den

Little Round
Top

Big Round
Top

Union signalers on Little Round Top see,
and can be seen by, *Longstreet's* column.

N

0   0.5   1 Mi

the rear and thus nearer the new route, to go first while McLaws turns around. But McLaws is in a terrible mood over the mix-ups and insists on keeping the lead. Vexedly, *Longstreet* lets him. Hood waits while McLaws turns around. Needless hours are added. Thus—approximated—*Longstreet's* march:

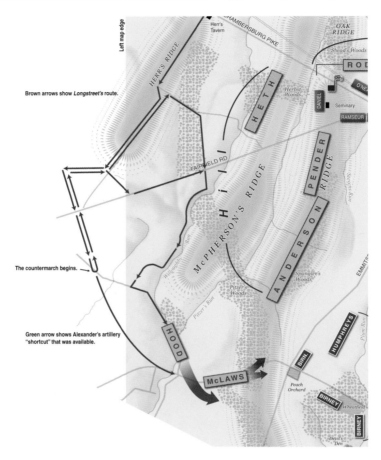

MEADE summons his generals for a consultation, from which *Sickles* asks to be excused. MEADE says no. *Sickles* arrives at MEADE's headquarters. MEADE has learned that *Sickles* has pushed out west all the way to the Peach Orchard. The famous MEADE temper goes into high gear; he rides behind *Sickles*, as if monitoring a child, south to *Sickles's* position.

Longstreet's long march finally begins to end, well past midafternoon, with the emergence of the first elements of McLaws's Division onto Seminary Ridge in front of the Peach Orchard. Since LEE has told McLaws, *Longstreet*, and Hood that they will, in attacking up the Emmitsburg Road, find MEADE's left dangling unanchored somewhere ahead, the Confederates are stunned to find *Sickles's* troops and guns seeming to teem before them. *Sickles's* fighters open fire on the Confederate arrival. The fight is on. Bitter it will be.

McLaws's Division begins to spread in battle array to meet the surprise of *Sickles's* units. (This will put McLaws in approximately the configuration *Long-street* delineated—and was overridden on by LEE—at their testy morning meeting.) Hood was, in the original plan, to deploy behind McLaws but now will be placed on McLaws's right, it being unclear when, how, or if *Longstreet* so decided.

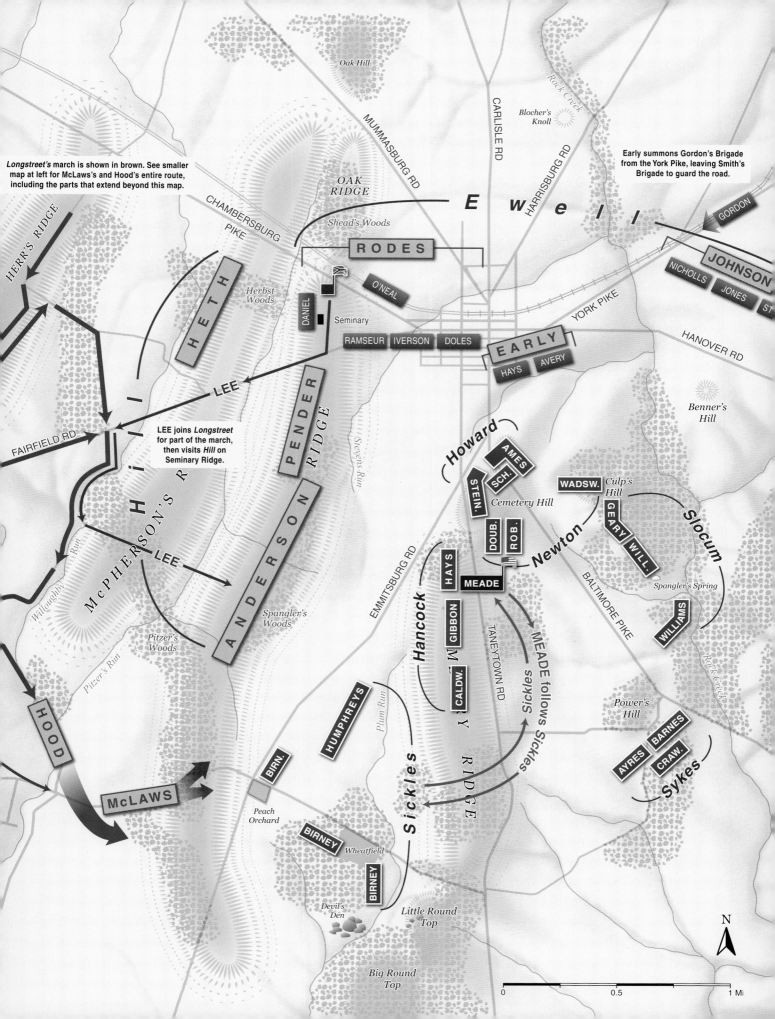

Longstreet's march is shown in brown. See smaller map at left for McLaws's and Hood's entire route, including the parts that extend beyond this map.

Early summons Gordon's Brigade from the York Pike, leaving Smith's Brigade to guard the road.

Oak Hill

Blocher's Knoll

MUMMASBURG RD

CARLISLE RD

HARRISBURG RD

Rock Creek

OAK RIDGE

CHAMBERSBURG PIKE

Shead's Woods

E w e l l

GORDON

RODES

O'NEAL

JOHNSON

NICHOLLS

JONES

ST

HERR'S RIDGE

HETH

Herbst Woods

DANIEL

Seminary

RAMSEUR   IVERSON   DOLES

EARLY

HAYS   AVERY

YORK PIKE

HANOVER RD

LEE

FAIRFIELD RD

LEE joins *Longstreet* for part of the march, then visits *Hill* on Seminary Ridge.

PENDER RIDGE

ANDERSON RIDGE

Stevens's Run

Benner's Hill

H i l l

McPHERSON'S RIDGE

LEE

Willoughby Run

Spangler's Woods

Pitzer's Woods

Pitzer's Run

Howard

AMES

SCH.

STEIN.

Cemetery Hill

WADSW.

Culp's Hill

DOUB.   ROB.

Newton

GEARY   WILL.

Slocum

Spangler's Spring

HAYS

MEADE

EMMITSBURG RD

GIBBON

Hancock

CALDW.

MEADE follows Sickles

Sickles

TANEYTOWN RD

BALTIMORE PIKE

WILLIAMS

Rock Creek

HOOD

McLAWS

BIRN.

HUMPHREYS

Plum Run

Peach Orchard

BIRNEY

Wheatfield

Sickles

Y RIDGE

Power's Hill

AYRES   BARNES   CRAW.

Sykes

BIRNEY

Devil's Den

Little Round Top

Big Round Top

N

0   0.5   1 Mi

The Confederates have found a Union position out of all conformation to what they expected. Instead of a vulnerable, full-of-holes Yankee left somewhere ahead up the Emmitsburg Road that they can blindside, they confront a heavy Union force smack in their faces where *Sickles* has pushed out west. (*Sickles* is indeed "full of holes," but this is not apparent to the Southerners in the initial moment.)

McLaws and Hood want to adjust, address the reality, attack intelligently.

To make an assault as planned, *up* the Emmitsburg Road, would be as if a boxer at close quarters turned sideways and flailed away at ninety degrees to his opponent.

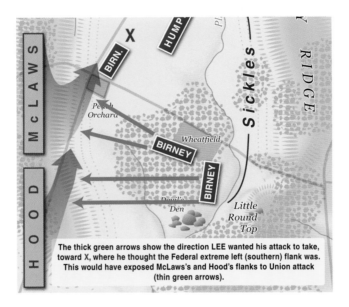

The thick green arrows show the direction LEE wanted his attack to take, toward X, where he thought the Federal extreme left (southern) flank was. This would have exposed McLaws's and Hood's flanks to Union attack (thin green arrows).

Longstreet peevishly rejoins no, LEE told us to attack up the road, we attack up the road. *Longstreet* is torn. There's no one way he feels. The experienced strategist wars with the loyal fighter; he knows all too well that LEE is thinking badly and acting vaguely; they could lose here. *Longstreet* was absent at the recent glory of Chancellorsville. Stuart and, immortally, *Jackson* pulled Chancellorsville off. Here at Gettysburg, *Jackson's* gone and Stuart absent-when-it-counted. LEE's working with "just *Longstreet*." If it's a defeat (and if it is, it could be a decisive one in the war), what will be said?

It's a sure thing they won't blame Bobby Lee.

During the fierce artillery duel, awaiting the attack order the Rebel foot soldiers shield themselves from the balls exploding around them, trying to become one with the earth, yearning for a command to advance—*anything* but this hapless waiting under air-bursting, dirt-furrowing fire.

Sickles, realizing his folly—the vulnerability of his unauthorized position—offers to withdraw. Too late. The guns have opened. MEADE tells *Sickles* he must fight. MEADE promises reinforcements. MEADE gallops off

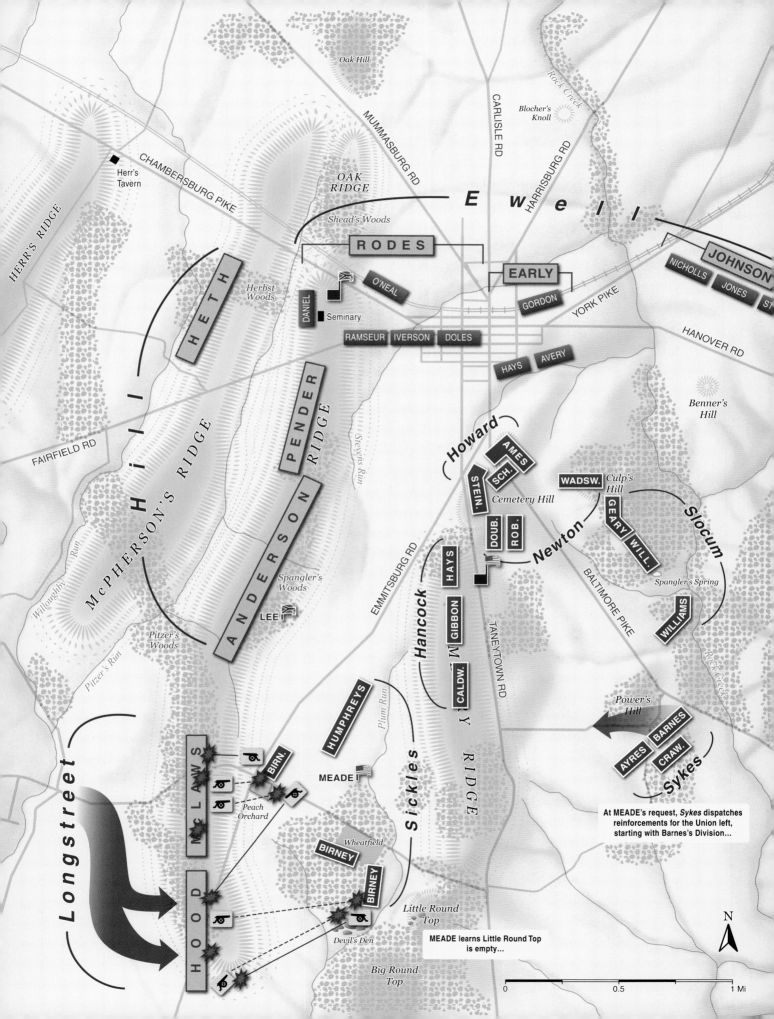

Herr's Tavern

CHAMBERSBURG PIKE

HERR'S RIDGE

Oak Hill

MUMMASBURG RD

OAK RIDGE

Shead's Woods

Herbst Woods

McPHERSON'S RIDGE

FAIRFIELD RD

Willoughby Run

Pitzer's Woods

Pitzer's Run

E   w   e   l   l

CARLISLE RD

Blocher's Knoll

Rock Creek

HARRISBURG RD

RODES

HETH

DANIEL

Seminary

O'NEAL

EARLY

GORDON

YORK PIKE

JOHNSON

NICHOLLS   JONES   ST

HANOVER RD

RAMSEUR   IVERSON   DOLES

HAYS   AVERY

PENDER

ANDERSON

RIDGE

Stevens Run

Spangler's Woods

LEE

Benner's Hill

Howard

AMES

STEIN.

SCH.

WADSW.

Culp's Hill

Cemetery Hill

GEARY   WILL.

Slocum

DOUB.   ROB.

Newton

Spangler's Spring

EMMITSBURG RD

Hancock

HAYS

GIBBON

CALDW.

BALTIMORE PIKE

WILLIAMS

Rock Creek

HUMPHREYS

MEADE

Sickles

Plum Run

RIDGE

Power's Hill

TANEYTOWN RD

BARNES

AYRES   CRAW.

Sykes

McLAWS

BIRN.

Peach Orchard

Wheatfield

BIRNEY

At **MEADE**'s request, *Sykes* dispatches reinforcements for the Union left, starting with Barnes's Division...

Longstreet

HOOD

BIRNEY

Little Round Top

Devil's Den

Big Round Top

MEADE learns Little Round Top is empty...

N

0   0.5   1 Mi

precipitously, briefly not in control of his spooked mount. A mistake has been made, a bad one. *Sickles* made it, MEADE will fix it, with ordered and unordered help from trusted subordinates. The afternoon's terrible business having begun, the coming hours will see some of the direst fighting of the war, the rolls of wounded and dead mounting by the minute.

Longstreet, not at the front, feels he has given McLaws a clear attack order. But McLaws sends a message to *Longstreet* to the effect that the Federals are in much greater number than we were told to expect. With screeching cannon fire crisscrossing overhead, McLaws prepares his division to attack this stronger, unanticipated Union force head on—*across* the road.

Back a message comes from *Longstreet*: Attack now; I'm sure it's a small number before you. Hearing no rifle fire such as signals an infantry attack, *Longstreet* repeats his message. McLaws, a corpulent, curly-haired and bearded Ghost-of-Christmas-Present look-alike, peevedly replies that he'll attack in five minutes. Before that short time is up, however, a new order arrives from *Longstreet*: Wait. Let Hood get all the way into position beside you.

An enthusiastic fighter, Hood is extremely reluctant to attack according to the original order, that is, directly up the Emmitsburg Road (see previous page). To do so would leave him defenseless against fire and attack from the side.

Hood has noticed Big Round Top, as it is called today. He's had it scouted. It's not occupied. There's a route over easy terrain by which one might get in around and behind the Union left flank—the actual one—and cause significant trouble, Hood feels. He asks permission to do this. *Longstreet* replies no, LEE ordered an attack *up* the road; that is what we must do.

Gibbon moves out two regiments to cover Humphreys's right. Union artillery chief *Hunt* bolsters *Sickles* with more cannon (right). MEADE is assiduously working to get still more reinforcements into *Sickles's* gaps.

Peach Orchard

Hood attacks. Not north-northeast, up the Emmitsburg Road, but, instead and rationally, going after the Yankees he sees before him: Birney's Federal infantry.

Hood's strike will hit Birney's left.

. . . fighting is first maneuvering to get—in relation to your foe—into the most advantageous position. Then you shoot at each other—artillery, rifles, mortars—hoping the combination of this and advantageous position will drive your foe away or to surrender. If not, you advance, charge, with or without firing. Closer, perhaps with bayonets fixed. If that doesn't work, you may be driven back yourself or else blade-fight, shoot at a range of mere feet, death-struggle hand-to-hand until one side runs or gives up . . .

Whether this attack is in defiance of *Longstreet's* order to attack up the road or occurs with *Longstreet's* sudden blessing, grudging or no, accounts do not make clear.

Law's Brigade leads.

It's 4:30.

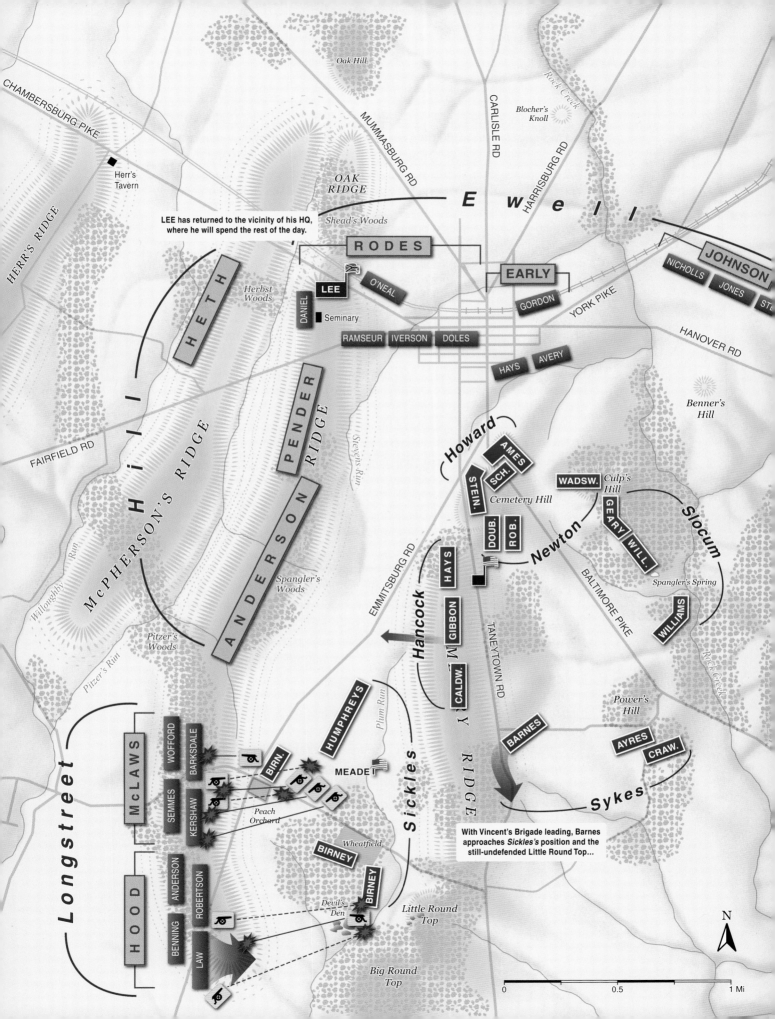

CHAMBERSBURG PIKE

Herr's Tavern

HERR'S RIDGE

Oak Hill

MUMMASBURG RD

CARLISLE RD

Blocher's Knoll

Rock Creek

HARRISBURG RD

E w e l l

OAK RIDGE

Shead's Woods

LEE has returned to the vicinity of his HQ, where he will spend the rest of the day.

RODES

EARLY

JOHNSON

NICHOLLS   JONES   STE...

HETH

Herbst Woods

DANIEL   LEE   O'NEAL

Seminary

GORDON

YORK PIKE

HANOVER RD

RAMSEUR   IVERSON   DOLES

HAYS   AVERY

PENDER

ANDERSON RIDGE

McPHERSON'S HILL

FAIRFIELD RD

Willoughby Run

Stevens Run

Spangler's Woods

Pitzer's Woods

Pitzer's Run

Benner's Hill

Howard

AMES

SCH.

STEIN.

WADSW.

Culp's Hill

Cemetery Hill

DOUB.   ROB.

Newton

GEARY   WILL.

Slocum

Spangler's Spring

EMMITSBURG RD

HAYS

GIBBON

CALDW.

Hancock

WILLIAMS

TANEYTOWN RD

Baltimore Pike

Rock Creek

Longstreet

McLAWS

WOFFORD   BARKSDALE

SEMMES   KERSHAW

HOOD

ANDERSON

BENNING   ROBERTSON   LAW

Peach Orchard

BIRN.

HUMPHREYS

MEADE

Plum Run

RIDGE

Sickles

BARNES

Power's Hill

AYRES   CRAW.

Sykes

With Vincent's Brigade leading, Barnes approaches *Sickles's* position and the still-undefended Little Round Top…

Wheatfield

BIRNEY

BIRNEY

Devil's Den

Little Round Top

Big Round Top

N

0   0.5   1 Mi

July 2, Late Afternoon

Over roller-coaster rocky farm fields, Law's Alabamans enthusiastically find footing. Clotting at, pouring over and around the stone and wood cross fences, reconstituting their formations they trot on. Passing barns and sheds. Quick-stepping through the grassy pastures. Descending soggy shade dells, clambering into the light again to hasten on. Union cannons find their range, belching fire across the sky into the oncoming gray infantry. Bones shatter. Whistling shells air-explode, driving fragments into flesh. Rows stagger, fall. The disciplined Yank gunners on their cramped ridges in the elevated little valley in the distance busily aim, load, fire. The shrieking shells arc—cracking Yankee rifles too as the distances start to close—dropping more and more men in the less and less symmetrical oncoming Rebel ranks. It's far stiffer resistance than anticipated.

The diverted portion of the advance (easier to re-task two-fifths of an advance-in-progress than all of it).

Law allows part of his advance to divert north to silence a battery of particularly lethally placed Union guns (Smith) above Devil's Den. Disconnecting from the extreme right of the Confederate assault (where the landscape is least passable and there are virtually no enemy), this tasked Rebel force proceeds north, crossing behind the rest of the Rebel advance, which pushes on.

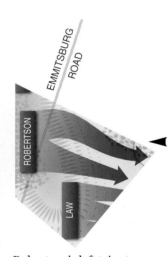

Robertson's left tries to hold to the Emmitsburg Road but is pulled away to the right with the rest of the brigade trying to keep connected to Law's left.

A beat later, on Law's left and to his immediate north, Robertson's Brigade of Texans moves out to the attack. Hood, standing kingly in his stirrups, adjures his riflemen to chase the Yankee defenders off their terrain. The Rebels move out. Their assigned direction is ambiguous. They've been told to keep their right in contact with Law's left and their left touching the Emmitsburg Road—an impossibility (lingering after-image of the original plan to attack *up* the road?) . . . Hood's assault is quickly beginning to lose its coherence.

Hood is wounded. Law must take over the division. Law initially omits to designate an interim brigade commander for himself, a bad oversight.

On Robertson's left, McLaws's Division awaits *Longstreet's* command to advance, this being the next step in the echelon tactic (attack-in-rapid-lateral-stages). Some of Robertson's advancing men look to their left and wonder where McLaws is (suggesting somebody's plan was a different one or somebody didn't get briefed).

Things have gotten off to a disjointed start for the Confederates. But the longer the fighting—no-holds-barred, remorseless—will go on, the clearer the magnitude of *Sickles's* error will become.

Little Round Top: Earlier MEADE responsibly sent his chief engineer, Warren, who was handy, to check on Little Round Top. Disconcerted to discover it empty save for a gaggle of Union signalmen, Warren reported the news to MEADE. MEADE at once made it a priority to occupy the priceless hill. Neither did it escape MEADE's ireful notice that if Little Round Top is unoccupied, *Sickles doesn't even have a* detachment *up there.* Told to rectify the situation— send a force up Little Round Top immediately—*Sickles* has pled Otherwise Occupied, being under attack . . . MEADE is trying to hurry *Sykes's* Corps to the area . . . couriers and aides bearing messages are galloping off every which way . . .

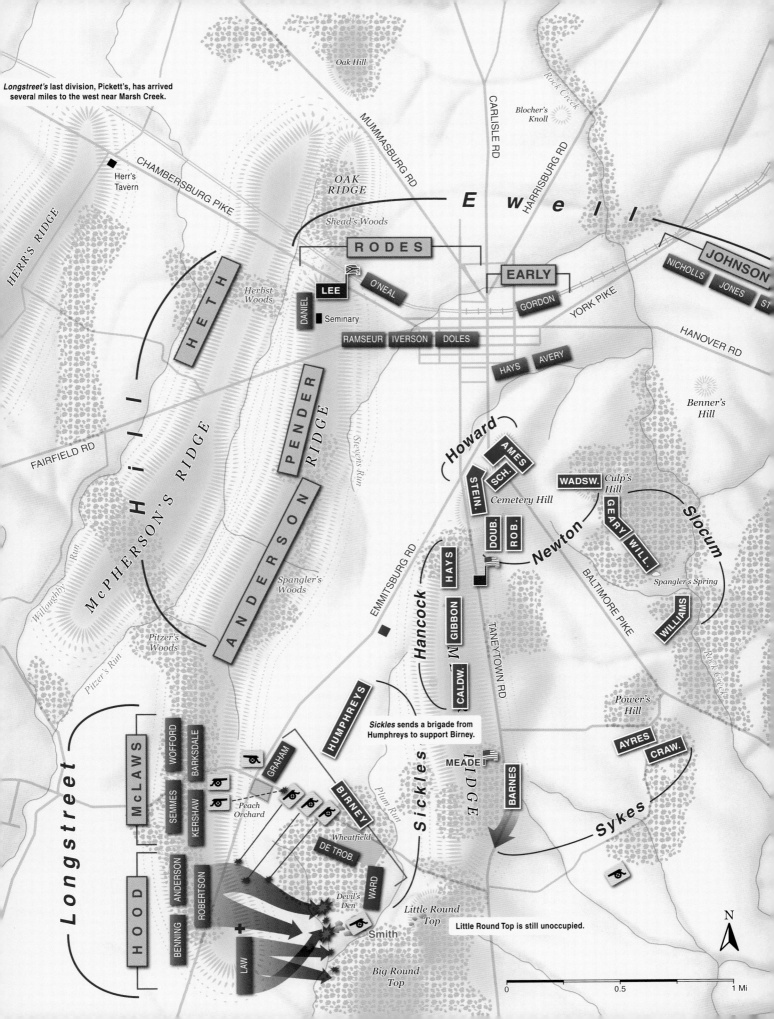

Longstreet's last division, Pickett's, has arrived several miles to the west near Marsh Creek.

Herr's Tavern

HERR'S RIDGE

CHAMBERSBURG PIKE

OAK RIDGE

Shead's Woods

MUMMASBURG RD

Oak Hill

CARLISLE RD

Blocher's Knoll

Rock Creek

HARRISBURG RD

E w e l l

RODES

JOHNSON

NICHOLLS   JONES   ST

Herbst Woods

HETH

LEE   O'NEAL

Daniel

■ Seminary

RAMSEUR   IVERSON   DOLES

EARLY

GORDON

YORK PIKE

HANOVER RD

HAYS   AVERY

FAIRFIELD RD

McPHERSON'S RIDGE

PENDER RIDGE

ANDERSON

Stevens Run

Benner's Hill

Howard

AMES

SCH.

STEIN.

WADSW.

Culp's Hill

Cemetery Hill

GEARY   WILL.

Slocum

Willoughby Run

Spangler's Woods

DOUB.   ROB.

Newton

Spangler's Spring

Pitzer's Woods

EMMITTSBURG RD

Hancock

HAYS

■

Rock Creek

WILLIAMS

Pitzer's Run

GIBBON

TANEYTOWN RD

Power's Hill

BALTIMORE PIKE

CALDW.

Sickles sends a brigade from Humphreys to support Birney.

Longstreet

McLAWS

WOFFORD   BARKSDALE

GRAHAM

HUMPHREYS

MEADE

AYRES

CRAW.

SEMMES   KERSHAW

Peach Orchard

BIRNEY

Plum Run

Sickles

IIDGE

BARNES

Sykes

HOOD

ANDERSON   ROBERTSON

Wheatfield

DE TROB.

WARD

BENNING

LAW

Devil's Den

Little Round Top

Little Round Top is still unoccupied.

Smith

Big Round Top

N

0   0.5   1 Mi

July 2, Late Afternoon

Key to the Union position, Little Round Top must be secured before Rebels get there. *Sykes* might not get men there quick enough. Overriding *Sickles*, who wants Humphreys out along the road, MEADE orders Humphreys, of *Sickles's* Corps, to move back—southeast—and occupy Little Round Top. Never mind *Sickles*.

Humphreys, his spread ranks in the middle of a positional advance toward the Emmitsburg Road, changes the direction of 3,500 men on a dime. They march southeast, for the hill. But *Sykes's* units will make it in time after all. Upon being reassured of this, MEADE orders Humphreys to go back to what he'd been doing (the unavoidable stop-go, seesaw nature of combat). Without complaint and drill-field smooth, Humphreys complies, his division's deft, responsive maneuvering under fire appreciated by their brother Federals looking on from Cemetery Ridge.

Little Round Top will be saved. *Sykes* rushes Barnes's Division there—or he is going to . . . or is he? MEADE has *Sykes's* Corps moving in the general Little Round Top direction, but the courier bearing the specific order to secure the hill can't find Barnes! Vincent, heading Barnes's lead brigade, felicitously runs into the flustered courier—presses him to reveal the order's contents. Hearing it's a command to occupy Little Round Top, Vincent takes it upon himself (at risk of court-martial) to take the prize. He does. Little Round Top is in Union hands. It's a very big deal. Credit will be rightly claimed for many—Warren, Vincent, alert aides, even *Sykes*. All deserve a share. But the achievement occurred under the guiding aegis of the attentive, high-strung soul running the show.

Sykes is sending still more Union brigades to the scene of *Sickles's* ungainly position: Sweitzer and Tilton (of Barnes) approach the Wheatfield. Ayres's Division is en route.

Per LEE's plan, Anderson is positioned to hit MEADE's center. (Anderson the division commander of Hill, not *Longstreet's* brigadier.)

Per LEE's plan, we see *Ewell* in the north facing Yankee-occupied Culp's and Cemetery Hills. He hears *Longstreet's* guns in the south, for which he was to listen—his cue to "demonstrate" against MEADE's right. *Ewell* authorizes his artillery to fire. Union guns on Culp's and Cemetery reply.

No sooner are Vincent's Federals in place on Little Round Top than Law's assault comes swarming out of the southwest following the winding watercourse of Plum Run, stepping through foothill forests of Big Round Top, negotiating the rocky wetland of hummocks and grouse bramble between Little Round Top and Devil's Den/Houck's Ridge. Soon after, Benning's Rebs advance, and Anderson's Brigade . . . for hours now, in legend and bloody fact, the Devil's Den/Plum Run swale earns the soubriquet "Slaughter Pen" and: "Valley of Death."

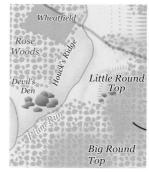

The Terrain

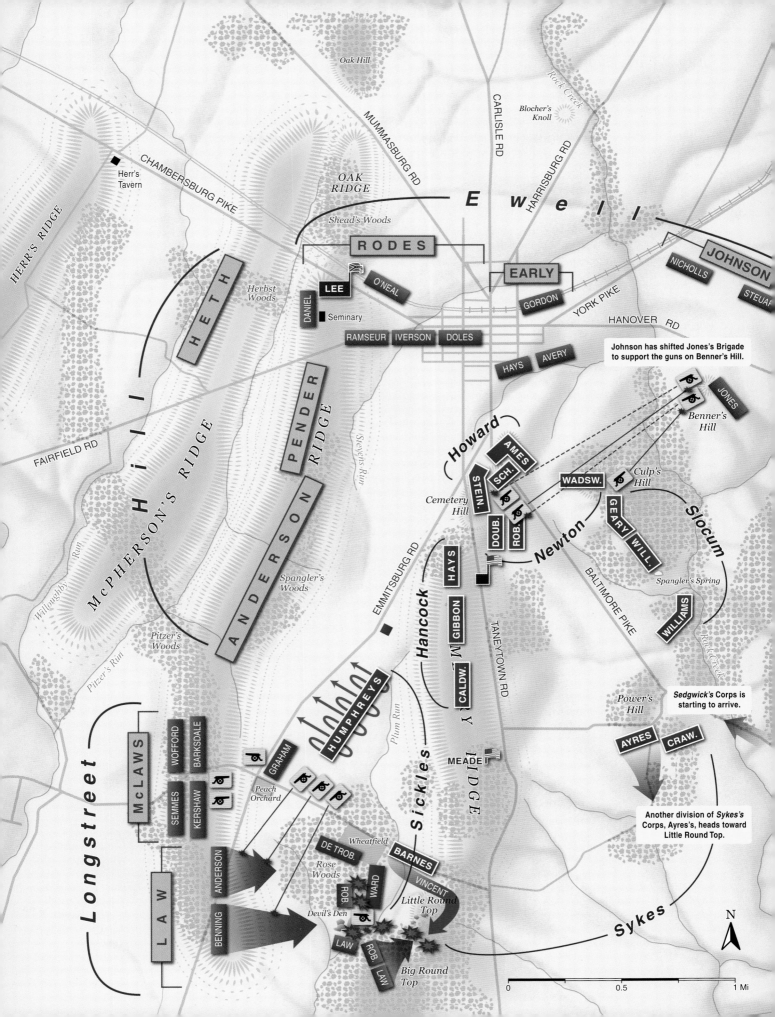

Herr's Tavern

CHAMBERSBURG PIKE

HERR'S RIDGE

Oak Hill

OAK RIDGE

MUMMASBURG RD

Shead's Woods

CARLISLE RD

Blocher's Knoll

Rock Creek

E   w   e   l   l

RODES

HETH

Herbst Woods

LEE

O'NEAL

DANIEL

Seminary

RAMSEUR   IVERSON   DOLES

EARLY

GORDON

YORK PIKE

HANOVER RD

JOHNSON

NICHOLLS

STEUAR

HAYS   AVERY

Johnson has shifted Jones's Brigade to support the guns on Benner's Hill.

McPHERSON'S RIDGE

PENDER

ANDERSON RIDGE

Steyens Run

Spangler's Woods

FAIRFIELD RD

Willoughby Run

Pitzer's Woods

Pitzer's Run

Howard

AMES

SCH.

STEIN.

Cemetery Hill

DOUB.

ROB.

HAYS

W GIBBON

CALDW.

MEADE

EMMITTSBURG RD

Hancock

Plum Run

RIDGE

TANEYTOWN RD

WADSW.

Culp's Hill

Newton

GEARY

WILL.

Slocum

Spangler's Spring

WILLIAMS

BALTIMORE PIKE

Rock Creek

Power's Hill

Sedgwick's Corps is starting to arrive.

AYRES   CRAW.

Another division of *Sykes's* Corps, Ayres's, heads toward Little Round Top.

JONES

Benner's Hill

Longstreet

McLAWS

WOFFORD   BARKSDALE

SEMMES   KERSHAW

LAW

ANDERSON

Peach Orchard

GRAHAM

HUMPHREYS

Sickles

DE TROB.

Wheatfield

Rose Woods

ROB.   WARD

Devil's Den

LAW

ROB.   LAW

Big Round Top

BARNES

VINCENT

Little Round Top

Sykes

N

0   0.5   1 Mi

Devil's Den is a boulder field. Masses of colossal shape and size pile and crowd, loom at angles, bigger than automobiles, create quasi-caves, precipitous crevices cool in summer. It's a sharpshooter's paradise. Dead-eye shots perch and hide, deliberately picking off their prey, prowl the surreal stone halls and walls and roofs, stalking human game.

The Confederates of Law's right flank charge again and again struggling to take Little Round Top. Benning's Brigade has advanced, shoring up Robertson's and Law's flagging initial effort at the Den. Their combined riflemen hit Ward's Union brigade of Birney's Division. Just to the north, Anderson is striking at Ward and De Trobriand (on Ward's right), drawing the fight deeper into Rose Woods, closer to the Wheatfield.

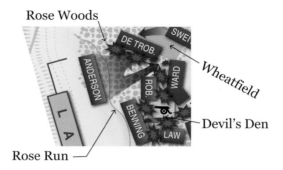

The pressure on *Sickles's* thin line anchored on Devil's Den is becoming irresistible, but Ward holds on, barely. The fight in the great rocks and out across the "Slaughter Pen" is savage, confused—"wild" in the word of one present. Capering on a boulder to draw fire, a Rebel dives to safety as his comrades blast the revealed Yank position. Units crisscross, gain ground, lose it, grapple close in, blades thrust, signals cross, misalignment, the air powder-dark, uncommon courage, explosive, enervating combat—the "above and beyond" common to war.

From the cover of the Den's massive stones, sniping up at Smith's Union cannons perched on the westernmost edge of Houck's Ridge just above the Den (and thus not able to train down on them), Confederate rifles harass the powerful Yankee artillery position, itself lately so effective as a spoiler of *Longstreet's* assault.

Anderson's Georgians slosh across Rose Run, bullets ripping, thudding, whizzing all around. De Trobriand bends but doesn't break, repulsing Anderson. The Wheatfield, a hole in *Sickles's* position, is safe.

Repeatedly the Rebels assail all-important Little Round Top. Its front, an open, rocky steep commandingly facing south-of-west all the way around to east-of-north, is impossible to fight one's way up under fire, though the Rebels more than once valiantly try. Meanwhile, storming the hill's forested elevations around to the south and "behind," other regiments of Law (acting division commander now) come closer to success. They take one pounding after another, withdraw to regroup for another go at the Michigan men, Pennsylvanians, and New Yorkers on the slope. The

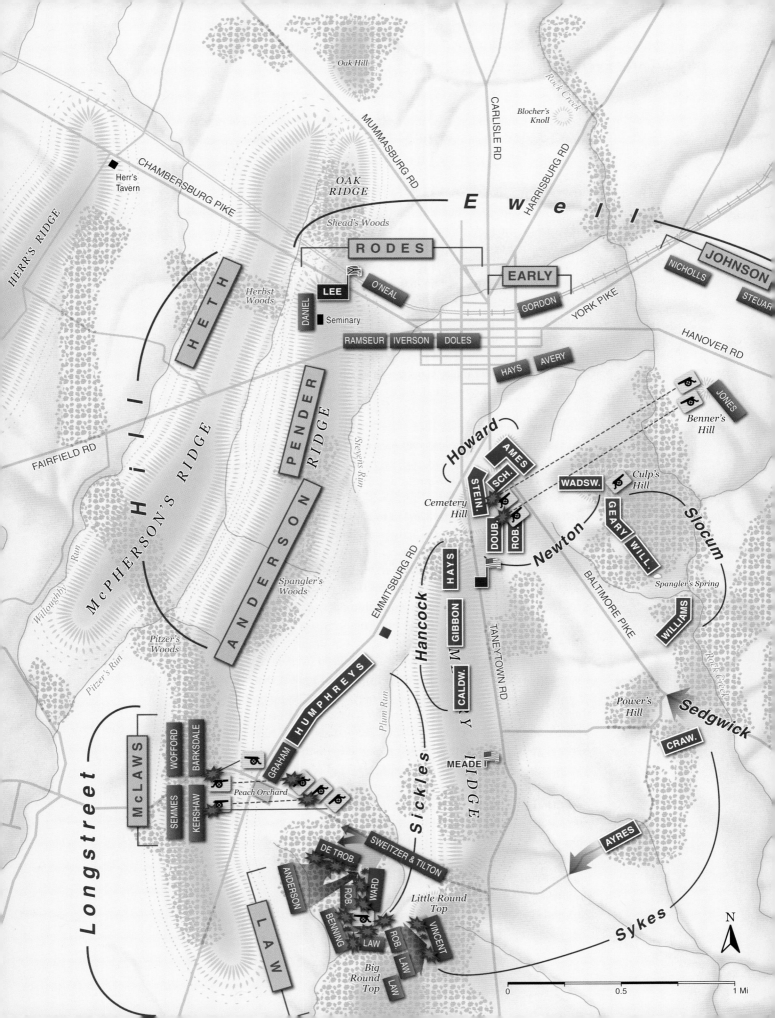

Herr's Tavern

CHAMBERSBURG PIKE

HERR'S RIDGE

Oak Hill

MUMMASBURG RD

OAK RIDGE

CARLISLE RD

Blocher's Knoll

Rock Creek

HARRISBURG RD

E w e l l

Shead's Woods

RODES

JOHNSON

NICHOLLS

STEUAR

HETH

Herbst Woods

LEE

O'NEAL

DANIEL

Seminary

EARLY

GORDON

YORK PIKE

McPHERSON'S RIDGE

PENDER RIDGE

RAMSEUR   IVERSON   DOLES

HANOVER RD

FAIRFIELD RD

ANDERSON

Stevens Run

HAYS   AVERY

JONES

Benner's Hill

Howard

AMES

Culp's Hill

WADSW.

Slocum

Spangler's Woods

SCH.

STEIN.

Cemetery Hill

Newton

GEARY   WILL.

DOUB.   ROB.

Willoughby Run

Pitzer's Woods

Spangler's Spring

EMMITSBURG RD

HAYS

BALTIMORE PIKE

WILLIAMS

Pitzer's Run

Hancock

GIBBON

Rock Creek

HUMPHREYS

CALDW.

Power's Hill

Sedgwick

Longstreet

McLAWS

WOFFORD   BARKSDALE

GRAHAM

Plum Run

MEADE

CRAW.

SEMMES   KERSHAW

Peach Orchard

Sickles

Y RIDGE

SWEITZER & TILTON

AYRES

DE TROB.

Little Round Top

ANDERSON

WARD

LAW

ROB.

BENNING

LAW

ROB. LAW

VINCENT

Sykes

Big Round Top

LAW

N

0   0.5   1 Mi

Yanks hold Little Round Top, at great cost, no unit showing more guts than the fabled 20th Maine of Joshua Chamberlain, manning the extreme left (southern extremity) of the Little Round Top position (and thus of MEADE's whole line running up the two miles and more to Cemetery and Culp's Hills).

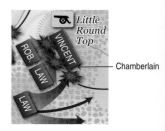

Little Round Top

Chamberlain

Part of the Rebel failure to carry Little Round Top involves Oates, whose responsibility for two of Law's regiments is imperfectly discharged. The lowest arrow on the map characterizes Oates's wandering, distracted route, contrasted with high command's intent for Oates's Alabamans.

Oates was supposed to swing left and north after his initial advance, head up to Little Round Top, and hit it. But he got distracted by some Yankee rifles on *Big* Round Top, which he diverted to chase up the wooded steep of Big Round Top with great difficulty in the heat. Five companies of Oates's skirmishers lose contact, end up on the side of Big Round Top away from the action—are never in the battle! Oates, a courageous fighter, is out of shape and, as a horse can't make it up the long, abrupt incline of forest, must be hauled up by helping hands at last to the top. The colonel is more exhausted even than his men, at least dozens of whom are out of it with heat prostration. Resting in the relative cool of the trees at the top of the wrong Round Top, Oates hears from Law by staff messenger—What are you *doing*? Attack!

With the portion of his men not misplaced or out of commission, Oates scrambles down, crosses the forested saddle between the Round Tops. On the way he spots a train of Union supply wagons down through the trees at the bottom. Still more men are diverted to capture these. They fail. They do not return. Oates bravely leads the Alabamans he has left up through the southern trees of Little Round Top against Chamberlain's Maine men in charge after charge. Little Round Top is vital to the entire battle.

At last McLaws attacks. His lead brigade—Kershaw—smartly steps out over lifting-plunging farm fields, through marshy defiles, over fencing, past barns and sheds. While Kershaw's right plunges straight ahead toward the Wheatfield, his left wheels north into a wall of Union artillery, twenty guns and more plugging the hole *Sickles's* error caused to gape east of the Peach Orchard. Kershaw can hear the "clatter of grape" against the sides of sheds and barns. Taking their losses, his men press on, not stopping to fire. Seeing the South Carolinians' grim approach, the Yankee cannoneers, unprotected by infantry, almost pull back. But an order for Kershaw's right half to shift farther to the right causes his left, wrongly, tragically, to do the same. They march like shooting-gallery ducks sidelong before a wall of enfilade, exposed utterly to the blinding Union muzzles. Marching Rebel hundreds wilt—one man in three. They will regroup . . . but not immediately. Following Kershaw, Semmes's Brigade of Georgians is also rocked back by the Blue artillery and will sit this fight out.

Kershaw's Left

Anderson renews his assault through Rose Woods toward the Wheatfield, joining the right wing of Kershaw. Birney's division is down to De Trobriand's Brigade, which bears the brunt of the encounter, with Ward tottering to the east and Graham up with Humphreys at the Emmitsburg Road. De Trobriand puts up a fight, reinforced by Sweitzer and Tilton (of Barnes).

Kershaw's Right

But Kershaw and Anderson are too much.

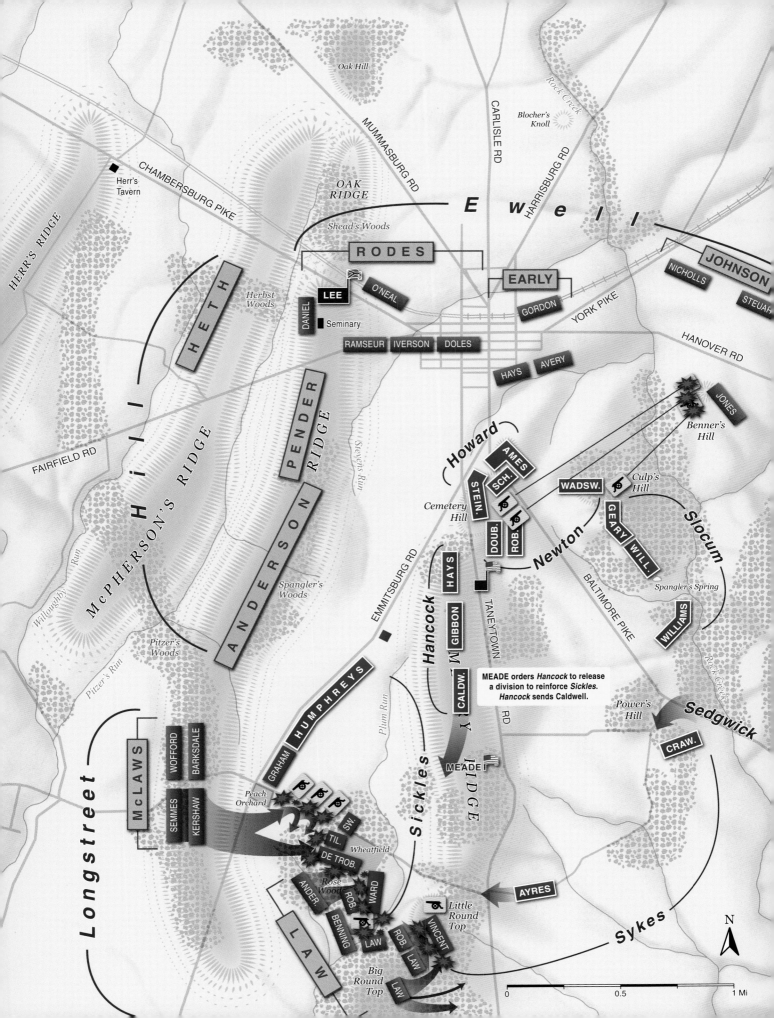

Herr's Tavern

CHAMBERSBURG PIKE

Oak Hill

MUMMASBURG RD

CARLISLE RD

Blocher's Knoll

Rock Creek

HARRISBURG RD

HERR'S RIDGE

OAK RIDGE

E w e l l

Shead's Woods

RODES

JOHNSON

NICHOLLS

STEUAR

HETH

Herbst Woods

LEE

O'NEAL

DANIEL

Seminary

EARLY

GORDON

YORK PIKE

HANOVER RD

RAMSEUR   IVERSON   DOLES

HAYS   AVERY

Benner's Hill

JONES

FAIRFIELD RD

PENDER RIDGE

Stevens Run

ANDERSON RIDGE

Howard

AMES

SCH.

STEIN.

WADSW.

Culp's Hill

GEARY   WILL.

Slocum

Cemetery Hill

DOUB.

ROB.

Newton

Spangler's Woods

Spangler's Spring

Willoughby Run

McPHERSON'S RIDGE

HAYS

GIBBON

TANEYTOWN

Hancock

BALTIMORE PIKE

WILLIAMS

Pitzer's Woods

Pitzer's Run

EMMITTSBURG RD

CALDW.

RD

Rock Creek

MEADE orders *Hancock* to release a division to reinforce *Sickles*. *Hancock* sends Caldwell.

Power's Hill

Sedgwick

MEADE

RIDGE

CRAW.

Longstreet

McLAWS

WOFFORD   BARKSDALE

HUMPHREYS

GRAHAM

SEMMES   KERSHAW

Peach Orchard

SW.

TIL.

DE TROB.

Wheatfield

Plum Run

Sickles

AYRES

Rose Wood

ANDER.

ROB.

WARD

Little Round Top

BENNING

LAW

ROB. LAW

VINCENT

LAW

Big Round Top

LAW

Sykes

N

0   0.5   1 Mi

July 2, Early Evening

Ward's Federals have put up an excellent fight, but Anderson's renewed attack on their right and Benning's and Robertson's continued assaults on their left are too much. Ward is thrown back, off Houck's Ridge. Smith's artillery is silenced. His crews are driven off and their guns captured by the Texans, Arkansans, and Georgians who have driven up through cramped wetlands and wooded gorges and up through the Den, having braved the blankets of minié balls raining out of the sulfurous smoke clouds obscuring Smith's sonorous cannons.

Pouring through the Den's dark outcroppings shooting, clambering, yelling, the men in gray plant their flag at the apex, where, through the great battle's climax tomorrow, they will stay, a backwater.

On Little Round Top, the 140th New York arrives in the nick of time to save Vincent's vulnerable right flank, under attack by Rebels whose way is cleared by Ward's withdrawal.

Along Birney's line to the west, De Trobriand, Sweitzer, and Tilton are driven back by Kershaw bolstered by Anderson from the south.

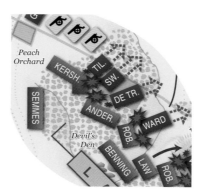

After a confused start, the Confederates have achieved their first significant successes of the day. They have driven in the center and left of *Sickles's* paper-thin line. Green arrows show what the Confederates could do now if unchecked—threaten Humphrey's rear (**1**) or roll up the flank of MEADE's Cemetery Ridge line (**2**). They control the Wheatfield and Rose Woods:

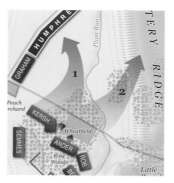

Not for long.

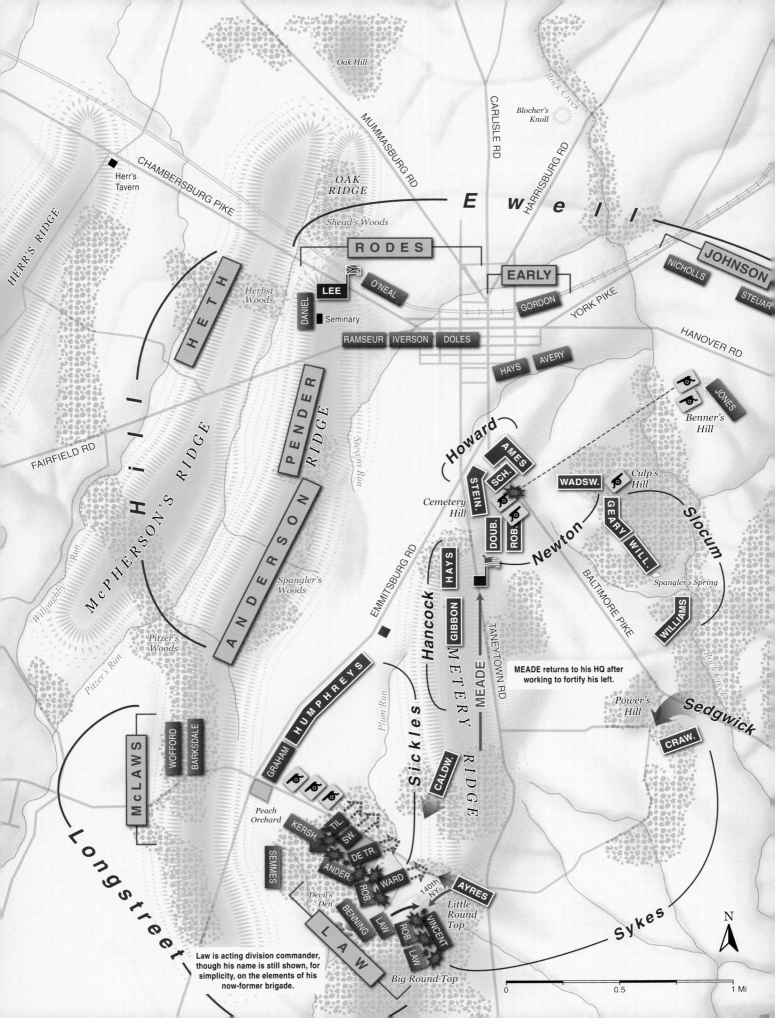

Herr's Tavern

CHAMBERSBURG PIKE

HERR'S RIDGE

Oak Hill

MUMMASBURG RD

CARLISLE RD

Blocher's Knoll

Rock Creek

HARRISBURG RD

E w e l l

OAK RIDGE

Shead's Woods

RODES

JOHNSON

NICHOLLS

STEUAR

HETH

Herbst Woods

LEE

O'NEAL

EARLY

GORDON

YORK PIKE

Daniel

Seminary

RAMSEUR IVERSON DOLES

HANOVER RD

PENDER RIDGE

HAYS AVERY

JONES

Benner's Hill

FAIRFIELD RD

McPHERSON'S RIDGE

ANDERSON RIDGE

Stevens Run

Howard

AMES

SCH.

WADSW.

Culp's Hill

STEIN.

Cemetery Hill

DOUB.

ROB.

Newton

GEARY WILL.

Slocum

Spangler's Woods

Willoughby Run

Pitzer's Run

Pitzer's Woods

Spangler's Spring

WILLIAMS

EMMITTSBURG RD

HAYS

Hancock

GIBBON

CEMETERY RIDGE

TANEYTOWN RD

MEADE

BALTIMORE PIKE

HUMPHREYS

Sickles

Rock Creek

MEADE returns to his HQ after working to fortify his left.

Power's Hill

Sedgwick

McLAWS

WOFFORD

BARKSDALE

GRAHAM

Plum Run

CALDW.

CRAW.

McLAWS

Peach Orchard

KERSH

TIL.

SW.

DE TR.

SEMMES

ANDER.

WARD

ROB.

Devil's Den

AYRES

Longstreet

BENNING

LAW

ROB.

LAW

140th NY

VINCENT

Little Round Top

Sykes

LAW

Law is acting division commander, though his name is still shown, for simplicity, on the elements of his now-former brigade.

Big Round Top

N

0   0.5   1 Mi

Caldwell's Division counterattacks. Hastened by Hancock, on MEADE's orders, to the fray of *Sickles's* predicament, Caldwell's four brigades begin pouring into the Wheatfield (in order Cross, Zook, Kelly's famed "Irish," with Brooke held back). Massing through the blond grain swearing, charging ablaze right into the Rebel ranks, wheat kernels bursting in the air and the dead growing in heaps, they will drive the Rebels back off their Rose Woods and Wheatfield gains.

Barksdale's attack has gotten underway. At McLaws's left front, Barksdale, a Mississippi legislator with debate skills running to fisticuffs, has been pleading to go: *Longstreet* lets him. Waving his hat, cornsilk white hair wild in the sun, Barksdale leads his rebel-yelling, blazing brigade across the Emmitsburg Road, rifles coming off shoulders like breaking beachcombers to fire.

Immediately to the north, *Hill's* Corps comes alive in the advance of Anderson's Division.

Against the beleaguered Humphreys and, on Humphreys's right, against Gibbon and Hays, Anderson is poised to strike with an impressive weight of five fresh brigades, all seeing action at Gettysburg for the first time.

It's been an hour and a half since *Longstreet* launched his assault. That's a long time for Anderson to have waited before "cooperating," as ordered, in echelon with *Longstreet's* attack. Yet, Anderson was told to launch in concert with *Longstreet's* northernmost attacking unit—that's Barksdale, who as we've seen has just gotten started. The elements of *Longstreet's* attack farther south (Hood/Law, then Kershaw and Semmes, of McLaws) have been attacking for an hour and a half before Barksdale starts. So, logically, Anderson's first brigades—Wilcox, Lang, and Wright—have not jumped off 'til now.

An attack in echelon, fine, but not so slow, so sluggish to unfold!

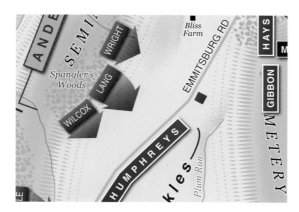

In the far south, at Little Round Top, Oates's Alabamans (Law's Brigade) with other regiments of Alabamans and Texans continue their fight against gravity and the Yankees shooting down at them.

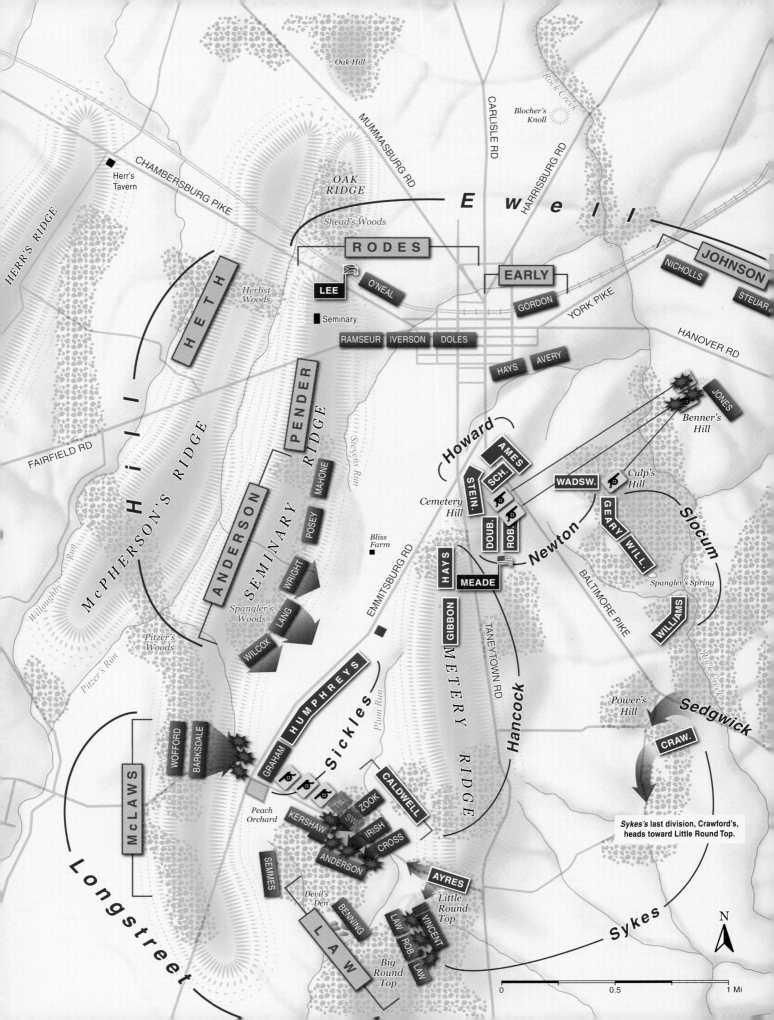

Herr's Tavern

CHAMBERSBURG PIKE

HERR'S RIDGE

Willoughby Run

McPHERSON'S RIDGE

HETH

Herbst Woods

OAK RIDGE

Oak Hill

MUMMASBURG RD

Shead's Woods

RODES

LEE

O'NEAL

Seminary

RAMSEUR IVERSON DOLES

CARLISLE RD

Blocher's Knoll

Rock Creek

HARRISBURG RD

E w e l l

EARLY

GORDON

YORK PIKE

HAYS AVERY

JOHNSON

NICHOLLS

STEUAR.

HANOVER RD

FAIRFIELD RD

PENDER RIDGE

Stevens Run

MAHONE

POSEY

ANDERSON

SEMINARY

WRIGHT

Spangler's Woods

LANG

WILCOX

Pitzer's Woods

Pitzer's Run

Bliss Farm

EMMITSBURG RD

Plum Run

Howard

AMES

SCH.

STEIN.

Cemetery Hill

DOUB.

ROB.

HAYS

GIBBON

MEADE

Newton

CEMETERY RIDGE

TANEYTOWN RD

Hancock

WADSW.

Culp's Hill

GEARY WILL.

Slocum

Spangler's Spring

BALTIMORE PIKE

WILLIAMS

Benner's Hill

JONES

Rock Creek

Power's Hill

Sedgwick

CRAW.

Sykes's last division, Crawford's, heads toward Little Round Top.

McLAWS

WOFFORD

BARKSDALE

Longstreet

Peach Orchard

GRAHAM

SEMMES

Devil's Den

BENNING

LAW

Big Round Top

HUMPHREYS

Sickles

TIL.

SW.

ZOOK

IRISH

CROSS

CALDWELL

KERSHAW

ANDERSON

AYRES

Little Round Top

LAW

ROB.

VINCENT

LAW

Sykes

N

0   0.5   1 Mi

Barksdale slams into Graham. Graham, the last remnant of Birney's pulverized division, which has not been whole on our map for some time, with his left exposed and under attack by one of the Confederacy's finest brigades, can't last.

In Rose Woods and the expanse of the Wheatfield, bordered by green groves (a killing field, a deathly stage where ranks enter, exit contesting and re-enter), the fighting is ferocious. Standing to, at sword-command discharged weaponry explodes in the grimacing faces shooting back from a coin-toss away. Cross, Zook, and the Irish drive Kershaw and Anderson before them. Cross, at odds with his men due to behavior such as ordering them to ford a creek without removing their footgear, falls mortally wounded. Likewise Zook, a Pennsylvania German and descendant of Mennonites, shot in the spine while rallying his men against horrific Rebel fire. Their ammunition running low, the Yankees start to slow down. Caldwell has Brooke in reserve, sends him in, relieving Cross (first in, first out). In a charge through the waist-high wheat, Brooke hits Anderson's tired Rebs, forcing them back through the woods yet again.

Zook falls

Cross falls

With Wilcox and Lang barreling down on his division, Humphreys asks *Hancock* for a brigade. *Hancock* has Gibbon dispatch two regiments to the area between Humphreys's right and the men Gibbon already has out at the road. To send more would expose Gibbon to a threat worse than the grave one he faces already.

His position collapsing, *Sickles* is wounded, carried off the field dramatically like a rajah on his stretcher, puffing an apocryphal cigar. Off the map for the rest of the battle, he will enter history (a checkered one), devoting the rest of his days to trying to turn posterity against MEADE.

MEADE orders *Hancock* to assume command of *Sickles's* Corps in addition to his own. *Hancock*, vital to rallying two defeated Union corps on Cemetery Hill yesterday, throws himself, with coolness and more than a little profanity, into this unenviable situation. MEADE has requested a brigade to reinforce his left. One of *Hancock's* first actions as commander of two corps is to lead Willard's all–New York brigade down the Taneytown Road.

Reinforcements continue to race toward the embattled Union left on MEADE's orders. From Ayres's Division Burbank's and Day's Brigades of U.S. Regulars approach the Wheatfield while Weed's Brigade has joined its 140th New York on Little Round Top. *Sykes's* last division, under Crawford, nears the front, with *Sedgwick's* Corps waiting for the order to go.

The Confederates are fighting like men convinced of their invincibility, pressing every advantage, exploiting every Union misstep. But behind them are no such readily available reserves as MEADE is ramming into one breach after another.

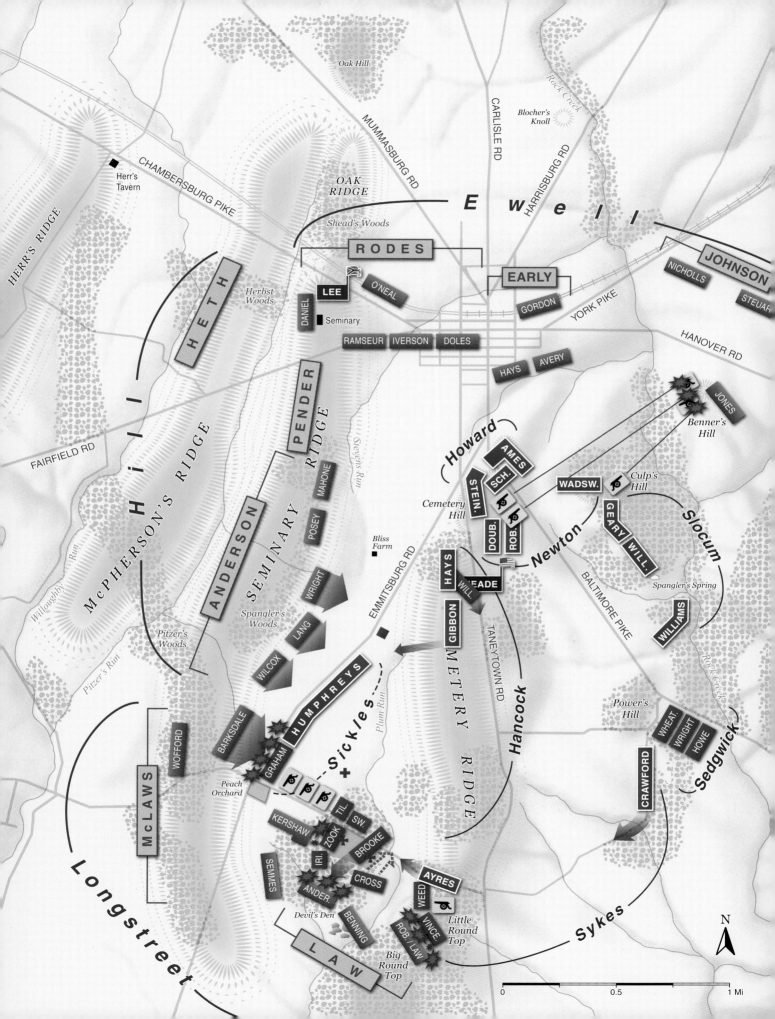

Herr's Tavern

CHAMBERSBURG PIKE

HERR'S RIDGE

Oak Hill

OAK RIDGE

Shead's Woods

MUMMASBURG RD

CARLISLE RD

HARRISBURG RD

Rock Creek

Blocher's Knoll

E w e l l

RODES

JOHNSON

NICHOLLS

STEUAR

HETH

Herbst Woods

LEE

O'NEAL

DANIEL

Seminary

EARLY

GORDON

YORK PIKE

HANOVER RD

RAMSEUR   IVERSON   DOLES

HAYS   AVERY

PENDER

RIDGE

MAHONE

Stevens Run

JONES

Benner's Hill

Howard

ANDERSON

SEMINARY

POSEY

Bliss Farm

AMES

SCH.

STEIN.

Culp's Hill

WADSW.

Cemetery Hill

GEARY   WILL.

Slocum

WRIGHT

LANG

Spangler's Woods

EMMITTSBURG RD

DOUB.

ROB.

Newton

WILCOX

Willoughby Run

McPHERSON'S RIDGE

FAIRFIELD RD

Pitzer's Woods

Pitzer's Run

Spangler's Spring

WILLIAMS

HAYS

MEADE

WILL.

GIBBON

METERY RIDGE

TANEYTOWN RD

BALTIMORE PIKE

Rock Creek

Power's Hill

Plum Run

HUMPHREYS

Sickles

BARKSDALE

WOFFORD

McLAWS

GRAHAM

Peach Orchard

TIL.   SW.

KERSHAW   ZOOK

SEMMES

IRI.

BROOKE

CROSS

ANDER.

WEED

AYRES

Devil's Den

BENNING

ROB / LAW

VINCE

Little Round Top

Longstreet

L A W

Big Round Top

Sykes

WHEAT.   WRIGHT   HOWE

CRAWFORD

Sedgwick

Hancock

N

0   0.5   1 Mi

July 2, Evening

The Wheatfield. As if in a suspension, out of time, the din and blast become as a silence around you as you grapple. For three straight hours—late afternoon to evening—the confused lines of attack form and reform to charge in shellburst, flame in your eye, damp thud. Small arms crackle in smoke zephyr-drifting through the thousands grim in their lines going for each other under the wildly churning big flags.

One volley drops young humans in a row as one in wool with their weapons. In the tawny soft grain more shout, spring, fire wild-eyed. Sweaty musket wood slips. Gleaming sword and stained bayonet aim. In no order and without respite, into the gravity hole of contested farm acreage suck regiments, battalions, brigades. They rush from all sides out of the tall green trees to enter the smoke, black, lung-searing, grunting, thudding, skull-cracking, flame-exploding scuffling . . .

Battle flags get yanked and yanked back, the dead underfoot. Living wounded underfoot. Fresh assaults spell shattered units who gratefully invite their replacements to march literally over their backs. Everywhere are acts of gallantry, bravery beyond imagining, not recorded. Some—there are always a few—slink, edging back a space with unloaded weapon lifted to pretend. A squad tries to squeeze a water break in! Dying last words are heard or drown in the tornadic roar, become as a dullness in your ringing ears. A rank fires too high over the heads of foe whose aiming eyes, in a row, won't miss.

Cross, Zook, Kelly with his famed Irish Brigade, Brooke, Kershaw, Anderson, Wofford, Sweitzer, Burbank, Day . . . hats bobbing in seas.

Two who will never be known and who bear each other no ill will, grimed, blind with honor, choke, are hands—four—at two throats. By them a soot-faced gent with silver shoulders calmly trains his pistol on the sergeant, level-lidded, similarly about to fire. There are pockets of stillness, bizarre blank stares across the corpse field. Blood-bobbled ramrods weakly reload. Officer Yell. And yet another charge assembles, goes, tinking tin cups, into musketry flame. A moan is by you.

Through the tumult you glimpse a buddy before he can spin and topple.

In the spattered piling forms, the lumped blue-gray, eyes shut or open forever under the blocked sun, blood, inching from the fallen, writes the first words of history's greatest address by a head of state.

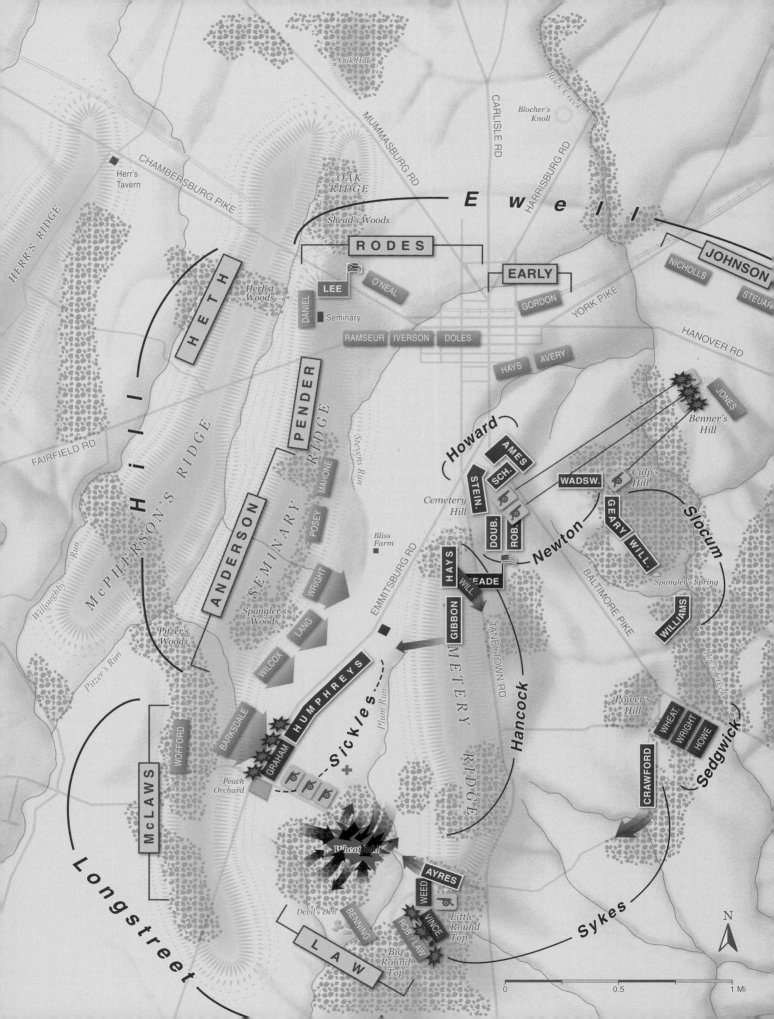

Herr's Tavern

CHAMBERSBURG PIKE

HERR'S RIDGE

Oak Hill

OAK RIDGE

MUMMASBURG RD

CARLISLE RD

Blocher's Knoll

Rock Creek

HARRISBURG RD

Ewell

Shead's Woods

RODES

JOHNSON

NICHOLLS

STEUAR

HETH

Herbst Woods

LEE

O'NEAL

EARLY

DANIEL

Seminary

GORDON

YORK PIKE

HANOVER RD

McPHERSON'S RIDGE

PENDER

RIDGE

RAMSEUR IVERSON DOLES

HAYS AVERY

McPherson Hill

Stevens Run

JONES

Benner's Hill

FAIRFIELD RD

ANDERSON

MAHONE

Howard

AMES

SCH.

WADSW.

Culp's Hill

SEMINARY

POSEY

STEIN.

Cemetery Hill

GEARY WILL.

Slocum

Willoughby Run

Spangler's Woods

WRIGHT

Bliss Farm

DOUB.

ROB.

Newton

Spangler's Spring

Pitzer's Woods

LANG

EMMITSBURG RD

HAYS

WILL.

WILLIAMS

WILCOX

MEADE

Pitzer's Run

GIBBON

BALTIMORE PIKE

HUMPHREYS

Sickles

Plum Run

TANEYTOWN RD

Rock Creek

Longstreet

WOFFORD

BARKSDALE

GRAHAM

Power's Hill

WHEAT WRIGHT HOWE

McLAWS

Peach Orchard

CEMETERY RIDGE

Hancock

CRAWFORD

Sedgwick

Wheatfield

AYRES

WEED

Devil's Den

BENNING

VINCE

ROB. LAW

Little Round Top

Sykes

LAW

Big Round Top

N

0   0.5   1 Mi

Barksdale's storming Mississippians are charging into the artillery fire that was shelling them during their unnerving wait. They knock aside skirmishers sent to slow them. Loading and firing as they go, they swipe aside the brave 114th Pennsylvania Zouaves in their fezes and russet baggy pants. They chase the Union cannons off their west-facing position at the road, hurling Graham's Brigade back off Humphreys's left, and, their blood up, are game for more.

Ewell ends his artillery "demonstration." More numerous and better positioned Yankee batteries have turned the Confederate position on Benner's Hill into a "hell infernal."

Little Round Top continues hotly contested.

On the heels of Barksdale's attack, Wofford's Brigade has jumped off and is swinging below Barksdale's unbrookable advance to press toward Rose Woods . . .

Barksdale splits his brigade. Part surges up the Emmitsburg Road, collapsing Humphreys's left; part thrusts east toward Plum Run and Cemetery Ridge: MEADE's main line. The Yankee gun line between the Peach Orchard and the Wheatfield is falling like dominoes as Barksdale approaches.

Caldwell's Division still pushes against the Rebels in Rose Woods but is beginning to peter out. The line of South Carolinians and Georgians opposing them now includes Semmes's Brigade. On the Confederate left Wofford is about to join in while on the right Anderson's Brigade threatens to overwhelm Caldwell's left flank. Caldwell's position is precarious.

Burbank's and Day's Union reinforcements loom at the edge of the Wheatfield.

In staggered fashion Anderson's Division (of *Hill*) attacks in mile-broad array. A staggered assault is the idea of the attack-in-echelon. Keep the enemy off balance—keep him from knowing when and where to reinforce.

But Anderson's advance is distracted and incomplete.

Anderson's rightmost brigade—Wilcox—hits Humphreys's front. Next Lang bites at Humphrey's front and right, even as Barksdale's euphoric charge up the road is staving in Humphreys's left:

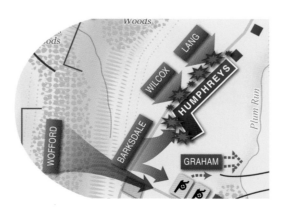

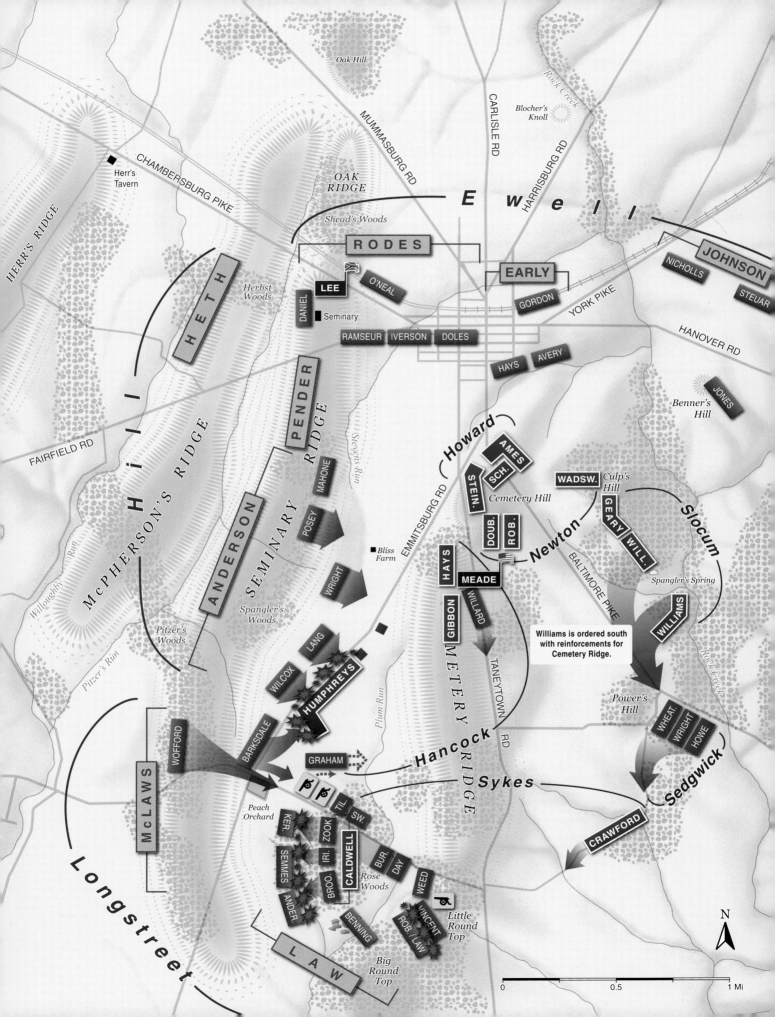

Herr's Tavern

CHAMBERSBURG PIKE

HERR'S RIDGE

Oak Hill

MUMMASBURG RD

CARLISLE RD

Rock Creek

Blocher's Knoll

HARRISBURG RD

OAK RIDGE

Shead's Woods

E w e l l

RODES

JOHNSON

NICHOLLS

STEUAR

HETH

Herbst Woods

LEE   O'NEAL

DANIEL

Seminary

EARLY

GORDON

YORK PIKE

HANOVER RD

RAMSEUR IVERSON DOLES

HAYS AVERY

JONES

Benner's Hill

PENDER

RIDGE

MAHONE

POSEY

Stevens Run

FAIRFIELD RD

ANDERSON

SEMINARY

Howard

AMES

SCH.

WADSW.

Culp's Hill

GEARY

WILL.

Slocum

STEIN.

Cemetery Hill

WRIGHT

Spangler's Woods

Bliss Farm

EMMITTSBURG RD

DOUB.

ROB.

Newton

HAYS

MEADE

Spangler's Spring

Baltimore Pike

WILLIAMS

Willoughby Run

Pitzer's Woods

LANG

WILCOX

HUMPHREYS

GIBBON

WILLARD

Williams is ordered south with reinforcements for Cemetery Ridge.

Plum Run

METERY

TANEYTOWN RD

Power's Hill

Rock Creek

Pitzer's Run

WOFFORD

BARKSDALE

GRAHAM

Hancock

RIDGE

WHEAT. WRIGHT HOWE

Sedgwick

McLAWS

Sykes

Peach Orchard

TIL. SW.

KER. IRI. ZOOK

SEMMES

BROO.

CALDWELL

Rose Woods

BUR. DAY

WEED

CRAWFORD

Longstreet

ANDER.

BENNING

ROB./LAW

VINCENT

Little Round Top

LAW

Big Round Top

N

0   0.5   1 Mi

Next up Anderson's mighty line, Wright's Georgians, who had farther to go to arrive at their attack point (Gibbon's Division), engage, overrunning the two Yankee regiments Gibbon has out west of Cemetery Ridge on the Emmitsburg Road. Also neutralizing Gibbon's artillery there, Wright attacks on toward the ridge itself, the center of MEADE's line (generally toward which Barksdale is attacking from the south).

Next up Anderson's line, the brigade of Posey is supposed to be driving east, shoulder-to-shoulder with Wright.

They aren't.

Posey's advance has gotten halted in a tangle of heavy skirmishing with Union riflemen at the Bliss Farm.

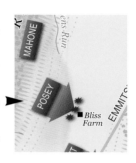

An island of fighting in and around the cover afforded by the large Bliss barn and other farm structures midway between the two great armies in a kind of open no-man's-land, the spot was earlier contested by a few skirmishers from both sides. When neither Blue nor Gray saw fit to withdraw, more and more troops were sent. An exchange of shots turned into a knot of stubborn, at times almost heavy combat. Here virtually Posey's entire brigade gets hung up and will remain so, never to get anywhere near Wright's attacking left. Worse, to Posey's left rear and at the top of Anderson's divisional array back on Seminary Ridge, Mahone, prodded by messenger from Anderson to attack, refuses. Bewilderingly badly coordinated by Anderson and his corps commander, *Hill*, Anderson's divisional advance ends up at scarcely more than half total strength. A "What-If" of import.

North of Anderson, the full division of Pender is not used. Clockwise, on around LEE's loose curving five-mile line, *Ewell*, his artillery "demonstration" having been silenced, is still awaiting his opportunity to make a "real attack," per LEE's orders of this morning.

Commanders' and historians' accounts differ as to whether a staggered attack, unfolding in stages clockwise from the Plum Run area, was LEE's intent. That this is what happened, however, and that its successive stages ignited far too sluggishly is not in dispute. We have: LEE's intent, *Longstreet's* mindset, what *Longstreet* did, and what actually happened. No two are the same.

Sweitzer's Federals, requested by Caldwell to cover Caldwell's right, reenter the Wheatfield amidst Caldwell's withdrawing troops and face southwest. Wofford's Georgians trample the twigs of Rose Woods, bursting forth to violently surprise Sweitzer's right. The Wheatfield is a maelstrom, acrid gunsmoke so thick you see only shoes in places, a spinning, devouring death whorl neither side can quit.

Sickles is a lost soul, off the grid, lucky to be wounded, his Swiss-cheese position penetrated, leveraged and about to be thrown for a total loss, all the way back to Cemetery Ridge. The considerable reinforcements MEADE has been at pains to rush to the area of *Sickles's* plight,

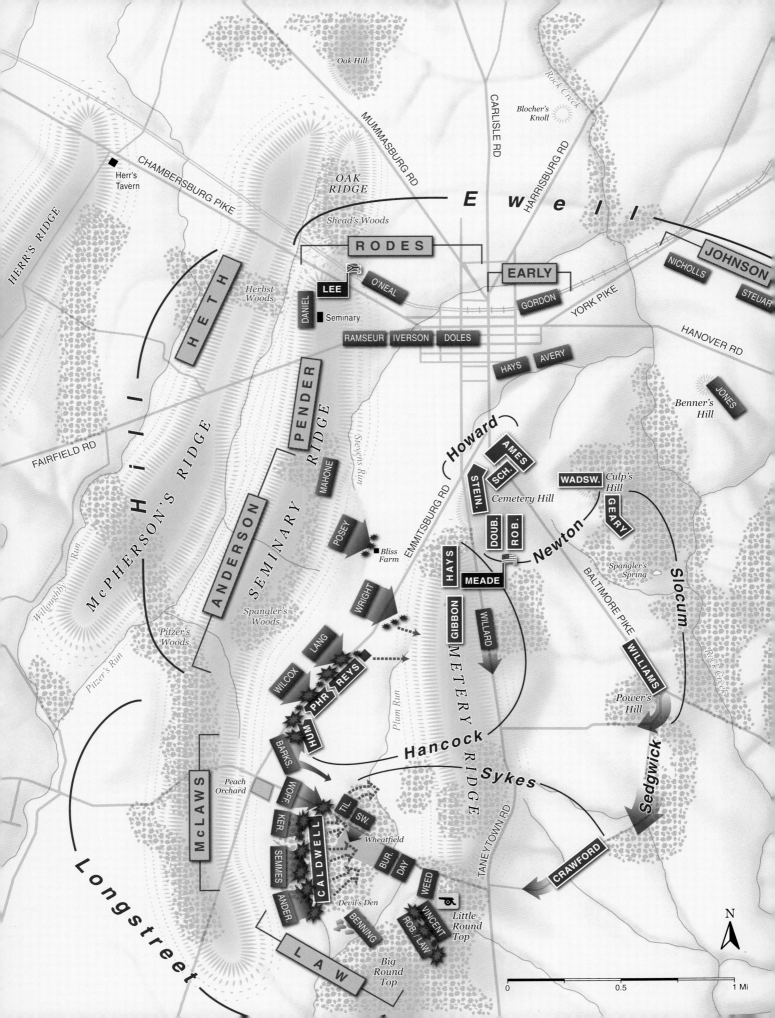

Herr's Tavern

CHAMBERSBURG PIKE

HERR'S RIDGE

Oak Hill

OAK RIDGE

MUMMASBURG RD

CARLISLE RD

Blocher's Knoll

Rock Creek

HARRISBURG RD

E w e l l

Shead's Woods

RODES

JOHNSON

NICHOLLS

STEUAR

HETH

Herbst Woods

LEE

O'NEAL

EARLY

GORDON

YORK PIKE

DANIEL

Seminary

RAMSEUR IVERSON DOLES

HANOVER RD

McPHERSON'S RIDGE

FAIRFIELD RD

PENDER RIDGE

MAHONE

Stevens Run

HAYS AVERY

Benner's Hill

JONES

ANDERSON

SEMINARY

POSEY

Bliss Farm

Howard

AMES

SCH.

STEIN.

WADSW. Culp's Hill

GEARY

Cemetery Hill

Newton

Willoughby Run

Pitzer's Woods

Spangler's Woods

WRIGHT

EMMITSBURG RD

DOUB. ROB.

Spangler's Spring

Slocum

Pitzer's Run

WILCOX

LANG

PHR REYS

HUM

HAYS

MEADE

GIBBON

WILLARD

METERY RIDGE

BALTIMORE PIKE

WILLIAMS

Power's Hill

Plum Run

BARKS.

Hancock

Sykes

Rock Creek

McLAWS

WOFF.

Peach Orchard

KER.

TIL.

SW.

Wheatfield

Sedgwick

SEMMES

CALDWELL

BUR DAY

TANEYTOWN RD

CRAWFORD

ANDER.

BENNING

Devil's Den

WEED

VINCENT ROB./LAW

Little Round Top

Longstreet

LAW

Big Round Top

N

0   0.5   1 Mi

facilitated by MEADE's short interior lines, are nevertheless delayed by having to march through the "air" *Sickles* opened behind him. Also they perforce arrive in order of availability and thus riddled with confusion as to who is to position where and who report to whom.

Bigelow's 9th Massachusetts—six big Napoleon cannons and their gun carriages, horses, and crews—after participating in the bitter fighting near the Peach Orchard are the last Federals to leave the area. Firing as they retreat, Bigelow's Yankees find themselves at the Trostle Farm, backed into a ninety-degree V of stone fence. Barksdale sets upon them, joined by sharpshooters from Kershaw. Ordered to make a stand so their brother retreating Federals can race back to get dug in on the elevated Cemetery Ridge defense line, Bigelow's men load and discharge their big pieces, firing scattershot, grapeshot, canister into the incredible bravery of Barksdale's and Kershaw's charging Rebels who duck to within feet of the flaming bronze.

Bigelow's tight quarter-circle of guns gets tighter with each discharge, recoiling backward with no time to reposition.

Lacking infantry protection, Bigelow's 9th Massachusetts makes its stand in the face of the inevitable, black-smeared, pouring sweat, serving one hornet-cloud of canister after another into Barksdale's and Kershaw's swarming infantry. Bigelow is badly wounded. At last, leaving behind a carnage of horses and humans, the 9th Massachusetts, breaking around the stone wall and through it, abandons the strewn field of their high endeavor.

Barksdale—plus Anderson's brigades of Wilcox/Lang/Wright—plus Kershaw, Semmes, and Anderson in Rose Woods and the Wheatfield—plus Wofford—with, always, the raggy, seasoned, big-hearted Rebel foot soldier carrying victory wings on his pack—begins to sweep the countryside clear of Yankees west of MEADE's Cemetery Ridge position.

Except for—noteworthily—Little Round Top.

In the thinning daylight Wright's Brigade gets up onto the ridge. Battling their way up into Gibbon's center and trying to get around his left and into the empty space beyond, Wright's men create an opportunity, if supported, to shake MEADE, can-open and expand their transitory wound in MEADE's shield, unravel the Yankee matrix.

It's their chance. The Confederate States of America are a beat away, a pair of fresh, seasoned brigades away, a stroke of good fortune, a genius commander—blood up, at the front—away from turning it. Here, now, with Humphreys collapsed (through no fault of his), the Wheatfield about to fall, Little Round Top under pressure, Culp's Hill weak, and at least a division's worth of idle, capable regiments scattered around the field, is LEE's moment.

He remains near his headquarters on Seminary Ridge, with *Hill*.

MEADE is sometimes at his headquarters, but mostly about the battlefield in the saddle. He orders reinforcements from *Newton*. At one famous juncture—about the time the tide of the Rebel assault is streaming up to Cemetery Ridge (and Wright penetrating the Union line), MEADE with his staff sits his horse on the ridge. He watches the gray wide lines of infantry charging

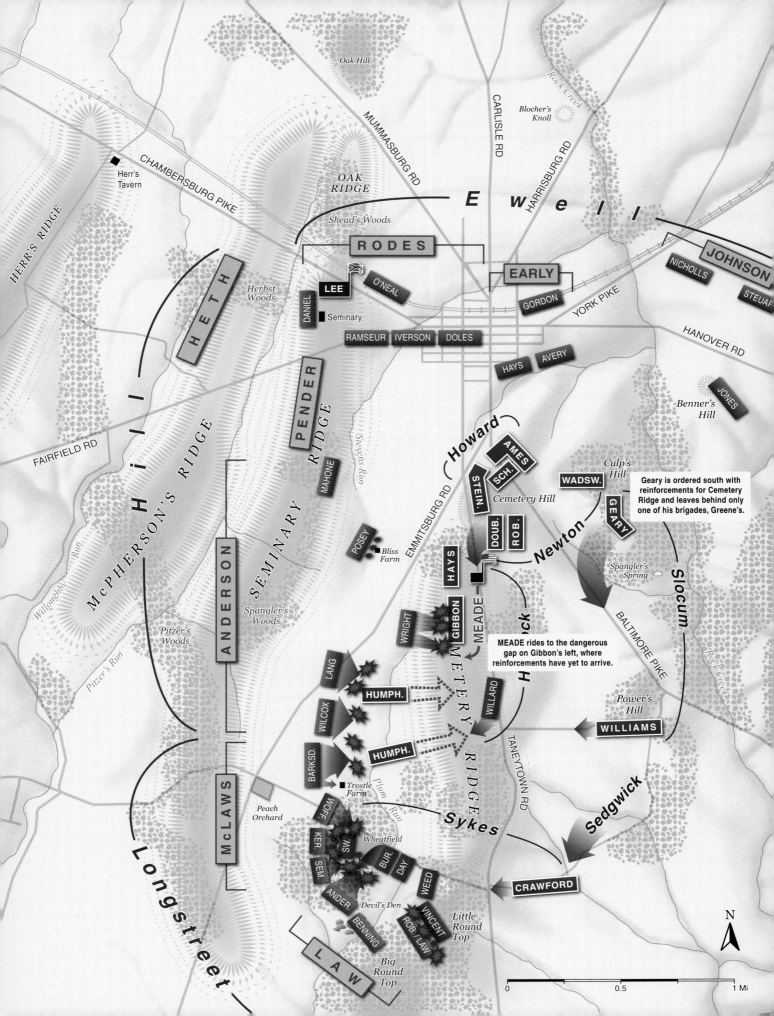

Herr's Tavern

CHAMBERSBURG PIKE

HERR'S RIDGE

Oak Hill

MUMMASBURG RD

OAK RIDGE

Shead's Woods

E w e l l

CARLISLE RD

Blocher's Knoll

Rock Creek

HARRISBURG RD

RODES

HETH

Herbst Woods

LEE

O'NEAL

DANIEL

Seminary

EARLY

GORDON

YORK PIKE

JOHNSON

NICHOLLS

STEUART

RAMSEUR   IVERSON   DOLES

HANOVER RD

HAYS   AVERY

FAIRFIELD RD

PENDER RIDGE

MAHONE

Stevens Run

JONES

Benner's Hill

Howard

AMES

SCH.

STEIN.

Cemetery Hill

WADSW.

Culp's Hill

Geary is ordered south with reinforcements for Cemetery Ridge and leaves behind only one of his brigades, Greene's.

GEARY

EMMITSBURG RD

POSEY

Bliss Farm

DOUB.

ROB.

Newton

HAYS

MEADE

Spangler's Spring

Slocum

MCPHERSON'S RIDGE

Willoughby Run

ANDERSON

SEMINARY

Spangler's Woods

WRIGHT

GIBBON

CETERY RIDGE

Hancock

MEADE rides to the dangerous gap on Gibbon's left, where reinforcements have yet to arrive.

Power's Hill

BALTIMORE PIKE

Rock Creek

Pitzer's Woods

LANG

HUMPH.

WILLARD

Pitzer's Run

WILCOX

WILLIAMS

McLAWS

BARKSD.

HUMPH.

Trostle Farm

Plum Run

Sykes

TANEYTOWN RD

Sedgwick

Peach Orchard

WOFF.

KER.

SW.

Wheatfield

BUR.

DAY

CRAWFORD

Longstreet

SEM.

ANDER.

Devil's Den

WEED

Little Round Top

BENNING

ROB./LAW

VINCENT

L A W

Big Round Top

N

0   0.5   1 Mi

toward him unchallenged.

He has ordered reinforcements from *Newton*. They've not arrived.

There is nothing between LEE's eastward-rolling lines and MEADE in the flesh, on his horse, with his staff. Stiffening on his mount, MEADE draws his sword.

Newton rides up, reporting as ordered with Doubleday's Division behind him in short order deploying to advance against the oncoming Confederates.

MEADE has a sip.

Incoming Rebel artillery tosses some dirt at him.

MEADE rides forward a bit with his Blue reinforcements' countercharge, shouting encouragement.

To the north Rodes observes a "stir" on Cemetery Hill, likely the departure of *Newton's* Corps. He informs *Ewell*, who takes this as his "opportunity" and orders Johnson to attack. Johnson swings his division down toward Benner's Hill.

Up in among the Blue on the ridge, Wright isn't supported. On Wright's left is empty air, Posey being still entangled in his fight back at the Bliss Farm—and Mahone nowhere.

On Wright's right, Lang and Wilcox fight on, and Wilcox had an opening momentarily, but, vigilantly, *Hancock* has plugged it with the 1st Minnesota. Charging bravely—but a few hundred against Wilcox's massed onslaught of greatly more than a thousand infantrymen—the Minnesotans close at a near-run with vertical bayonets. They are decimated: two-thirds and more killed or wounded in mere minutes. But their calm, steadied rush stops Wilcox in his tracks, deciding him to withdraw.

Like a mighty breaker exhausting to froth, the Confederate sweep eastward has run out of steam. The sun is under the horizon. Barksdale's Mississippians especially, after their stunning charges of the past hour like a scythe through the Yankees, are worn out.

The Union position on Cemetery Ridge is a strong one. It has held. MEADE has plenty of cannon and men to hold, reinforce, and defend the ridge—his intent and preoccupation all along. Yet, had the Rebel advance sweeping eastward been able to reach the ridge just half an hour sooner, they would have fallen upon a chaos of retreating and demoralized shards—*Sickles's* smashed elements mixed with the reinforcements MEADE had hoped might bail *Sickles* out, all in disarray. The Federals would have been vulnerable in the extreme, that single half hour earlier. A rout could well have poured backward up onto the ridge and spread farther, with imaginable consequence.

Thus the half hour bought by Bigelow's cannoneers at the Trostle Farm—that delay—deserves all the note and accolade forever since accorded the 9th Massachusetts.

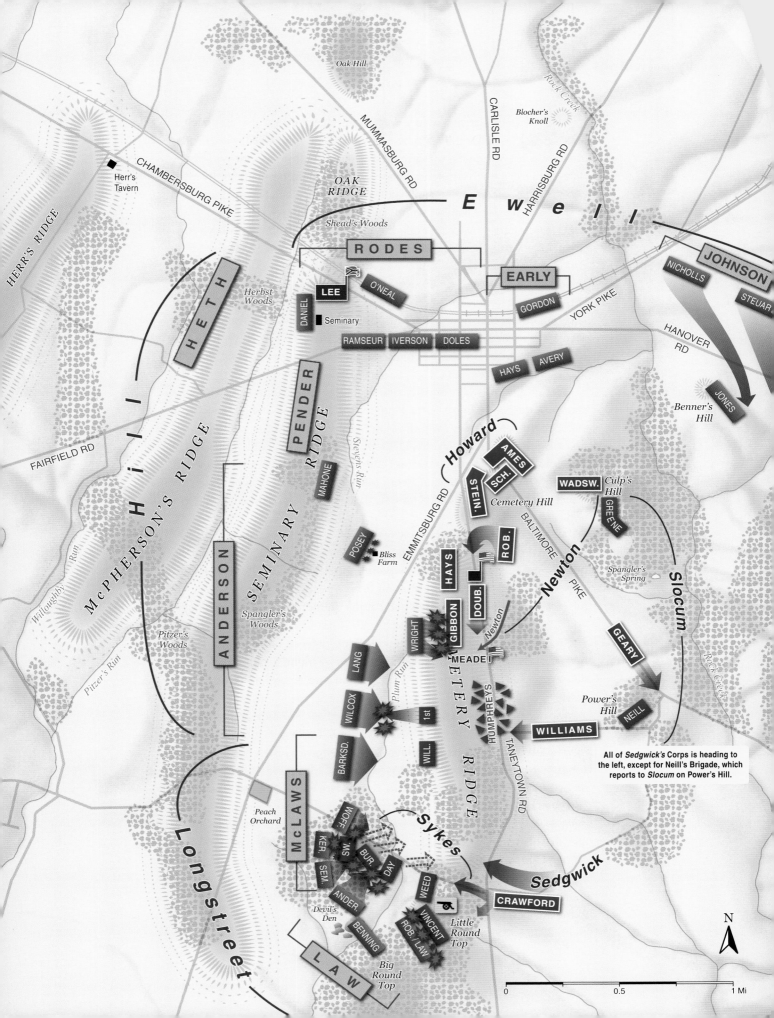

Herr's Tavern

CHAMBERSBURG PIKE

OAK RIDGE

Oak Hill

Blocher's Knoll

Rock Creek

MUMMASBURG RD

CARLISLE RD

HARRISBURG RD

E w e l l

Shead's Woods

RODES

JOHNSON

NICHOLLS

STEUAR.

HERR'S RIDGE

HETH

Herbst Woods

LEE

O'NEAL

DANIEL

Seminary

EARLY

GORDON

YORK PIKE

HANOVER RD

RAMSEUR   IVERSON   DOLES

HAYS   AVERY

Benner's Hill

JONES

FAIRFIELD RD

PENDER RIDGE

MAHONE

Stevens Run

McPHERSON'S RIDGE

Willoughby Run

SEMINARY

ANDERSON

Spangler's Woods

Pitzer's Woods

Pitzer's Run

POSEY

Bliss Farm

EMMITSBURG RD

Howard

AMES

SCH.

STEIN.

Cemetery Hill

BALTIMORE

WADSW.

Culp's Hill

GREENE

Spangler's Spring

Slocum

ROB.

HAYS

DOUB.

Newton

GEARY

Power's Hill

NEILL

LANG

WRIGHT

GIBBON

MEADE

CEMETERY RIDGE

WILCOX

1st

HUMPHREYS

WILLIAMS

BARKSD.

WILL.

Plum Run

TANEYTOWN RD

All of *Sedgwick's* Corps is heading to the left, except for Neill's Brigade, which reports to *Slocum* on Power's Hill.

McLAWS

Peach Orchard

WOFF.

KER.

MS

SEM

BUR

DAY

Sykes

ANDER.

WEED

Devil's Den

BENNING

ROB./LAW

VINCENT

Little Round Top

Sedgwick

CRAWFORD

LAW

Big Round Top

Longstreet

N

0   0.5   1 Mi

Little Round Top: repeated Confederate charges, into fire at times so intense their ascending lines bow and waver as if before an iron gale, fail. They try again, struggling up through the hardwood forest in the end-of-day dim. Chamberlain's thin defense line thins still more as his dead fall. By disciplined fire his depleted riflemen maintain a seamless front, aiming downward at the eerie yells and flaming barrels surging up at them in the gloam.

Oates's Alabamans and beside them the Texans of Robertson have tried the heights with repeated gallantry. But their earlier march to the field, then to Plum Run, then the divertive ascent of the near-vertical woods of Big Round Top (Oates), and now the strain of their charges up the Little Round Top steep—all have taken a toll. Oates will decline to attack again. Chamberlain can't know this; he must assume another charge is coming. His Maine men are dwindled awfully in their ranks, like so many units on both sides this day. They're out of ammo. They're used up. There's no retreat route. They are MEADE's left anchor.

Chamberlain's bayonet charge

Joshua Chamberlain finds it practicable to fix bayonets. He orders a charge. A desperate one it is, hurtling down the wooded steep through the shadows to catch Oates's withdrawing Southerners by utter surprise. It's a rout, legendary. Back on the hilltop in the dying light the last of Vincent's Brigade, bolstered by the 140th New York from neighboring Weed, breaks what will be the final Rebel assault against Little Round Top (by Robertson's Texans) with bullet swarms so dense "a man could hold out a hat and catch it full."

MEADE's left is secure. The Gray gave its all. The Federals likewise.

Near the darkling swale of Plum Run, Barksdale is discovered on the ground, nobody around him, his wound mortal. He lifts his head to accept some water, which, an instant after his drinking, ebbs from his chest. He will not last the night, his uniformed body at the mercy of momento-scavengers and hospital flies.

Now MEADE's reinforced Cemetery Ridge defense comes down off its high ground to drive the spent Confederates—Wright, Lang, Wilcox, Barksdale—back off their hard-won gains, toward and across the Emmitsburg Road.

Farther south, the brigades of Wofford, Kershaw, Semmes, and Anderson, exhausted by a long three hours of fighting, make a last-gasp advance toward Little Round Top's open face. Seeing *Sedgwick's* men flood the area, *Longstreet* orders a retreat. Wofford is furious. McCandless's Pennsylvania Reserves and Nevin's Brigade seal the Rebels' fate with a charge through the "Valley of Death."

A period has been put to the late-afternoon and summer-evening struggles, in which many a unit has lost over half its men. Casualties, so far this day: Confederates roughly 6,000 out of more than 17,000 men engaged; Union perhaps 9,000 out of at least 26,000.

Now in the northeast, *Ewell* advances Johnson's Division toward Culp's Hill to the attack, a futile postscript to LEE's failed plan.

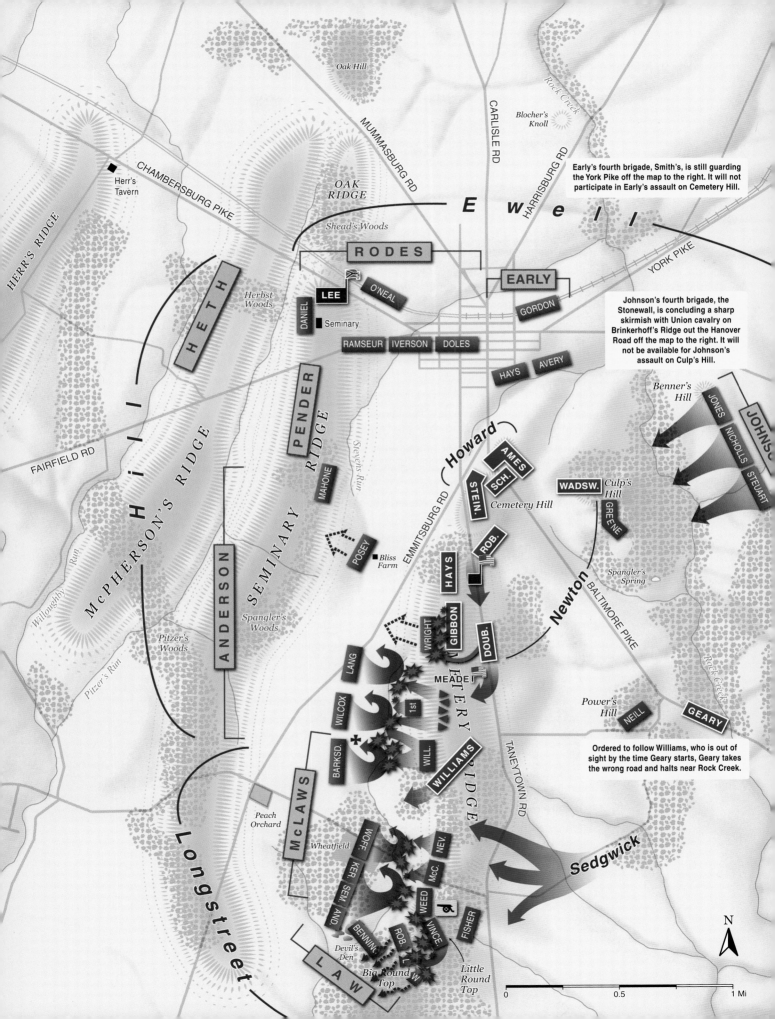

Herr's Tavern

CHAMBERSBURG PIKE

MUMMASBURG RD

CARLISLE RD

HARRISBURG RD

Oak Hill

Blocher's Knoll

Rock Creek

HERR'S RIDGE

OAK RIDGE

Shead's Woods

E   w   e   l   l

Early's fourth brigade, Smith's, is still guarding the York Pike off the map to the right. It will not participate in Early's assault on Cemetery Hill.

RODES

HETH

Herbst Woods

LEE

O'NEAL

EARLY

YORK PIKE

Daniel

Seminary

GORDON

Johnson's fourth brigade, the Stonewall, is concluding a sharp skirmish with Union cavalry on Brinkerhoff's Ridge out the Hanover Road off the map to the right. It will not be available for Johnson's assault on Culp's Hill.

RAMSEUR   IVERSON   DOLES

HAYS   AVERY

Benner's Hill

JONES   NICHOLLS   STEUART   JOHNSO

PENDER RIDGE

MAHONE

Stevens Run

Howard

AMES

SCH.

STEIN.

Cemetery Hill

WADSW.

Culp's Hill

GREENE

FAIRFIELD RD

McPHERSON'S HILL

Willoughby Run

Pitzer's Woods

ANDERSON

SEMINARY

POSEY

Bliss Farm

EMMITSBURG RD

ROB.

HAYS

Spangler's Spring

Newton

BALTIMORE PIKE

Rock Creek

Spangler's Woods

WRIGHT

GIBBON

DOUB.

MEADE

Power's Hill

NEILL

GEARY

Pitzer's Run

LANG

WILCOX

1st

WILL.

WILLIAMS

TANEYTOWN RD

Ordered to follow Williams, who is out of sight by the time Geary starts, Geary takes the wrong road and halts near Rock Creek.

BARKSD.

*

McLAWS

Peach Orchard

Wheatfield

WOFF.

KER.

SEM.

AND.

NEV.

McC.

WEED

VINCE

FISHER

Sedgwick

Longstreet

BENNIN.

ROB.   L   W

Devil's Den

LAW

Big Round Top

Little Round Top

N

0   0.5   1 Mi

This is the attack on MEADE's right that LEE had hoped would happen many hours earlier, in at least some sort of sync with the opening of *Longstreet's* late-afternoon assault on *Sickles* and Anderson's strike at the Union center.

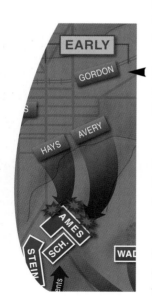

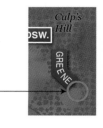

Johnson's advance on Culp's Hill is impeded by the crossing of Rock Creek, runs into stubborn Yankee skirmishers, and, upon reaching the near-sheer, bristling Union defense barriers—breastworks—which Confederate delay has allowed the Federals on Culp's to perfect, is thrown into two hours of the most deadly, snarling night combat. Union units (Geary, Williams) from this sector having earlier been sent south to help with the main fight, Culp's Hill is a thin, stretched defense, its right (southeast) line even empty in spots.

Reinforced by *Howard* and then by Wadsworth and benefitting from the rugged leadership of elderly, nails-tough Brigadier Greene, to whom the near-impregnability of the Union breastworks is to be credited, the Yankee position on Culp's Hill ends mainly as it began: secure . . . save for a single Rebel inroad, where Steuart's attacking brigade (STE.) achieves, chigger-like, a position. This happens where the above-mentioned spots, earlier emptied to rush reinforcements to *Sickles* and others, remained empty! On the southern/southeastern slope of Culp's, then, Steuart's Gray brigade will pass the night. It is a wedge, potentially significant, if small, in the righthand terminus of MEADE's upside-down-J line.

(Geary's Division, earlier ordered out of this sector and tasked with heading south to help reinforce the main fight, became lost and, unbelievably, wandered off course to hang around in a quiet backwater for considerable hours . . . Geary and Williams will return in the night. Looking to re-occupy their old position but finding it full of Rebs, they will decline, in the blackness, to attempt reclamation.)

As Johnson's night fight to take Culp's Hill is failing, over on Cemetery Hill Early's attack, with half his division, in more bitter hand-to-hand fighting in the flashing dark finds only short-lived success against positions reinforced by *Hancock*.

Early withdraws.

Rodes's Division, next to the west in *Ewell's* awkward line, took too long making preparations for *its* participation in the sector's action. Rodes's advance, supported by part of Pender, scarcely gets started before petering out.

A comedy of errors?

Combat can seem so. In accounts of it, combat can appear comical. Cataclysmic. Sublime. Human excellence in action. Valor. Command genius. Noble sacrifice. Moronic stupidity. This is because battle accounts tend naturally to describe extremes. Extremes are more interesting,

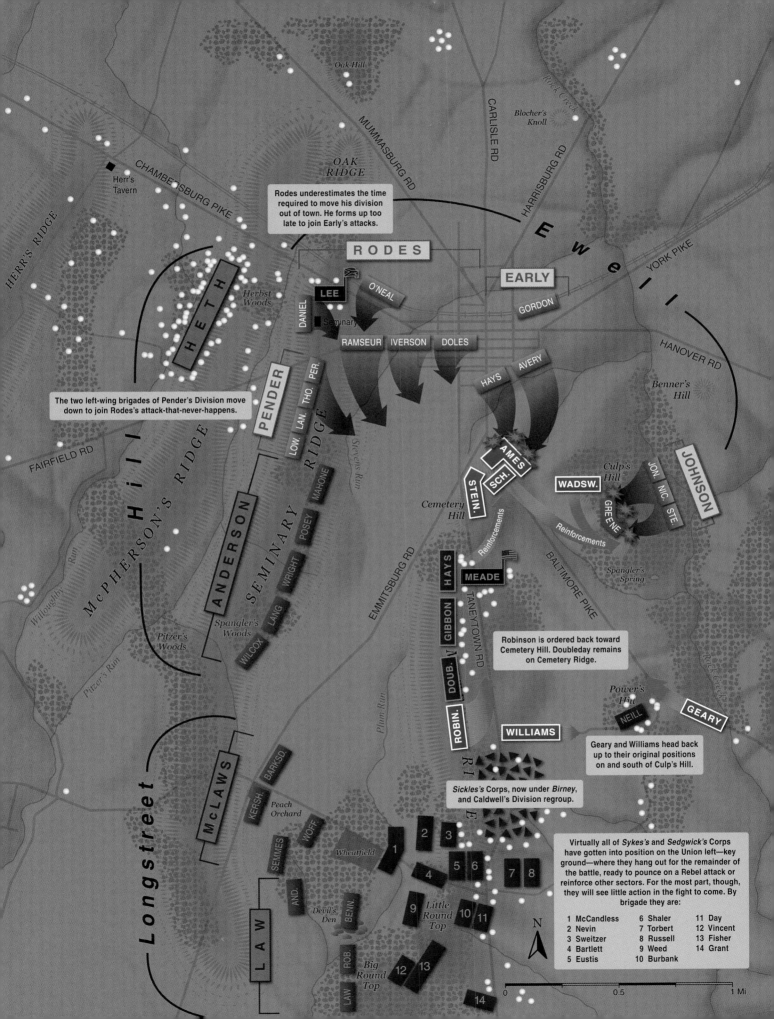

CHAMBERSBURG PIKE

Herr's Tavern

HERR'S RIDGE

OAK RIDGE

Oak Hill

MUMMASBURG RD

CARLISLE RD

Blocher's Knoll

Rock Creek

HARRISBURG RD

E
w
e
l
l

Rodes underestimates the time required to move his division out of town. He forms up too late to join Early's attacks.

RODES

HETH

Herbst Woods

LEE

O'NEAL

DANIEL

Seminary

RAMSEUR   IVERSON   DOLES

EARLY

GORDON

YORK PIKE

HANOVER RD

Benner's Hill

HAYS   AVERY

The two left-wing brigades of Pender's Division move down to join Rodes's attack-that-never-happens.

PENDER

LOW. LAN. THO. PER.

SEMINARY RIDGE

Stevens Run

McPHERSON'S RIDGE

FAIRFIELD RD

MAHONE

POSEY

WRIGHT

ANDERSON

LANG

Willoughby Run

Spangler's Woods

WILCOX

Pitzer's Woods

Pitzer's Run

McPherson Hill

AMES

SCH.

STEIN.

Cemetery Hill

WADSW.

Culp's Hill

GREENE

JON. NIC. STE.

JOHNSON

Spangler's Spring

Reinforcements

Reinforcements

HAYS

MEADE

GIBBON

TANEYTOWN RD

EMMITSBURG RD

DOUB. V

BALTIMORE PIKE

Robinson is ordered back toward Cemetery Hill. Doubleday remains on Cemetery Ridge.

ROBIN.

Power's Hill

NEILL

GEARY

Rock Creek

WILLIAMS

Plum Run

Geary and Williams head back up to their original positions on and south of Culp's Hill.

Longstreet

McLAWS

BARKSD.

KERSH.

Peach Orchard

WOFF.

SEMMES

R
I
E

Sickles's Corps, now under Birney, and Caldwell's Division regroup.

Wheatfield

AND.

Devil's Den

BENN.

ROB.

LAW

LAW

Big Round Top

Little Round Top

1

2   3

5   6

4

9

7   8

10 11

12   13

14

Virtually all of *Sykes's* and *Sedgwick's* Corps have gotten into position on the Union left—key ground—where they hang out for the remainder of the battle, ready to pounce on a Rebel attack or reinforce other sectors. For the most part, though, they will see little action in the fight to come. By brigade they are:

1 McCandless	6 Shaler	11 Day
2 Nevin	7 Torbert	12 Vincent
3 Sweitzer	8 Russell	13 Fisher
4 Bartlett	9 Weed	14 Grant
5 Eustis	10 Burbank	

N

0   0.5   1 Mi

more exciting, and they have more effect on outcome. But the preponderance of battle is a process of normal folk going about the terrifying workaday business of trying to kill and survive. Scared, staunch, average, unsung, the Unknown shoulder the massive weight of obedient routine.

Success is gained at the "bottom" by the faceless rifleman, the near-deaf gunner. By the cooks and drovers and medics who support them. The generals at the top indeed cast their spell for good or ill: no army succeeds without an informed plan, canniness, experience, and a dogged—merciless if need be—seeing to specifics.

MEADE holds another council of war. At his headquarters past ten o'clock with his top men, he decides to hold—defend the excellent high ground they have kept during the day's fight.

Hope LEE tries us again.

LEE at around the same time finalizes his desire, on the morrow, to attack MEADE's left (Little Round Top and environs) (lower green arrows) and right (Culp's Hill) (upper green arrow), early.

LEE wants Jeb Stuart at the same time to ride his 5,000 elite cavalrymen out into the east, seek opportunities to cause MEADE trouble from that direction.

LEE wants Pickett's fresh division to lead the attack in the Little Round Top sector, supported by McLaws and Law.

LEE believes he sensed, today, in the late afternoon and early evening, and most especially in the collapse of *Sickles*, MEADE's edifice totter.

LEE believes, and rightly so, in his fighting men's prowess and morale.

An early-morning attack if properly coordinated, with fresh brigades such as are available, will kick MEADE off his high ground in defeat.

On Day One LEE's infantry mauled two Union corps, sending them reeling. Today LEE obliterated *Sickles*, stung MEADE's center, got a toehold on Culp's. Tomorrow, with benefit of early-morning surprise:

Longstreet hits MEADE.

Ewell hits MEADE.

Hill is poised opposite MEADE's center.

Stuart is ready to exploit success.

LEE doesn't doubt the outcome. He outlines this plan for his commanders, not, however, meeting with them as a group.

A key will be Pickett's divisional attack on the Union right, first thing in the morning. Knowing this, *Longstreet*, as the night hours and wee morning hours of July 2–3 pass, omits to perform a routine task, the ordering of Pickett's Division forward and south, under cover of darkness, to approximately the jump-off position LEE has indicated for the morning attack. (Contrast with *Ewell*, who during these same hours, knowing *he* is to attack early, has reinforcing brigades on the move to Culp's Hill.)

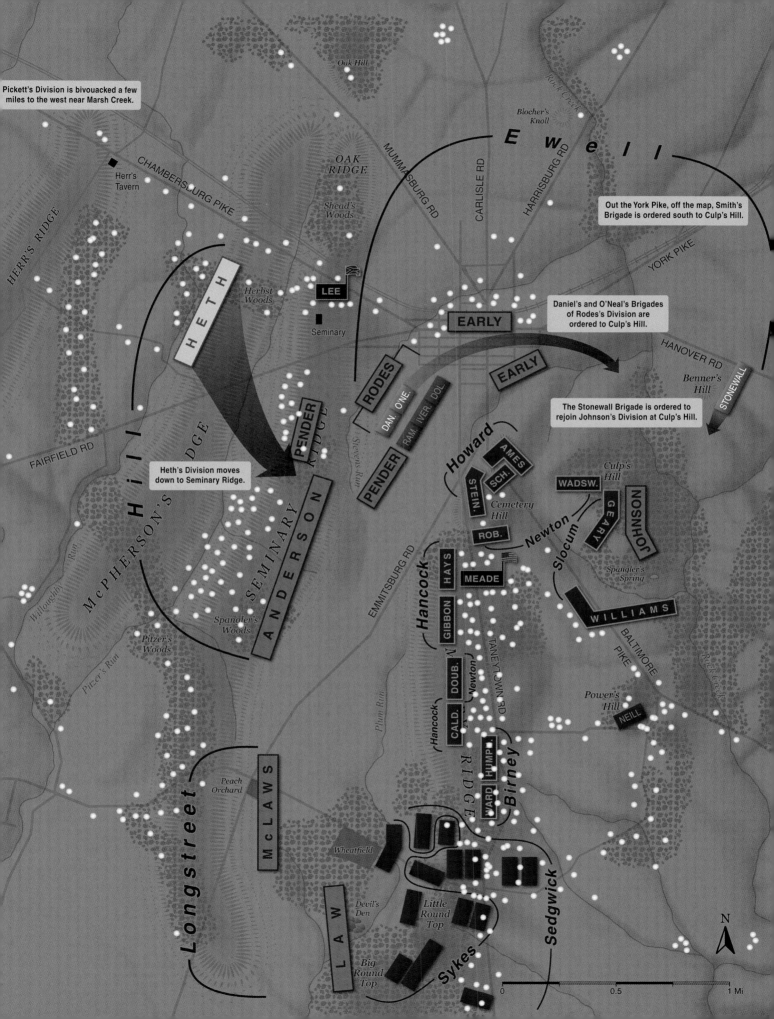

Pickett's Division is bivouacked a few miles to the west near Marsh Creek.

Out the York Pike, off the map, Smith's Brigade is ordered south to Culp's Hill.

Daniel's and O'Neal's Brigades of Rodes's Division are ordered to Culp's Hill.

The Stonewall Brigade is ordered to rejoin Johnson's Division at Culp's Hill.

Heth's Division moves down to Seminary Ridge.

CHAMBERSBURG PIKE

Herr's Tavern

OAK RIDGE

Oak Hill

Blocher's Knoll

MUMMASBURG RD

CARLISLE RD

HARRISBURG RD

Rock Creek

E w e l l

YORK PIKE

HANOVER RD

Benner's Hill

STONEWALL

HERR'S RIDGE

Shead's Woods

HETH

Herbst Woods

LEE

Seminary

EARLY

RODES

DAN. ONE.

RAM. IVER. DOL.

EARLY

FAIRFIELD RD

PENDER RIDGE

SEMINARY RIDGE

McPHERSON'S RIDGE

Willoughby Run

Pitzer's Run

PENDER

PENDER

Stevens's Run

Howard

AMES

SCH.

STEIN.

Cemetery Hill

ROB.

Newton

WADSW.

Culp's Hill

GEARY

JOHNSON

Spangler's Spring

Slocum

BALTIMORE PIKE

Rock Creek

ANDERSON

Spangler's Woods

Pitzer's Woods

EMMITTSBURG RD

Hancock

HAYS

GIBBON

MEADE

DOUB.

Newton

CALD.

Hancock

TANEYTOWN RD

HUMP.

WARD

Birney

RIDGE

WILLIAMS

Power's Hill

NEILL

Longstreet

McLAWS

Peach Orchard

Wheatfield

Plum Run

Devil's Den

LAW

Little Round Top

Big Round Top

Sykes

Sedgwick

N

0   0.5   1 Mi

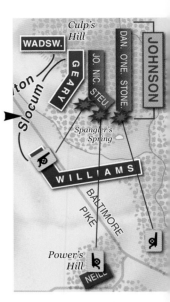

Gray predawn shows the ridge crests and wooded hills. A rumbling of artillery is coming from the vicinity of Culp's Hill.

The Yankees want their wedge of right flank back.

Where Steuart's Brigade has spent the night, holding their sylvan sliver of Culp's Hill's lower slope, now in the warming dawn a blizzard of screaming shells of deadly variety arcs down. From in-range Union batteries—especially on Power's Hill—the bombardment tells ruinously on Johnson's Rebs, who cringe in the formerly Union breastworks of branch, stone, detritus, and earth.

LEE and *Longstreet* hear it, statuesque on their horses on Seminary Ridge: to their ears an unmistakable if distant booming (to Steuart's infantrymen a deafening, banshee, ceaseless hail-cloud of defoliating, flesh-rending missiles).

The gunfire means *Ewell* is in a fight. Not the dawn attack doubly and simultaneously on MEADE's right and left that LEE had in mind. That plan is not going to eventuate. This steady, distant boom and rumble from *Ewell's* sector means the balloon, in some fashion, is up there. Here in the south, however, where LEE and *Longstreet* sit erect in their saddles across from MEADE's left, *Longstreet's* Corps is not remotely ready to attack.

Uneasy with each other, the two great generals sit their horses on the ridge.

Before dawn, *Longstreet* rode northeast to here from his headquarters.

LEE rode south to here from his headquarters.

They met as the sun rose.

It's the first in-person meeting the two have had since yesterday afternoon.

Last night, when LEE issued his orders for the simultaneous double attack on MEADE's flanks, to happen at first light, *Longstreet* wasn't present. *Longstreet* did not follow his customary practice of riding to LEE at the end of a day's fight. Nor did LEE require it. Neither, in fact, has *Ewell* been in personal consultation with LEE. Both corps commanders received their orders for today from LEE by courier during the night. (Years later, *Longstreet* will maintain he never received such orders, an untruth.)

LEE is greatly disconcerted. There will be no dawn attack here on MEADE's left such as he'd envisioned. Pickett's fresh division—a key, LEE thought he made clear—is hours away from its attack position. This should have been taken care of overnight (a tactical basic).

LEE demands an explanation.

Longstreet launches into a spiel about how he's had scouts out all night investigating MEADE's lines. He expresses his confidence that a maneuver in force, rather than a direct attack—an expedition in around

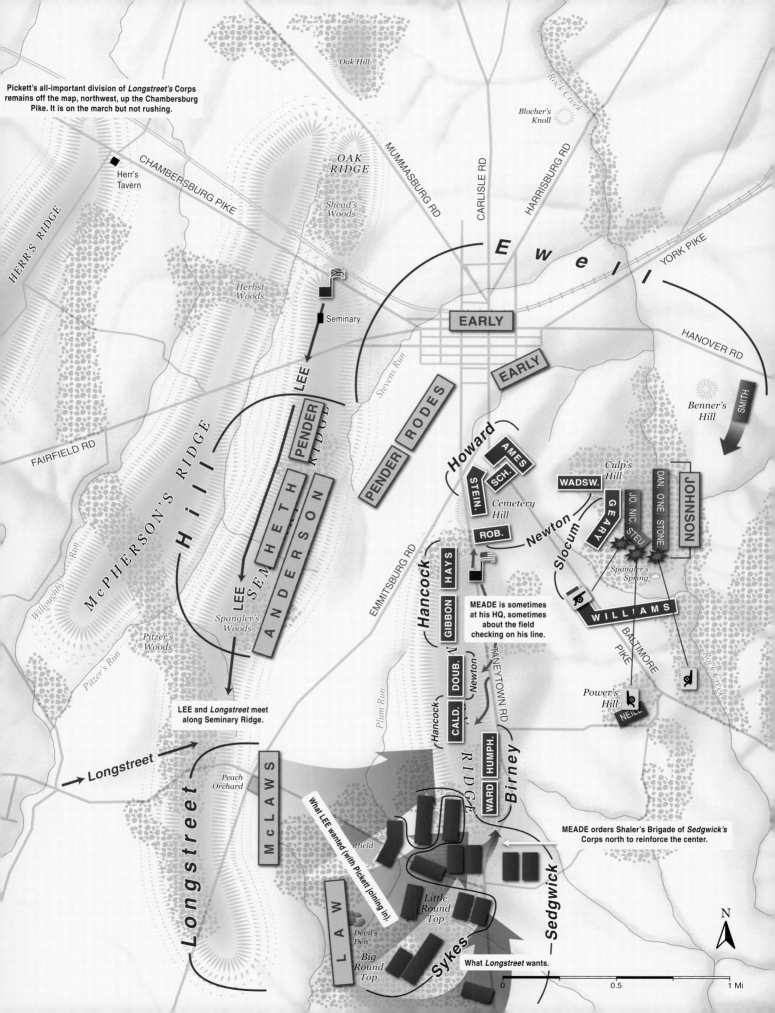

Pickett's all-important division of *Longstreet's* Corps remains off the map, northwest, up the Chambersburg Pike. It is on the march but not rushing.

Herr's Tavern

CHAMBERSBURG PIKE

HERR'S RIDGE

Oak Hill

OAK RIDGE

MUMMASBURG RD

CARLISLE RD

HARRISBURG RD

Rock Creek

Blocher's Knoll

Shead's Woods

E w e l l

YORK PIKE

Herbst Woods

Seminary

LEE

EARLY

EARLY

HANOVER RD

Benner's Hill

SMITH

FAIRFIELD RD

McPHERSON'S RIDGE

Hill

Willoughby Run

PENDER

RIDGE

PENDER

RODES

Howard

AMES

SCH.

STEIN.

Cemetery Hill

ROB.

Newton

Slocum

WADSW.

Culp's Hill

JO. NIC. STEU

DAN. O'NE. STONE

JOHNSON

Spangler's Spring

WILLIAMS

BALTIMORE PIKE

Rock Creek

LEE

HETH

ANDERSON

Spangler's Woods

Pitzer's Woods

Pitzer's Run

Plum Run

EMMITSBURG RD

Hancock

HAYS

GIBBON

MEADE is sometimes at his HQ, sometimes about the field checking on his line.

DOUB.

Newton

Hancock

CALD.

TANEYTOWN RD

Power's Hill

NEILL

LEE and *Longstreet* meet along Seminary Ridge.

Longstreet

Longstreet

Peach Orchard

McLAWS

HUMPH.

WARD

Birney

RIDGE

MEADE orders Shaler's Brigade of *Sedgwick's* Corps north to reinforce the center.

What LEE wanted (with Pickett joining in).

LAW

Wheatfield

Little Round Top

Sedgwick

Devil's Den

Big Round Top

Sykes

What *Longstreet* wants.

N

0   0.5   1 Mi

and *behind* MEADE's left flank, below the Round Tops—can succeed. This *Longstreet* has been preparing for, he informs the gray-white, ramrod-straight, gentlemanly living legend in the saddle beside him.

LEE lifts his fist.

Looking eastward at MEADE's defense line on Cemetery Ridge, LEE repeats his intent (not for the first time) to attack.

Not in *behind* anything.

From the sound of things, *Ewell's* already in a fight or about to be.

Longstreet won't be ready to attack for who knows how long. He's been organizing an attack LEE doesn't want. And Pickett's not up.

LEE decides to modify his plan to hit MEADE's flanks. He begins thinking about MEADE's center.

Meanwhile, *Longstreet's* excellent artilleryman, Alexander, entrusted by *Longstreet* (over certain of Alexander's superiors) to oversee the all-important placement of *Longstreet's* artillery here in the southern sector of LEE's position, has been up since before dawn diligently seeing to his batteries, their position, their ammo supply, their angle, range, interrelation. At first light, seeing right off, and with consternation, a line of twelve cannon by the Peach Orchard placed so as to be vulnerable to deadly at-the-diagonal Yankee fire, Alexander rapidly realigned the guns. Diligently he has been continuing his preparations the while . . .

MEADE too, up early and in the saddle, visits his positions with characteristic nervous energy seeing to disposition and role. More than one subordinate will later speak of MEADE's seeming glow of confidence.

Perhaps the famed MEADE temper crackles as well. If so, not surprising . . . but MEADE's wrath, when it flares, is in the service neither of legend nor bombast but, rather, in the service of seeing happen what he wants to have happen.

Jeb Stuart is getting underway for his assigned ride eastward, off the map, to get into position to menace MEADE's rear east of the Cemetery Ridge defense line.

Hill . . . is a cipher. LEE has spent more time in the company of *A. P. Hill* than of any other of his corps commanders, probably not despite his doubts about *Hill* but because of them. (Also conceivably because *Hill* is passive—unlike *Ewell* and *Longstreet* tends not to say no.)

LEE and *Longstreet*, on foot (somewhere around **[1]**), glass the Union defenses. *Hill* and others join the group. LEE still wants *Longstreet's* Corps to play a major role, namely all three of *Longstreet's* divisions, McLaws, Law (formerly Hood), and Pickett when he shows up. LEE wants to hit MEADE's center now. LEE points to approximately **[2]**. *Longstreet* protests that in addition to McLaws's and Law's hard fight of yesterday, if he sends them up that way (toward MEADE's center), they will be mortally exposed to Union attack and fire on their right **[3]**. LEE: all

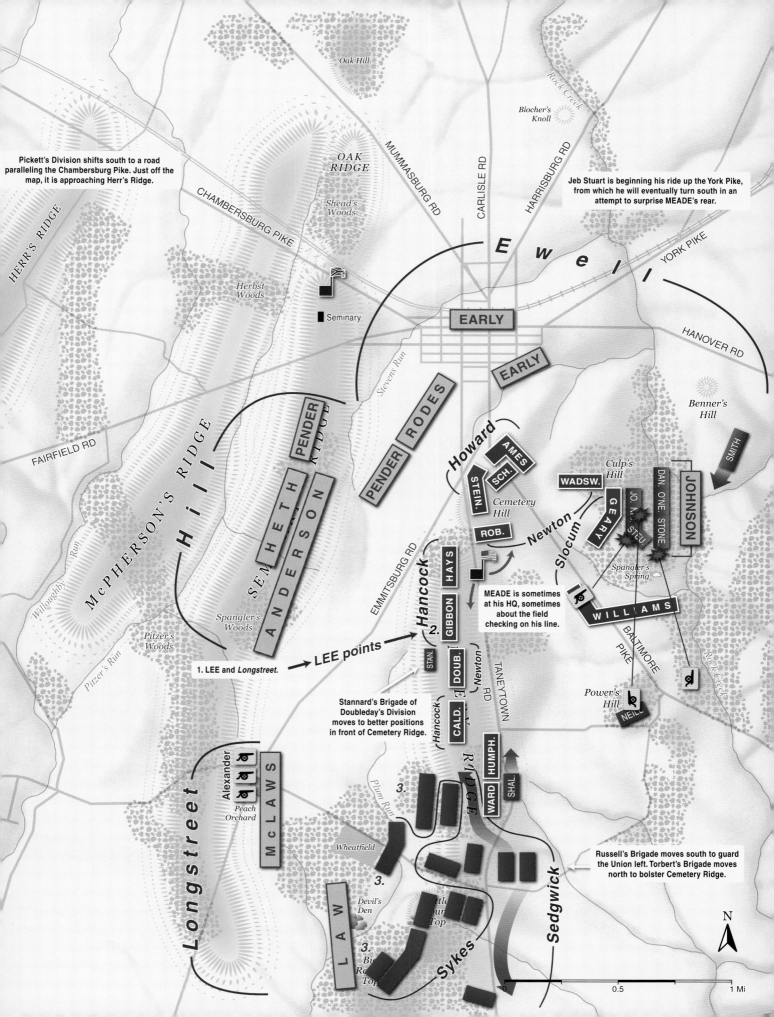

Pickett's Division shifts south to a road paralleling the Chambersburg Pike. Just off the map, it is approaching Herr's Ridge.

Jeb Stuart is beginning his ride up the York Pike, from which he will eventually turn south in an attempt to surprise MEADE's rear.

Oak Hill

Blocher's Knoll

Rock Creek

OAK RIDGE

MUMMASBURG RD

CARLISLE RD

HARRISBURG RD

Shead's Woods

CHAMBERSBURG PIKE

E   w   e   l   l

YORK PIKE

Herbst Woods

HERR'S RIDGE

Seminary

EARLY

EARLY

HANOVER RD

Benner's Hill

FAIRFIELD RD

PENDER

PENDER RIDGE

RODES

Howard

AMES

STEIN.

SCH.

Cemetery Hill

SMITH

Culp's Hill

WADSW.

GEARY

JO. M.

DAN. O'NE. STONE.

JOHNSON

Stevens Run

M c PHERSON'S RIDGE Hill

SEM

HETH

ANDERSON

Spangler's Woods

Pitzer's Woods

Willoughby Run

ROB.

Newton

Slocum

STEU

Spangler's Spring

WILLIAMS

BALTIMORE PIKE

Rock Creek

EMMITSBURG RD

Hancock

HAYS

GIBBON

2.

MEADE is sometimes at his HQ, sometimes about the field checking on his line.

1. LEE and *Longstreet*. ➔ LEE points ➔

STAN.

DOUB.

Newton

Hancock

Stannard's Brigade of Doubleday's Division moves to better positions in front of Cemetery Ridge.

CALD.

TANEYTOWN RD

Power's Hill

NEILL

Pitzer's Run

Longstreet

Alexander

McLAWS

Peach Orchard

Plum Run

WARD

HUMPH.

SHAL.

RIDGE

Russell's Brigade moves south to guard the Union left. Torbert's Brigade moves north to bolster Cemetery Ridge.

Wheatfield

3.

3.

LAW

Devil's Den

Little Round Top

Sedgwick

3.

Big Round Top

Sykes

N

0   0.5   1 Mi

right, then keep McLaws and Law where they are. Attack MEADE's center with Pickett. As overall commander of the attack, which I appoint you, you—*Longstreet*—will use half of *Hill's* Corps (Heth's Division, led by Pettigrew; part of Pender's Division, under Trimble) next to Pickett in the main attack. Wilcox's and Lang's Brigades, from Anderson's Division, will support the attack's right. McLaws and Law will play a supporting role. As will, on the left, beyond your (*Longstreet's*) command, Anderson's remaining three brigades, two from Pender, and even three from Rodes if opportune. *Or so LEE believes he has ordered.* Thus "Pickett's Charge."

Preparatory to which, LEE decrees an artillery barrage. It will be colossal when it comes, thundering from the top of the map to the bottom, the greatest concentration of cannon fire in the Western Hemisphere ever.

Longstreet continues unenthusiastic. *"Pete" Longstreet*, whom LEE affectionately refers to as "my old war horse," is a seasoned, proven fighter. *Longstreet* is a man of considerable courage, as well as stamina. Anything but flamboyant, a careful soul, much given to mulling before taking action, he dreads sending soldiers to their possible death in an attack plan he more than doubts—is certain will fail. Decades later *Longstreet* will write that LEE "should have put an officer in charge who had more confidence in his plan." A remark the unworthiness of which, the more the words are considered, is breathtaking.

Starting before sunrise and continuing through the morning, across the gently rolling expanse of the battlefield, in its woods and grain fields and along its open inclines, the usual scattered flurries of rifle fire and musketry break out, densifying and as quickly dying to silence as skirmishers from both sides go about the screening, testing, taunting, probing work in the no-man's-land between the waiting, bristling masses of divisions and corps.

The hard action is on Culp's Hill. There an infantry attack against the Union defense lines (who thought *they* were going to attack first) is initiated by Johnson—*Ewell's* left jab to accompany *Longstreet's* right, which *Ewell* believes will begin any minute two miles to the southwest.

Johnson's frontline brigades of Steuart, Nicholls, and Jones open fire and press up the wooded, rocky slope **[1]**, trying to expand the toehold of Union breastworks won by Steuart last night. Walker's famed Stonewall Brigade advances in support **[2]**. It's a game attack, but without satisfaction.

Ewell learns that *Longstreet* won't get started for hours, but it's too late to stop Johnson.

Between attacks Johnson keeps the Yankees uphill from him, on Culp's, under heavy rifle and sniper fire, in time ordering O'Neal's Brigade (which arrived overnight from Rodes's Division) into attack line for a second Rebel surge **[3]**. O'Neal's men pass through Johnson's first line, moving out smartly toward the Union Culp's Hill defenders, only to be halted by more devastating cannon and rifle fire.

At the Bliss Farm, on its no-man's-land expanse of open terrain midway between the two great armies, yesterday's back-and-forth deadly quarrel persists, now drawing in artillery fire which comes to nothing (and to Alexander, observing from the south, constitutes a waste of precious ammunition).

Bliss Farm

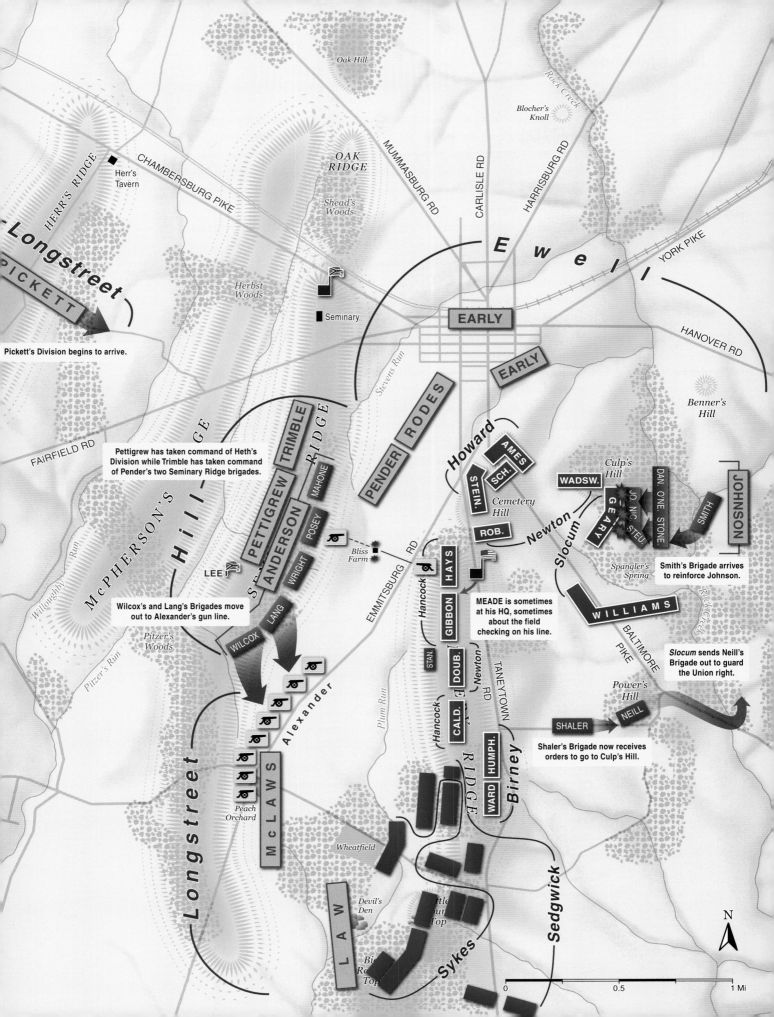

Herr's Tavern

CHAMBERSBURG PIKE

HERR'S RIDGE

Oak Hill

OAK RIDGE

MUMMASBURG RD

CARLISLE RD

HARRISBURG RD

Blocher's Knoll

Rock Creek

YORK PIKE

E w e l l

Longstreet

PICKETT

Pickett's Division begins to arrive.

Shead's Woods

Herbst Woods

Seminary

Seminary

EARLY

EARLY

HANOVER RD

Benner's Hill

PENDER

RODES

Howard

TRIMBLE

RIDGE

Pettigrew has taken command of Heth's Division while Trimble has taken command of Pender's two Seminary Ridge brigades.

MAHONE

PETTIGREW

ANDERSON

POSEY

WRIGHT

LEE

McPHERSON'S HILL

Willoughby Run

Wilcox's and Lang's Brigades move out to Alexander's gun line.

Pitzer's Woods

Pitzer's Run

WILCOX

LANG

Alexander

Bliss Farm

Emmitsburg RD

Stevens Run

AMES

STEIN.

SCH.

Cemetery Hill

ROB.

Newton

WADSW.

GEARY

JO. NIC. STEU

DAN. ONE. STONE.

SMITH

JOHNSON

Smith's Brigade arrives to reinforce Johnson.

Culp's Hill

Slocum

Spangler's Spring

Rock Creek

HAYS

Hancock

GIBBON

MEADE is sometimes at his HQ, sometimes about the field checking on his line.

WILLIAMS

BALTIMORE PIKE

STAN.

DOUB.

Newton

Hancock

CALD.

HUMPH.

WARD

Birney

RIDGE

TANEYTOWN RD

Slocum sends Neill's Brigade out to guard the Union right.

Power's Hill

SHALER

NEILL

Shaler's Brigade now receives orders to go to Culp's Hill.

McLAWS

Peach Orchard

Wheatfield

Devil's Den

Little Round Top

LAW

Big Round Top

Sykes

Sedgwick

FAIRFIELD RD

N

0   0.5   1 Mi

Longstreet makes his expectations for the coming cannonade clear. *Longstreet* wants Alexander's guns to "cripple the enemy," preparatory to the 13,000-man infantry assault over a half mile of open fields smack in the face of MEADE's arrayed artillery and riflemen. *Longstreet* wants a barrage that will achieve far more than merely to soften the Yankees up (a further reflection of *Longstreet's* doubts).

Alexander continues diligently placing his cannon for maximum tactical effect. To his north, Walker, for *Hill's* Corps, does the same. North of town, Brown, in charge of *Ewell's* "Arty.", is doing likewise. Neither as capably or effectively as Alexander, however (nor with much oversight from their superiors).

Up above the Rebels on Culp's Hill, from behind breastworks and boulders, Union soldiers pour murderous volleys downslope. Blue regiments rotate into and out of the firing line: spent units pull back to rest cramped, sweaty bodies and replenish ammunition while fresh men and muskets take their places. The constant fire has blunted two Confederate attacks and shows no signs of letting up.

Johnson orders Steuart's and Daniel's Brigades to make an all-out charge: take Culp's Hill from MEADE once and for all. Both commanders, neither prone to shirk from a good fight, say it's suicide.

Johnson won't hear of it. Following orders, Steuart quits the shelter of the "wedge" of captured Yankee breastworks and moves south, where his brigade is to make the main effort. Daniel forms up on Steuart's right. The Stonewall Brigade comes in on Daniel's right to support the attack.

Through an open field Steuart charges his men **[1]** into a Union fusillade from three sides including rifle fire and artillery canister of such blizzard-like, unremitting density that whole ranks of gray are scythed down at a stroke. The brave Steuart is reduced to tears—"My poor boys."

Though less exposed than Steuart, and having to cover less ground, Daniel and the Stonewall meet a wall of blasting musketry **[2]**. They too are repulsed.

MEADE tends to detail with nervous energy, receiving reports, issuing orders, moving between his little headquarters building and various outdoor vantage points from which he can view the field. He consults with key subordinates personally: *Newton, Hancock, Howard . . .*

Pickett is at Spangler's Woods. His division is finally near, though still not at, his designated jump-off area for the great charge to come.

LEE tours his lines, passes among the resting foot soldiers and wheeling bronze guns, sometimes with *Longstreet*, sometimes not, checking (one assumes) like MEADE the detail of his forces' disposition and orders. It is a fact that there are many, many more orders issued by MEADE this morning, as well as during the course of the entire battle, than by LEE.

The Bliss Farm contest ends in a consummation of flame when Union General Hays, tired of the distraction (and potential obstruction to future crucial lines of fire), orders the farm buildings burned to the ground.

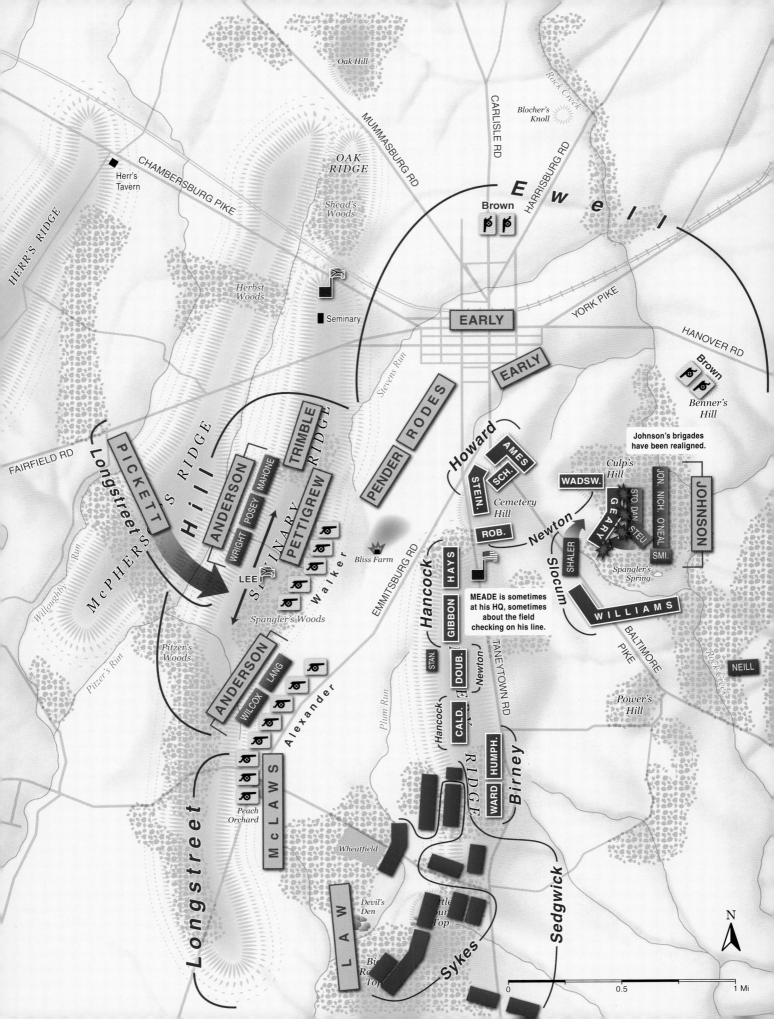

Herr's Tavern

CHAMBERSBURG PIKE

HERR'S RIDGE

Oak Hill

OAK RIDGE

MUMMASBURG RD

CARLISLE RD

Blocher's Knoll

Rock Creek

HARRISBURG RD

E w e l l

Brown

Shead's Woods

Herbst Woods

Seminary

Stevens Run

EARLY

YORK PIKE

EARLY

HANOVER RD

Brown

Benner's Hill

RODES

PENDER

Howard

AMES

SCH.

STEIN.

Cemetery Hill

ROB.

Newton

WADSW.

Culp's Hill

Johnson's brigades have been realigned.

STO. DAN. STEU

GEARY

JON. NICH. O'NEAL

SMI.

JOHNSON

Spangler's Spring

TRIMBLE

PICKETT

RIDGE

Hill

McPHERSON'S

Willoughby Run

Longstreet

ANDERSON

WRIGHT POSEY MAHONE

SEMINARY RIDGE

PETTIGREW

Walker

LEE

Spangler's Woods

Bliss Farm

EMMITSBURG RD

Slocum

SHALER

WILLIAMS

NEILL

Pitzer's Woods

ANDERSON

WILCOX LANG

Alexander

Pitzer's Run

Hancock

STAN.

GIBBON HAYS

MEADE is sometimes at his HQ, sometimes about the field checking on his line.

Power's Hill

BALTIMORE PIKE

Rock Creek

Hancock

CALD. DOUB.

Newton

E.

TANEYTOWN RD

HUMPH.

Birney

WARD

RIDGE

McLAWS

Wheatfield

Peach Orchard

Longstreet

LAW

Devil's Den

Little Round Top

Big Round Top

Sedgwick

Sykes

N

0   0.5   1 Mi

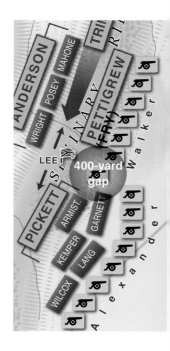

Alexander continues the careful placement of each of *Longstreet's* cannons as they are rolled forward. North of Alexander, only two-thirds of *Hill's* and fewer than half of *Ewell's* available cannons are being readied for use, the rest to be kept in reserve (one might ask for what). Sometime late morning, Alexander reports to *Longstreet* that the placement of his guns is complete. Approximately 160 Confederate cannon are ready.

Touring his lines, LEE either doesn't notice the 400-yard gap between Pettigrew's right (Fry) and Pickett's left (Garnett), or doesn't mind. (A massive frontal infantry charge with a big hole in its middle is a terrible idea.) LEE and *Longstreet* seem unaware of the severely degraded condition of much of Pettigrew's Division (formerly the wounded Heth's). The division is a third short of men after much tough fighting. Pettigrew has green colonels heading several of his brigades, rather than experienced brigadiers, and himself has never commanded a division (until two days ago). If LEE/*Longstreet* know about all this, they don't mind. If they don't know, they didn't ask. If *Hill* knows (he should: it's his corps), he doesn't tell. Others have fresher units with more seasoned commanders at the helm. These will not be used. Instead LEE selects Pettigrew, who happens to be near where LEE wants to attack.

Two brigades of Pender's Division, led by Trimble in place of the mortally wounded Pender, are to advance directly behind Pettigrew—behind Pettigrew's right, not his weaker left. One of even *these* brigades has lost almost half of its men, including most of its field officers. Trimble, belly-fire aggressive, eager to get into this fight since before it began, not having commanded a unit in battle for ten months, now, mere hours before the attack, takes over two brigades who don't know him and whom *he* doesn't know.

As Johnson is being repulsed at Culp's Hill, *Slocum*, without consulting or informing his subordinate, Williams, orders a Union counterattack on Johnson's brigades. The order is either garbled in transmission or misunderstood. One of the Federal officers tasked to carry out the attack calls it murder. And so it is, an assault without a prayer [1] (left)—useless bloody sacrifice . . .

Pickett's Division is finally in its pre-attack position.

The fight for Culp's Hill has ended. Six bitter hours of it. The woods there are lifeless, leafless, tree trunks filled with lead, bloated bodies askew. The Rebels have been pushed out of their wedge of advantage in MEADE's right.

A quiet descends. From Oak Hill to Big Round Top, the foot soldier seeks shade, snacks, naps, whiles his time. Odor, in oven-hot air, of thousands upon thousands of dead horses and humans across the countryside of yesterday's fight mingles with a sergeant's barked command, the chirp of a brave bird, snores from under shade trees, the nervy click, *snick* of fiddled-with rifles.

Longstreet as assigned tactical chief for the coming effort tends to his own corps, but not to *Hill's* (Pettigrew, Trimble). There is weakness on Pettigrew's left, where Brockenbrough's Brigade is a mess. The gap between Pickett and Pettigrew is a weakness, as is the lack of assigned flank-protection for the huge charge's left [1] and right [2] flanks, which will be "in the air". Weakness: the shortage of Rebel artillery ammo. Weakness: LEE's indifferent cannon placement (except for Alexander). All this, unnoticed or unattended to as the minutes pass, becomes irretrievably built in.

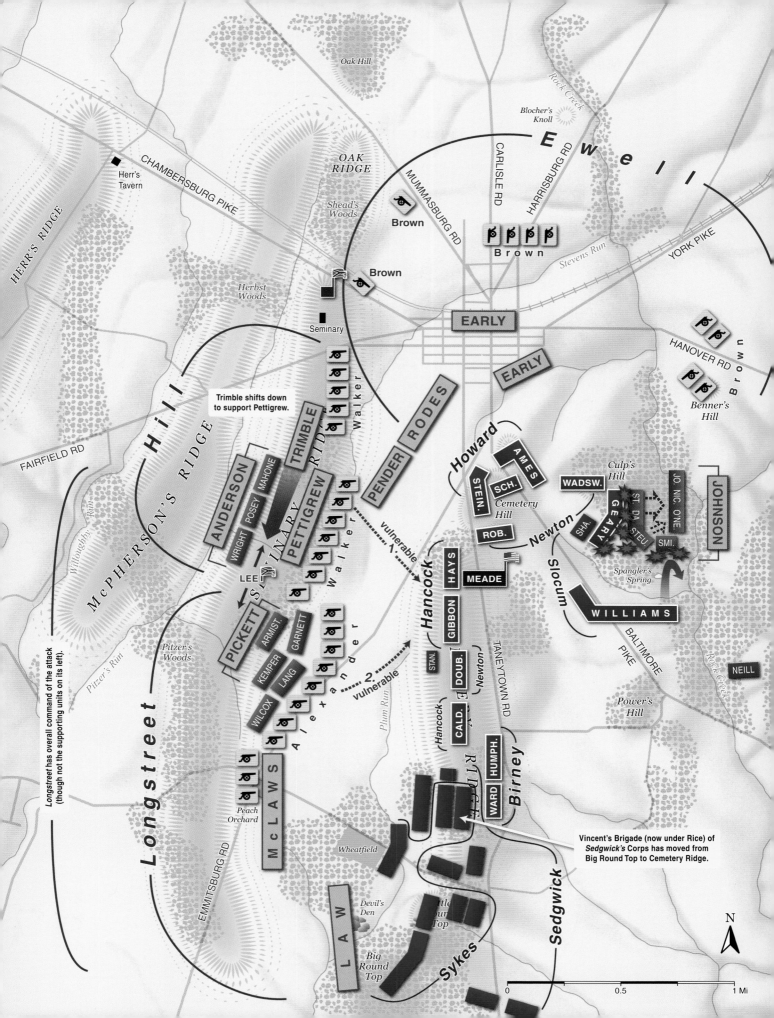

Longstreet has overall command of the attack (though not the supporting units on its left).

Trimble shifts down to support Pettigrew.

Vincent's Brigade (now under Rice) of *Sedgwick's* Corps has moved from Big Round Top to Cemetery Ridge.

CHAMBERSBURG PIKE

Herr's Tavern

HERR'S RIDGE

FAIRFIELD RD

Willoughby Run

McPHERSON'S RIDGE

Hill

Pitzer's Run

Pitzer's Woods

EMMITSBURG RD

Longstreet

Peach Orchard

Wheatfield

Devil's Den

LAW

Big Round Top

Sykes

Oak Hill

OAK RIDGE

Shead's Woods

Herbst Woods

Seminary

MUMMASBURG RD

Brown

Brown

Brown

Walker

TRIMBLE

SEMINARY RIDGE

ANDERSON

MAHONE
POSEY
WRIGHT

PETTIGREW

Walker

LEE

Walker

PICKETT

ARMIST.
KEMPER
GARNETT
LANG
WILCOX

Alexander

McLAWS

PENDER

RODES

EARLY

EARLY

CARLISLE RD

HARRISBURG RD

Blocher's Knoll

Rock Creek

Ewell

Stevens Run

YORK PIKE

HANOVER RD

Brown

Benner's Hill

Howard

AMES

STEIN.

SCH.

Cemetery Hill

ROB.

WADSW.

Newton

GEARY

ST. DA.
SHA.
STEU.
SMI.

JO. NIC. ONE.

Culp's Hill

Spangler's Spring

JOHNSON

Slocum

WILLIAMS

BALTIMORE PIKE

Rock Creek

NEILL

Power's Hill

TANEYTOWN RD

MEADE

Hancock

HAYS

GIBBON

STAN.

DOUB.

Newton

CALD.

E.

Hancock

RIDGE

WARD

HUMPH.

Birney

Sedgwick

vulnerable 1.

vulnerable 2.

N

0   0.5   1 Mi

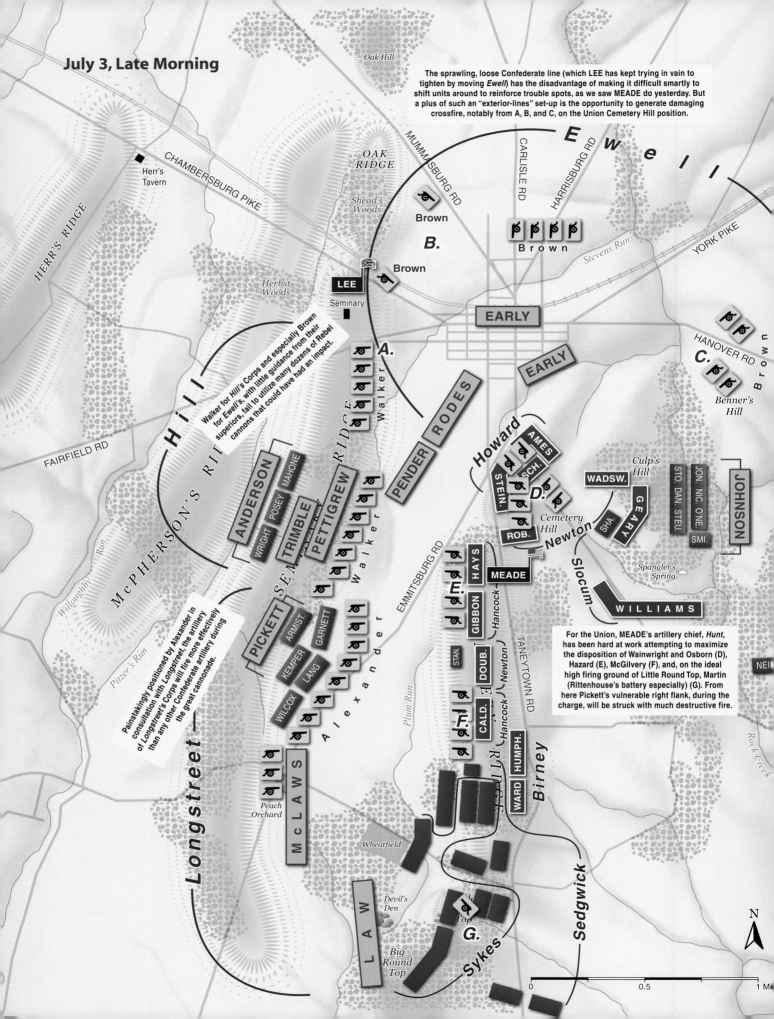

July 3, Late Morning

The sprawling, loose Confederate line (which LEE has kept trying in vain to tighten by moving *Ewell*) has the disadvantage of making it difficult smartly to shift units around to reinforce trouble spots, as we saw MEADE do yesterday. But a plus of such an "exterior-lines" set-up is the opportunity to generate damaging crossfire, notably from A, B, and C, on the Union Cemetery Hill position.

Walker for *Hill's* Corps and especially Brown for *Ewell's*, with little guidance from their superiors, fail to utilize many dozens of Rebel cannons that could have had an impact.

Painstakingly positioned by Alexander in consultation with Longstreet, the artillery of Longstreet's Corps will fire more effectively than any other Confederate artillery during the great cannonade.

For the Union, MEADE's artillery chief, *Hunt*, has been hard at work attempting to maximize the disposition of Wainwright and Osborn (D), Hazard (E), McGilvery (F), and, on the ideal high firing ground of Little Round Top, Martin (Rittenhouse's battery especially) (G). From here Pickett's vulnerable right flank, during the charge, will be struck with much destructive fire.

Herr's Tavern

CHAMBERSBURG PIKE

HERR'S RIDGE

Oak Hill

OAK RIDGE

MUMMASBURG RD

Shead's Woods

Brown

B.

Brown

Herbst Woods

LEE

Brown

Seminary

McPHERSON'S RIDGE

FAIRFIELD RD

Willoughby Run

A.

Walker

SEMINARY RIDGE

Hill

ANDERSON

WRIGHT   POSEY   MAHONE

TRIMBLE

PETTIGREW

PENDER

RODES

Walker

CARLISLE RD

HARRISBURG RD

E

Ewell

Brown

Stevens Run

YORK PIKE

EARLY

EARLY

HANOVER RD

C.

Benner's Hill

Brown

Howard

AMES

SCH.

STEIN.

D.

ROB.

Cemetery Hill

Newton

WADSW.

Culp's Hill

GEARY

STO. DAN. STEU.

JON. NIC. ONE.

SMI.

JOHNSON

Slocum

Spangler's Spring

WILLIAMS

PICKET

ARMIST.

KEMPER   GARNETT

LANG

WILCOX

Alexander

Pitzer's Run

Longstreet

McLAWS

Peach Orchard

EMMITSBURG RD

MEADE

E.

HAYS

GIBBON

Hancock

STAN.

DOUB.

CALD.

F.

WARD

HUMPH.

BIRNEY

Hancock

Newton

Hancock

TANEYTOWN RD

RIDGE

Sedgwick

Rock Creek

NEI

Wheatfield

LAW

Devil's Den

...le Top

G.

Big Round Top

Sykes

0   0.5   1 Mi

N

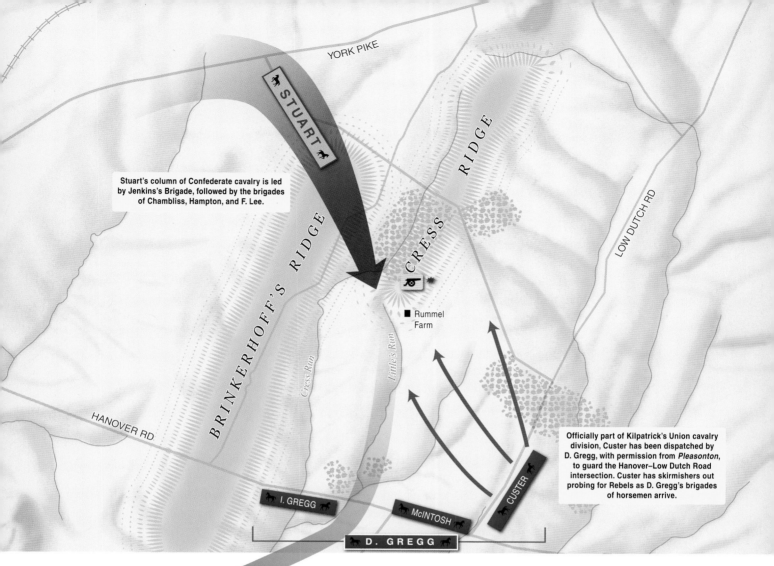

Stuart's column of Confederate cavalry is led by Jenkins's Brigade, followed by the brigades of Chambliss, Hampton, and F. Lee.

YORK PIKE

STUART

CRESS RIDGE

BRINKERHOFF'S RIDGE

LOW DUTCH RD

Cress Run

Little's Run

Rummel Farm

HANOVER RD

Officially part of Kilpatrick's Union cavalry division, Custer has been dispatched by D. Gregg, with permission from *Pleasonton*, to guard the Hanover–Low Dutch Road intersection. Custer has skirmishers out probing for Rebels as D. Gregg's brigades of horsemen arrive.

I. GREGG

McINTOSH

CUSTER

D. GREGG

Stuart's potential threat to the Union rear.

July 3, Late Morning

Left: *Hunt*, MEADE's talented artillery chief, has been actively seeing to the Federal guns all morning. This in unflattering contrast to LEE's top artillery man, Pendleton, nickname "Granny," of whom we see and hear next to nothing, for good reason.

Map Above: East Cavalry Field (to-scale eastward extension of main map). Jeb Stuart arrives in the Rummel Farm area, having, per plan, led his elite mounted cavalry far out and around to MEADE's northeast. Numbering as many as 5,000—perhaps one and a half times the size of the Yankee force that will oppose him—Stuart's brigades are to be taken seriously. The open farmland to their south affords Stuart a clear path (green arrow) to MEADE's vulnerable rear, his supply trains, retreat route, even the unsuspecting back of MEADE's Cemetery Ridge infantry and guns.

Instead of sending out scouts, Stuart has cannon shots fired in various directions. Why? To signal LEE he's in place? Odd if so, for how could LEE be certain, miles off? And what would LEE do differently as a result? Or does Stuart want to smoke out any Union forces that may be in the vicinity? If so, that works, as now David Gregg's Federal cavalry, which have just joined horsemen commanded by one General Custer, already forewarned of the likelihood of Rebel horsemen in the area, know it for a fact.

MEADE, sitting on an emptied cracker box set on its side, relaxes with some of his generals over a repast of potatoes, buttered bread, and stewed chicken, which a servant of Gibbon has promoted. Thanking Gibbon for the feast, MEADE orders all provost guards forward from their assigned rear-guard duty (snaring cowards) to rejoin their regular units for what's surely to come. MEADE's reasoning is that some of the finest fighters are assigned to provost rear-guard duty, while cowards who flee aren't worth catching. MEADE rides off to inspect Hays's Division.

When Alexander reported to *Longstreet* that his artillery was ready, *Longstreet* allowed as how the infantry needed more time to finalize its preparations and positioning for the charge.

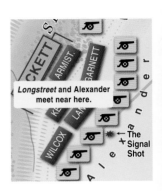

Longstreet and Alexander meet near here.

The Signal Shot

Near noon, Alexander receives this message from *Longstreet*:

> If the artillery fire does not have the effect to drive off the enemy, or greatly demoralize him, so as to make our effort pretty certain, I would prefer that you should not advise General Pickett to make the charge. I shall . . . expect you to let General Pickett know when the moment offers [to make the charge].

Unbelievably, LEE's designated chief for the great attack is in effect telling a colonel, one of three artillery superintendents (an unofficial one at that) of LEE's three corps, to decide when and whether to make Pickett's Charge! Furthermore, how is Porter Alexander supposed to decide if the artillery barrage has made the success of the charge "pretty certain"?

Immensely worried, Alexander sends a message back to *Longstreet* saying, in so many words, that once we've done the shelling, we'll have no more ammunition, so if you want to consider an alternative to this charge, the time for that is now.

Longstreet, who if not abashed should be, sends back a message little different from his first one. In it the words "advise General Pickett" make it unambiguously clear that *Longstreet* is putting his own responsibility off on Alexander, with no mention or hint of "advise *me*."

In the midday summer heat the battlefield quiet extends.

The minutes tick off . . .

A cannon barrel flares. Echoes: a signal shot. The first of two.

Longstreet has given the order: "Let the batteries open."

For a beat the quiet continues.

The cause of the South is not lost.

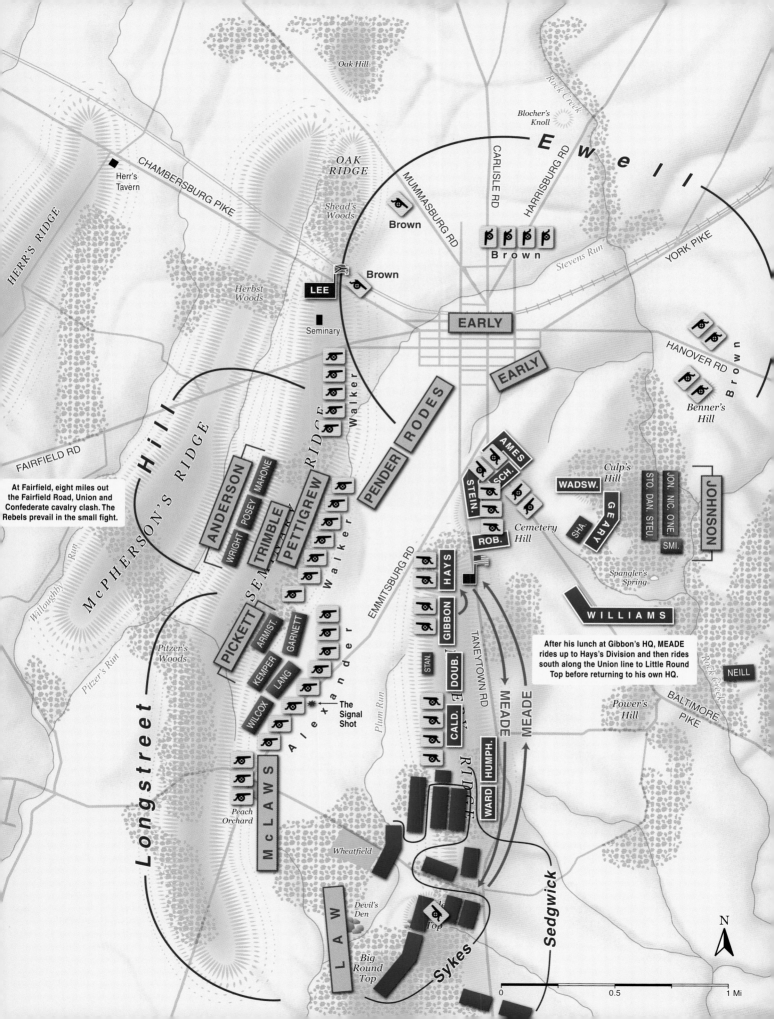

At Fairfield, eight miles out the Fairfield Road, Union and Confederate cavalry clash. The Rebels prevail in the small fight.

After his lunch at Gibbon's HQ, MEADE rides up to Hays's Division and then rides south along the Union line to Little Round Top before returning to his own HQ.

The Signal Shot

Herr's Tavern

CHAMBERSBURG PIKE

HERR'S RIDGE

FAIRFIELD RD

Willoughby Run

McPHERSON'S RIDGE

Pitzer's Woods

Pitzer's Run

Peach Orchard

Wheatfield

Devil's Den

Big Round Top

Longstreet

LAW

McLAWS

PICKETT

ARMST.
GARNETT
KEMPER LANG
WILCOX

Alexander

ANDERSON
WRIGHT POSEY MAHONE
TRIMBLE
PETTIGREW

Walker

SEMINARY RIDGE

Herbst Woods

LEE

Seminary

OAK RIDGE

Shead's Woods

Oak Hill

Brown

Brown

PENDER | RODES

EMMITSBURG RD

STAN.
WARD HUMPH.

CEMETERY RIDGE

TANEYTOWN RD

GIBBON
DOUB.
CALD.

HAYS

MEADE MEADE

AMES
SCH.
STEIN.
ROB.

Cemetery Hill

WADSW.

Culp's Hill

GEARY
SHA.

STO. DAN. STEU.
JON. NIC. ONE.
SMI.

JOHNSON

Spangler's Spring

WILLIAMS

Power's Hill

NEILL

Rock Creek

BALTIMORE PIKE

MUMMASBURG RD

CARLISLE RD

HARRISBURG RD

Rock Creek

Blocher's Knoll

Stevens Run

Ewell

EARLY

EARLY

Brown

YORK PIKE

HANOVER RD

Benner's Hill

Brown

Plum Run

Sedgwick

Sykes

N

0   0.5   1 Mi

July 3, Early Afternoon

The thundering roar can be heard twenty towns away. Square miles of sky fill with smoke and crisscrossing shrieks, streaking fused shells, cannons booming on top of each other by the hundreds. Human limbs cartwheel, horses fly, ammo wagons blow, big ground rocks are cloven. Hissing projectiles chug and explode. Your arms-covered head, if you're infantry, maddens with the airbursts and ground-bursts mere yards from you (if you're fortunate).

Hays [1], a bluff and sentimental, much-beloved general, riding among his cowering Federal riflemen sings out encouragement. He has his infantry gather up abandoned long arms, clean, load, set them within neat reach by the low stone wall where the charge will come.

Gibbon's Division finds itself in hell [2], taking devastating fire. Horses on their backs kick and expire, human entrails drape from a fence rail, faces, bones, torsos in red splinter in the smoking crashing. Calm Gibbon stands with folded arms, looking west, showing his men how to be.

Frontal fire

Union gunners on Cemetery Hill [3] serve their pieces under a hurricane of enfilade fire from [4] and [5]. Enfilade (fire from a side), such as the wraparound Confederate northern line affords ideal conformation to deliver, is multi-deadly. It's the difference between rolling a bowling ball straight, frontally, at a dozen pins side-by-side in two rows . . . and rolling the same ball at that same formation from the side. (Even better to hit from the front and side at once.)

Enfilade fire

Much Confederate fire flies long, over the Yankee infantry and guns that LEE's barrage is intended to incapacitate. Faulty fuses and sighting difficulty due to the deceptive rolls of the fields and the thickening smoke cause this overshooting. Though missing its target, it wreaks havoc with the Union supply, medical, horse-team, headquarters, and ammo reserves to MEADE's rear, around the Taneytown Road. MEADE is persuaded to abandon his battered little headquarters house. Out back some of his staff are taking shelter, more imagined than real, against the house's weather-beaten wood walls. MEADE puts them at ease with a story from the Mexican War, then sets off for the refuge of a barn farther to the south.

Hunt has ordered the Union guns to wait fifteen minutes. Then, carefully, targeting each firing Rebel piece one at a time, concentrate on a specific target, judging each shot's result. But *Hancock*, cussing and blaspheming, cannot stand the thought that his infantry should cringe under the Rebel holocaust without hearing their own artillery boom in reply. He furiously tours the lines: Return fire goddammit! Hazard (around [2]) obeys. McGilvery (south of Hazard) refuses, citing *Hunt*. Precious ammunition is conserved, for which McGilvery will find a use soon enough.

The Rebel guns on Benner's Hill are silenced by excellent cannon work. This lessens the enfilade pressure on the Yankee guns on Cemetery Hill.

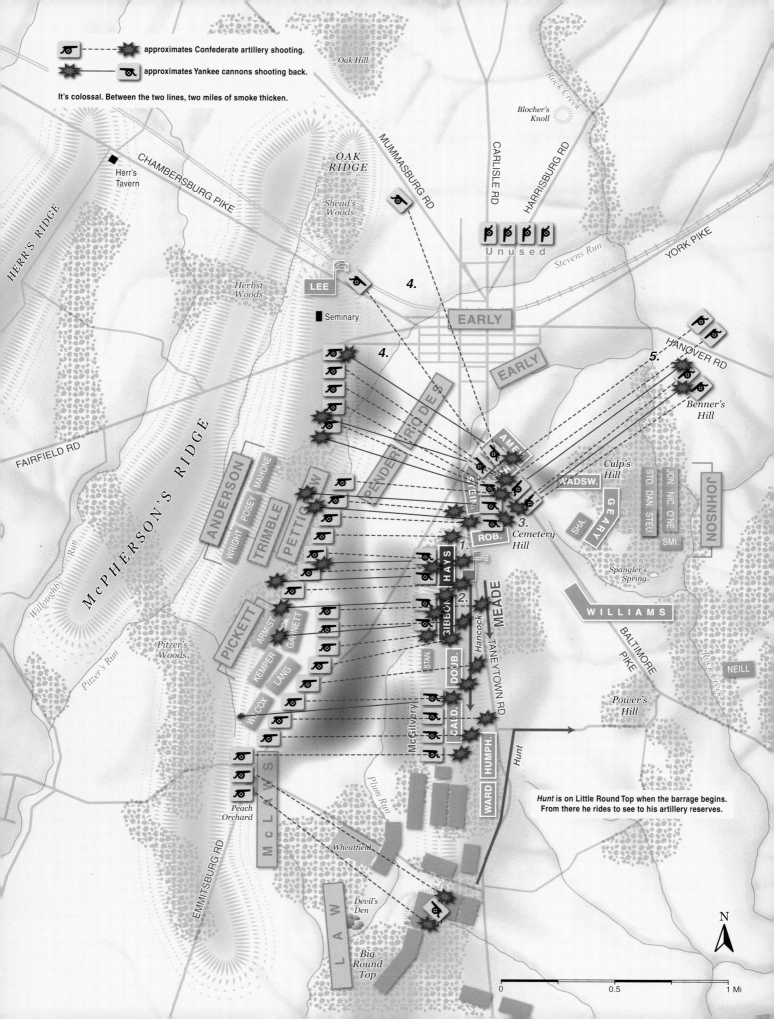

approximates Confederate artillery shooting.

approximates Yankee cannons shooting back.

It's colossal. Between the two lines, two miles of smoke thicken.

Herr's Tavern

CHAMBERSBURG PIKE

HERR'S RIDGE

FAIRFIELD RD

Herbst Woods

LEE

Seminary

Shead's Woods

OAK RIDGE

MUMMASBURG RD

CARLISLE RD

HARRISBURG RD

Blocher's Knoll

Rock Creek

Oak Hill

Unused

Stevens Run

YORK PIKE

4.

EARLY

EARLY

4.

McPHERSON'S RIDGE

Willoughby Run

Pitzer's Woods

Pitzer's Run

ANDERSON

WRIGHT   POSEY   MAHONE

TRIMBLE

PETTIGREW

PENDER

PICKETT

ARMIST.

KEMPER   LANG

GARNETT

W. COY

McLAWS

EMMITSBURG RD

Peach Orchard

LAW

Plum Run

Wheatfield

Devil's Den

Big Round Top

AMES

STEIN.

WADSW.

ROB.

Cemetery Hill

3.

Culp's Hill

GEARY

STO. DAN. STEU

JON. NIC. ONE.

SHA.

SMI.

Spangler's Spring

JOHNSON

HANOVER RD

5.

Benner's Hill

1.

HAYS

2.

GIBBON

Hancock

STAN.

DOUB.

McGilvery

CAI. D.

WARD

HUMPH.

MEADE

TANEYTOWN RD

WILLIAMS

BALTIMORE PIKE

Power's Hill

NEILL

Rock Creek

Hunt

Hunt is on Little Round Top when the barrage begins. From there he rides to see to his artillery reserves.

N

0   0.5   1 Mi

Better planning (and guncraft) might have maximized Rebel enfilade opportunities against Cemetery Hill. (See note on map, top right.)

With nothing coming from McGilvery, Alexander's Rebel gunners pour their fire northeast, on poor Gibbon at the Union center. It seems to Gibbon's gunners as if they've been singled out by the entire Confederate cannon line. Gibbon's Yankee gun crews grimly, heroically serve their pieces amid a focused storm of destruction and death . . . hand-passing the heavy ammo, bleeding from your ears, adjust the elevation screw, sight through the slit, sponge the scalding bronze. Load, ram, stand back. An officer snips the shell's detonation fuse to burn, when airborne, just long enough. Lanyard yanked: the terrific thunder and percussion. By the numbers back to work, same drill. Through field glasses an officer squints, struggling to ascertain effect thousands of feet away through the smoke pall and confusion.

Life ends around you again and again as you praise the Lord and pass the ammunition. Re-sight, swab, load, ramrod home, prime, stand back. The incoming rounds whizz over, or, chugging, go off close. If you're still at your sweaty work after the blast, you're alive. The grass at your feet smolders. Fire!

For the huddled infantryman with nothing to do, it is psychologically almost worse (than for the artillery gunner) to exist in this eternity of detonations. It's like being forced to play Russian roulette nonstop for an hour . . . longer . . .

Longstreet rides his lines, magnificent under fire, trotting his horse through the worst of it unhurried, poker-faced, upright, looking not left, not right, showing his bravery like a hole card.

For all the death and havoc it rains on particular Union loci, the Rebel cannonade is not effective. Not in terms of its stated goals.

Ammo is depleted that could later be used to help cover Pickett's Charge.

A dearth of hands-on tactical coordination and adjustment from LEE or *Longstreet* results in available Confederate cannon languishing unused, or used to subpar effect.

As well, the Federal return fire tells on the Southern gun batteries, not to mention the foot soldier in gray cowed in the uncool shade of Seminary Ridge. (After the war a Confederate combatant, asked how the invincible South could have lost at Gettysburg, will answer, "I always thought the Yankees had something to do with it.")

MEADE, finding little protection at the barn, heads rearward to Power's Hill. But his Cemetery Ridge forces are neither driven off, demoralized in any lasting way, nor do they suffer many casualties all in all—at most several hundred out of over 6,000 Federals where the Southern waves of infantry will hit. By now MEADE has reinforcements approaching the ridge: Ward's Division and Eustis's Brigade from the south; Shaler's Brigade from the northeast. MEADE suspects with increasing certainty that LEE is going to strike his center, but he is also preparing for other possibilities. Robinson's Division moves up in case the Rebs try Cemetery Hill again.

LEE is at his headquarters.

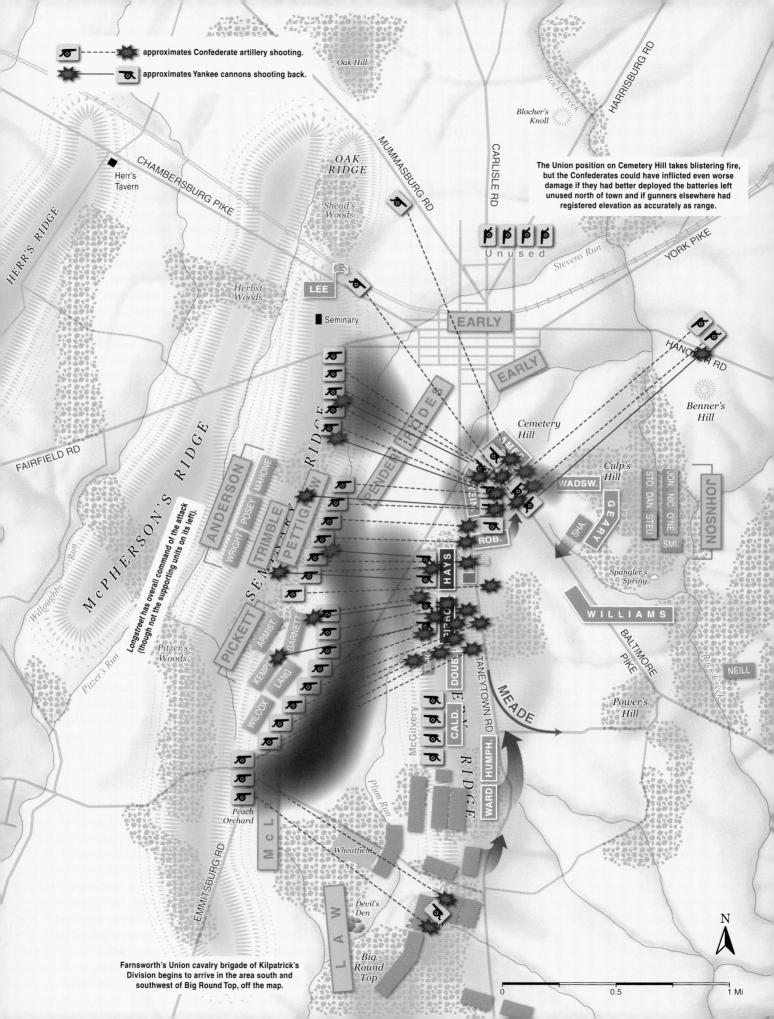

approximates Confederate artillery shooting.

approximates Yankee cannons shooting back.

Herr's Tavern

CHAMBERSBURG PIKE

HERR'S RIDGE

Oak Hill

OAK RIDGE

MUMMASBURG RD

Shead's Woods

CARLISLE RD

Blocher's Knoll

Rock Creek

HARRISBURG RD

The Union position on Cemetery Hill takes blistering fire, but the Confederates could have inflicted even worse damage if they had better deployed the batteries left unused north of town and if gunners elsewhere had registered elevation as accurately as range.

Unused

Stevens Run

YORK PIKE

Herbst Woods

LEE

Seminary

EARLY

EARLY

Cemetery Hill

HANGER RD

Benner's Hill

FAIRFIELD RD

McPHERSON'S RIDGE

Willoughby Run

ANDERSON

WRIGHT   POSEY   MAHONE

TRIMBLE

SEMINARY RIDGE

PETTIGREW

PENDER

RODES

Culp's Hill

WADSW.

STO. DAN. STEU

JON. NIC. ONE

SMI.

JOHNSON

Longstreet has overall command of the attack (though not the supporting units on its left).

PICKETT

ARMST.   GARNETT

KEMP.   LANG

WILCOX

Pitzer's Woods

Pitzer's Run

ROB.

HAYS

SHA.

GEARY

Spangler's Spring

WILLIAMS

BALTIMORE PIKE

Rock Creek

Power's Hill

NEILL

MEADE

McGivery

CALD.   DOUB.

HUMPH.

WARD

STAN.

TANEYTOWN RD

CEMETERY RIDGE

EMMITSBURG RD

McL

Peach Orchard

Plum Run

Wheatfield

LAW

Devil's Den

Big Round Top

Farnsworth's Union cavalry brigade of Kilpatrick's Division begins to arrive in the area south and southwest of Big Round Top, off the map.

0   0.5   1 Mi

N

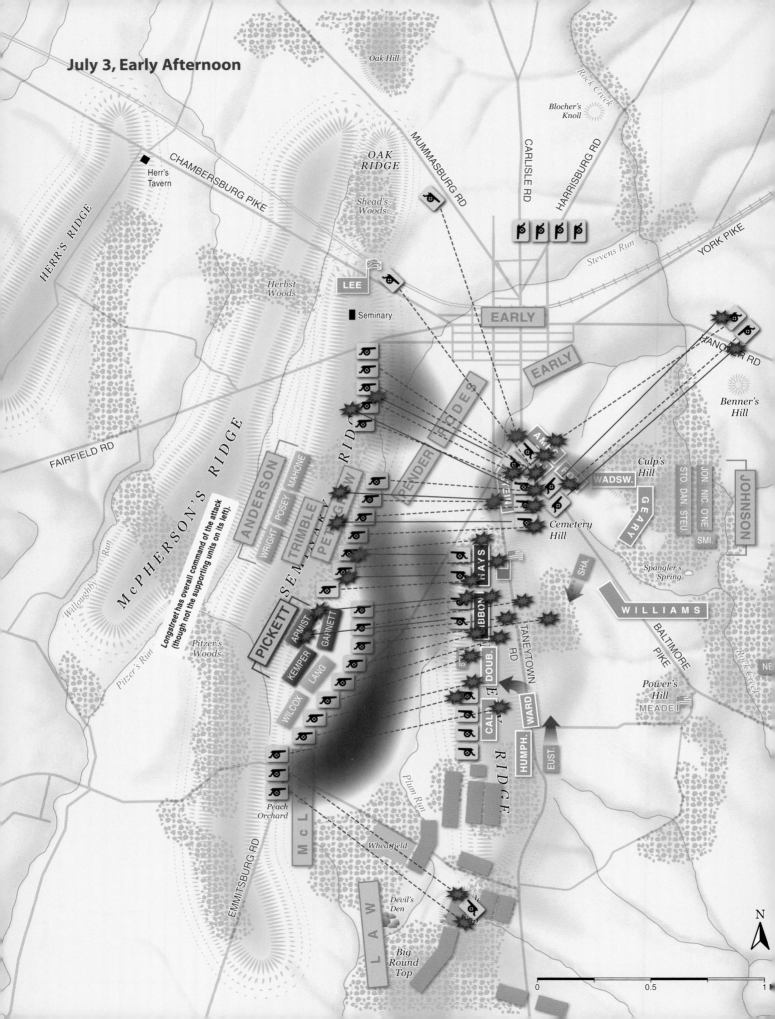

July 3, Early Afternoon

Herr's Tavern

CHAMBERSBURG PIKE

HERR'S RIDGE

OAK RIDGE

Oak Hill

MUMMASBURG RD

Blocher's Knoll

Rock Creek

CARLISLE RD

HARRISBURG RD

Stevens Run

YORK PIKE

Shead's Woods

Herbst Woods

LEE

Seminary

EARLY

EARLY

HANOVER RD

Benner's Hill

McPHERSON'S RIDGE

Willoughby Run

FAIRFIELD RD

Longstreet has overall command of the attack (though not the supporting units on its left).

ANDERSON

WRIGHT · POSEY · MAHONE

TRIMBLE

PENDER'S RIDGE?

PETTIGREW

SEMINARY RIDGE

PICKETT

ARMIST.

GARNETT

KEMPER · LANG

WILCOX

Pitzer's Woods

Pitzer's Run

WADSW.

Cemetery Hill

Culp's Hill

GEARY

STO. DAN. STEU.

JON. NIC. ONE.

SMI.

JOHNSON

HAYS

GIBBON

SHA.

Spangler's Spring

WILLIAMS

DOUB.

TANEYTOWN RD

SMY.

CALD.

WARD

HUMPH.

EUST.

BALTIMORE PIKE

Power's Hill

MEADE

Rock Creek

NE

RIDGE

Peach Orchard

McL

Wheatfield

Plum Run

EMMITSBURG RD

LAW

Devil's Den

Big Round Top

N

0   0.5   1

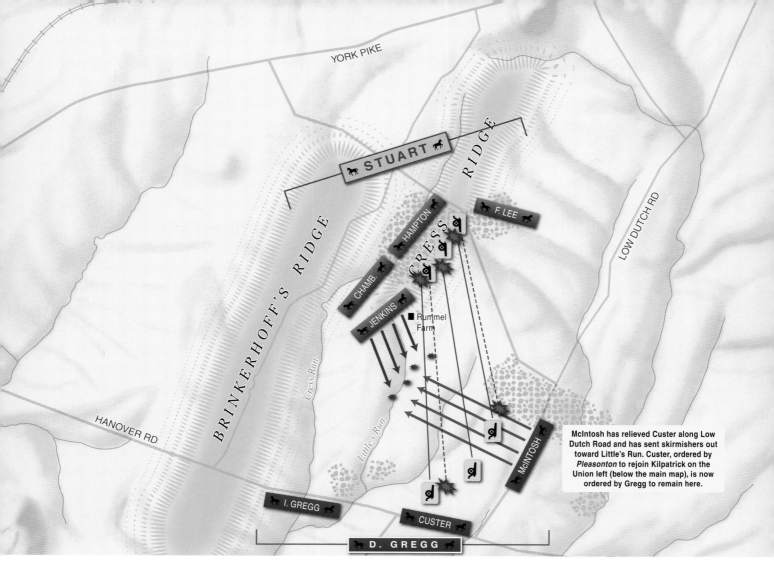

July 3, Early Afternoon

Left: Midway through the great cannonade, Porter Alexander sends a message to Pickett: "If you are to advance at all, you must come at once." The Union fire hasn't slackened, but Alexander knows too well the dangerously low and rapidly dwindling level of remaining artillery rounds. He wants desperately to have some left after the barrage, to cover the huge lines of gray that will be marching out over the gentle rise of open, undulating fields. Pickett takes Alexander's note to *Longstreet*, who glumly nods—wordless: *Go on. Make the charge.*

Longstreet rides to Alexander. When Alexander bemoans the low ammo situation, and what it bodes, *Longstreet's* surprised. Grasping for an excuse to call the attack off, *Longstreet* says halt Pickett, we'll replenish our ammo chests. Alexander informs *Longstreet* that there *are* no ammo reserves anywhere near. *Longstreet* or LEE should have looked into this. (MEADE did.)

Map Above: East Cavalry Field (to-scale eastward extension of main map). The hours-long cavalry face-off turns into a fight. Stuart counters Union artillery fire with cannon of his own and pushes out foot soldiers. McIntosh throws out skirmishers. D. Gregg's superior Yankee cannons prevail. (Their booms are as nothing compared to the earth-shuddering, titanic roar in the west.)

Longstreet, Pickett, and Alexander are moving about this part of the field.

113

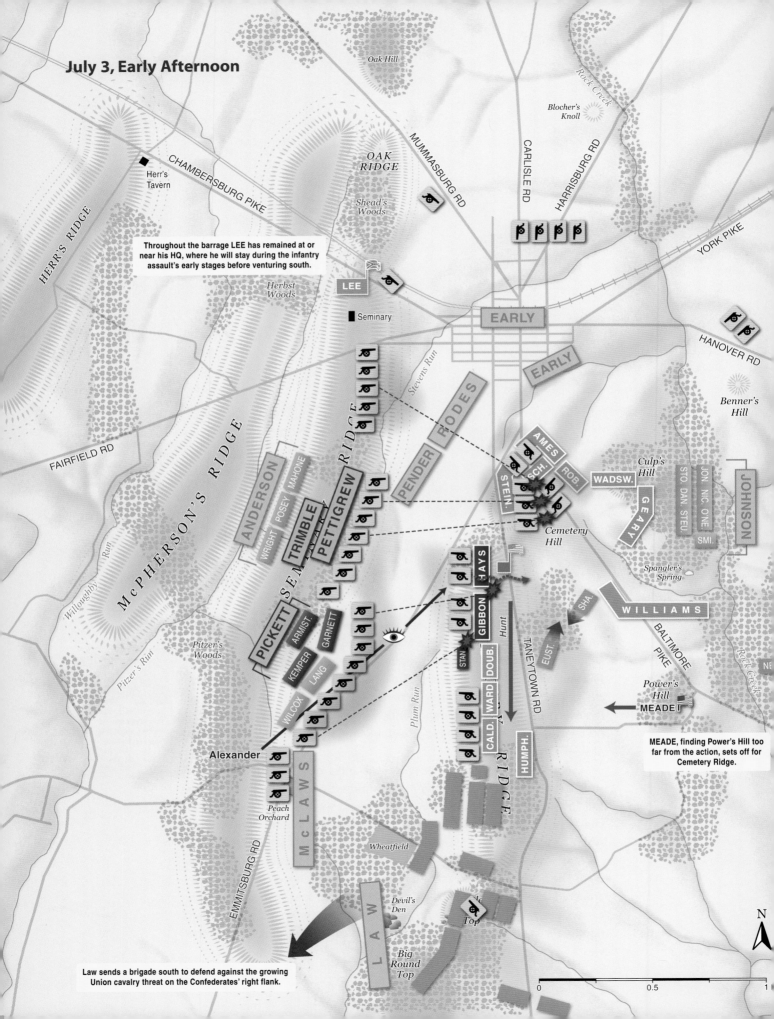

July 3, Early Afternoon

Herr's Tavern

CHAMBERSBURG PIKE

HERR'S RIDGE

Oak Hill

OAK RIDGE

MUMMASBURG RD

Blocher's Knoll

Rock Creek

CARLISLE RD

HARRISBURG RD

Shead's Woods

YORK PIKE

Throughout the barrage LEE has remained at or near his HQ, where he will stay during the infantry assault's early stages before venturing south.

Herbst Woods

EARLY

EARLY

LEE

Seminary

Benner's Hill

HANOVER RD

FAIRFIELD RD

McPHERSON'S RIDGE

Stevens Run

PENDER

RODES

AMES

Culp's Hill

JOHNSON

ANDERSON

WRIGHT POSEY MAHONE

TRIMBLE

PETTIGREW

SEMINARY RIDGE

SCH. ROB.

STEIN.

WADSW.

STO. DAN. STEU

JON. NIC. ONE

GEARY

SMI.

Cemetery Hill

Spangler's Spring

Willoughby Run

PICKETT

ARMIST.

GARNETT

KEMPER LANG

WILCOX

Pitzer's Woods

HAYS

GIBBON

Hunt

SHA.

WILLIAMS

EUST

BALTIMORE PIKE

Rock Creek

STAN. DOUB.

WARD

CALD.

HUMPH.

TANEYTOWN RD

RIDGE

Power's Hill

MEADE

Alexander

McLAWS

Pitzer's Run

Plum Run

MEADE, finding Power's Hill too far from the action, sets off for Cemetery Ridge.

Peach Orchard

EMMITSBURG RD

Wheatfield

LAW

Devil's Den

Top

Big Round Top

N

Law sends a brigade south to defend against the growing Union cavalry threat on the Confederates' right flank.

0   0.5   1

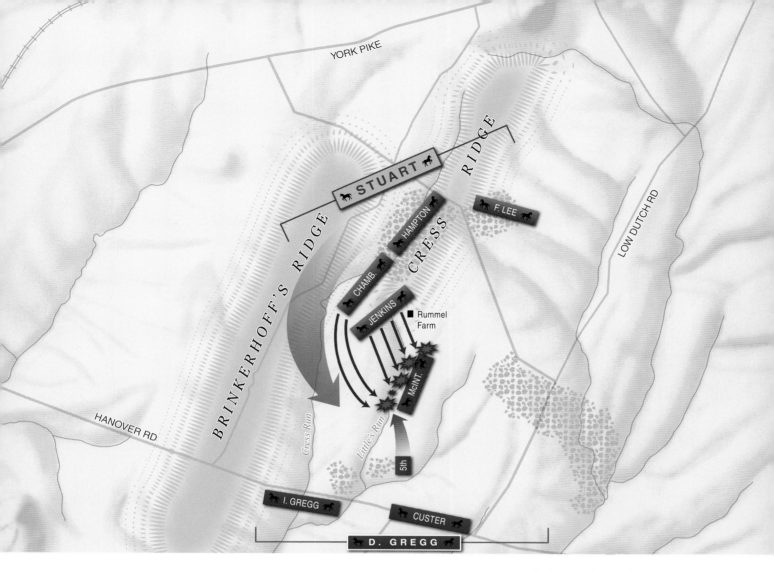

July 3, Early Afternoon

Left: On Gibbon's left, Stannard has pushed some of his brigade a bit farther out west of the Union line, where a bit of stony terrain affords cover.

Hunt, who at West Point taught many of the Rebel gunners shooting at him, cocks a critical eye at his former pupils' skills. He and several Union generals, MEADE included, semi-independently decide it would be a good idea to cease all artillery fire. The ensuing quiet might fool LEE & Co. into believing they've taken the Union guns out—the preponderance of them anyway . . . and so, the Union cannons fall silent.

It's an old trick. Alexander notes the sudden halt. He also has observed some Union cannon being wheeled back off the ridge at the Yankee center (it's replacement, not retreat, but Alexander can't know this). Whether or not he is exactly *fooled*, still he knows it has got to be now or never. It can't be never. Is he singlehandedly going to gainsay ROBERT E. LEE? Where *is* Pickett? "For God's sake," Alexander scribbles to him, "come on quick or we cannot support you ammunition nearly out."

Map Above: East Cavalry Field. Stuart pushes more fighters south (Jenkins, with Chambliss extending the line). They'll hold McIntosh by the nose while a Reb flanking force (green arrow) will move around his left. Stiff Union resistance stymies Stuart: he's surprised. D. Gregg has advanced a regiment from Custer, the 5th Michigan, to bolster McIntosh: heavy fighting.

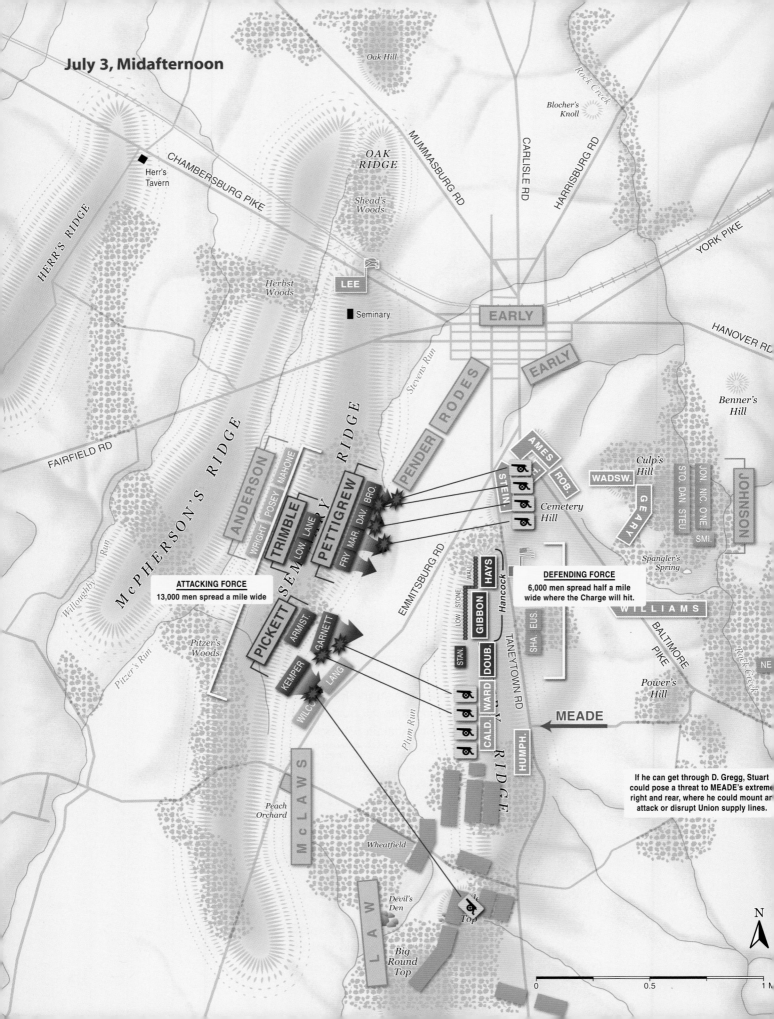

July 3, Midafternoon

Herr's Tavern

CHAMBERSBURG PIKE

HERR'S RIDGE

Oak Hill

OAK RIDGE

MUMMASBURG RD

Shead's Woods

Blocher's Knoll

Rock Creek

CARLISLE RD

HARRISBURG RD

YORK PIKE

FAIRFIELD RD

Herbst Woods

LEE

Seminary

Stevens Run

EARLY

EARLY

HANOVER RD

Benner's Hill

McPHERSON'S RIDGE

Willoughby Run

ANDERSON

MAHONE
POSEY
WRIGHT

TRIMBLE

LOW. LANE

PENDER

RODES

PETTIGREW

RIDGE

FRY. MAR. DAV. BRO.

SEMINARY

AMES
ROB.
STEIN.

Culp's Hill

WADSW.

STO. DAN STEU
JON. NIC. ONE
SMI.

GEARY

JOHNSON

Cemetery Hill

Spangler's Spring

EMMITTSBURG RD

WALL
STONE
LOW.
HAYS
GIBBON
DOUB.
STAN.
WARD
CALD.
Hancock
SHA. EUS.
HUMPH.

WILLIAMS

BALTIMORE PIKE

Rock Creek

ATTACKING FORCE
13,000 men spread a mile wide

PICKETT

ARMIST.
GARNETT

KEMPER

WILCOX
LANG

Pitzer's Woods

Pitzer's Run

DEFENDING FORCE
6,000 men spread half a mile wide where the Charge will hit.

Power's Hill

TANEYTOWN RD

RIDGE

◄── **MEADE**

McLAWS

Peach Orchard

Plum Run

If he can get through D. Gregg, Stuart could pose a threat to MEADE's extreme right and rear, where he could mount an attack or disrupt Union supply lines.

Wheatfield

LAW

Devil's Den

le Top

Big Round Top

N

0   0.5   1

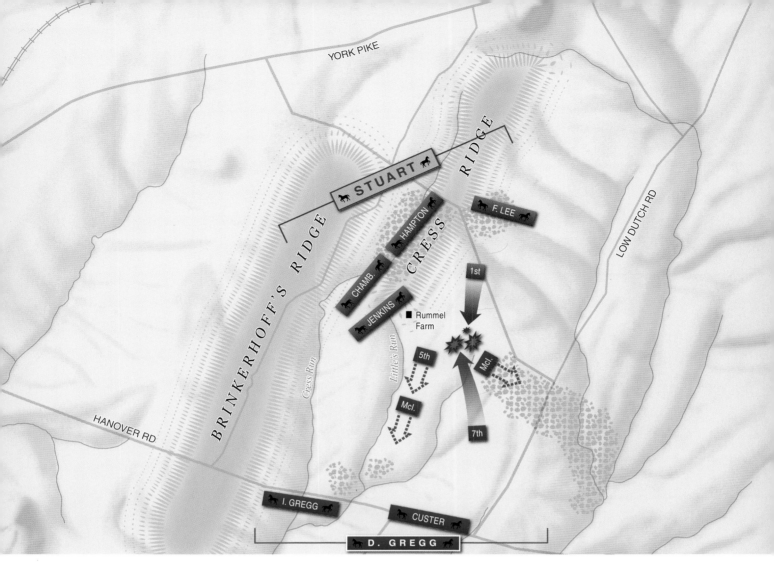

July 3, Midafternoon

Left: To bugles and even band music, the gray thousands step from the trees. They start their march up the gentle fields. Extreme heat drops some. Yankee divisions stare at them from behind the low stone wall half a mile away. Seventeen football fields wide, the array of Rebel infantry is a magnificence of ranks on ranks, towering flags, lines of slanted steel, mounted officers galloping up and back the impeccable formations—except for Pettigrew's left. There, Davis's brigade got off late. Just north of Davis, on the extreme left of the great charge, Brockenbrough's ill-used, depleted Southerners will get off later still and lag, angling northward, causing LEE's left to "droop."

Along the Union line in the suspended shreds of smoke, red tongues lick. MEADE's artillery begins tearing horrible human holes in the advancing gray—Pettigrew's brigades especially. (At MEADE's center, Hazard's guns are silent, however, being out of long-range ammo due to *Hancock's* testosterone.)

Above: East Cavalry Field. Stuart commits some of his Virginia cavalry. Charging at a gallop down through the farm fields, the gray *beaux sabreurs* of the 1st Virginia drive the Northerners south. At the head of a Yankee counter-charge by the 7th Michigan, romantic Custer, glory ever just within his reach, golden locks streaming, smashes into the Rebel assault in a crush of stamping warhorses, battle cries, swordplay, pistol and rifle cracks.

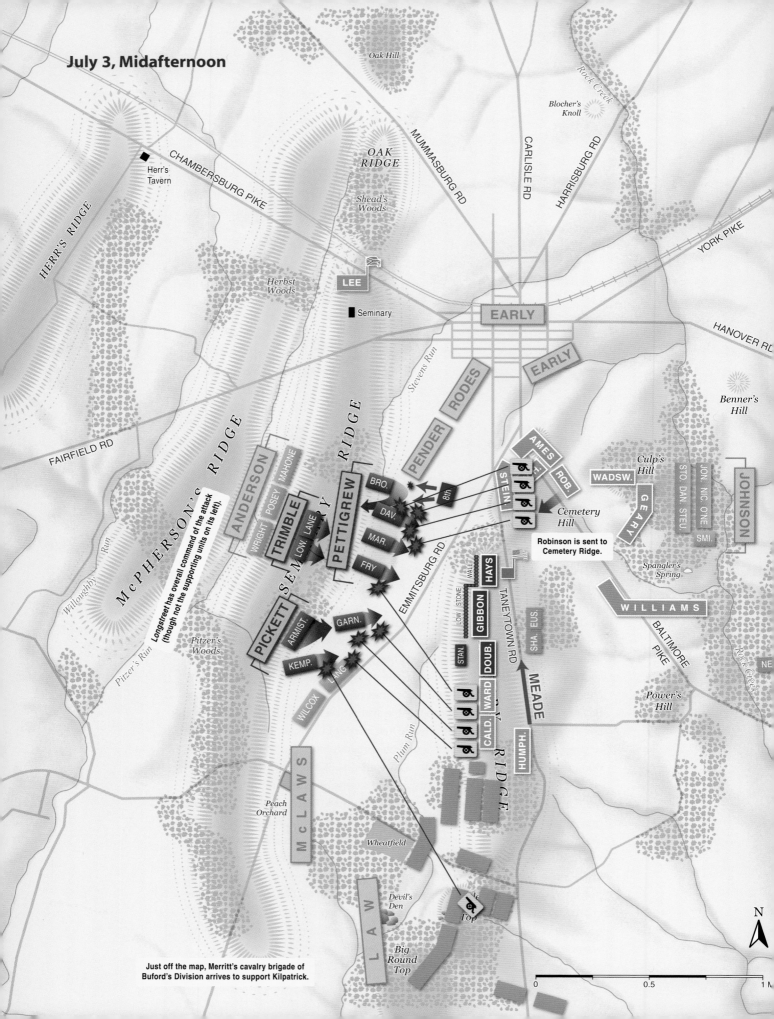

July 3, Midafternoon

Herr's Ridge

Herr's Tavern

CHAMBERSBURG PIKE

OAK RIDGE

Oak Hill

MUMMASBURG RD

CARLISLE RD

HARRISBURG RD

Blocher's Knoll

Rock Creek

Shead's Woods

Herbst Woods

LEE

Seminary

YORK PIKE

Stevens Run

EARLY

EARLY

HANOVER RD

Benner's Hill

McPHERSON'S RIDGE

Willoughby Run

FAIRFIELD RD

ANDERSON

WRIGHT | POSEY | MAHONE

TRIMBLE

LOW. | LANE

SEMINARY RIDGE

PENDER

RODES

BRO.

8th

DAV.

MAR.

FRY

EMMITSBURG RD

AMES

ROB.

STEIN.

Cemetery Hill

WADSW.

Culp's Hill

GEARY

STO. DAN. STEU

JON. NIC. ONE

SMI.

JOHNSON

Robinson is sent to Cemetery Ridge.

Longstreet has overall command of the attack (though not the supporting units on its left).

PICKETT

ARMIST.

GARN.

KEMP.

LING.

WILCOX

Pitzer's Woods

Pitzer's Run

WALL

LOW. STONE

HAYS

GIBBON

STAN.

DOUB.

WARD

CALD.

TANEYTOWN RD

SHA. EUS.

MEADE

HUMPH.

Spangler's Spring

WILLIAMS

BALTIMORE PIKE

Power's Hill

Rock Creek

NE

McLAWS

Peach Orchard

Plum Run

Wheatfield

CEMETERY RIDGE

LAW

Devil's Den

Top

Big Round Top

Just off the map, Merritt's cavalry brigade of Buford's Division arrives to support Kilpatrick.

N

0   0.5   1 M

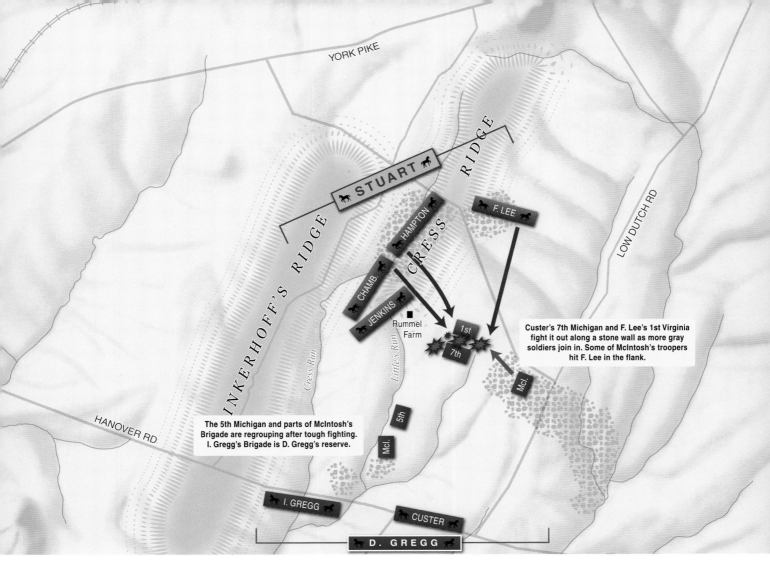

The 5th Michigan and parts of McIntosh's Brigade are regrouping after tough fighting. I. Gregg's Brigade is D. Gregg's reserve.

Custer's 7th Michigan and F. Lee's 1st Virginia fight it out along a stone wall as more gray soldiers join in. Some of McIntosh's troopers hit F. Lee in the flank.

July 3, Midafternoon

Left: Pickett's smartly stepping brigades (Garnett/Kemper/Armistead) take horrific fire from MEADE's Little Round Top guns and McGilvery's unleashed batteries. Where a second ago men marched, the Reb holes mend. The gap between Pickett's left and Pettigrew's right, there at the beginning, a vulnerability, begins strainingly to be closed.

On LEE's left, Brockenbrough, reeling from Union cannon fire, is hit by the flaming rifles of the 8th Ohio (not 160 Yanks against many times that number—but striking from the side!). Nerves shattered, Brockenbrough's men run away. The 8th Ohio plows right on, firing crisp volleys into Davis's and parts of Marshall's marching ranks. Davis, inexperienced, can't control his battle-excited brigade, which, having started slow, rushed to catch up and overran and must slow again, bunching. Marshall and Fry—Pettigrew's main body, professionally, excellently formed—step ahead into the crashing explosions. Under the mountains of smoke, Lowrance's and Lane's Brigades, of Trimble's Division, are coming on gallantly behind Marshall/Fry.

Drifting out of alignment, with Brockenbrough gone, Davis disordered, and Pickett's brigades struggling to close the hole between them and Pettigrew, the great advance commences to slow—show stress torque.

Above: East Cavalry Field. Stuart feeds more mounted squadrons into the fray. Foot soldiers in the bargain. Will the Yanks stand up to it?

119

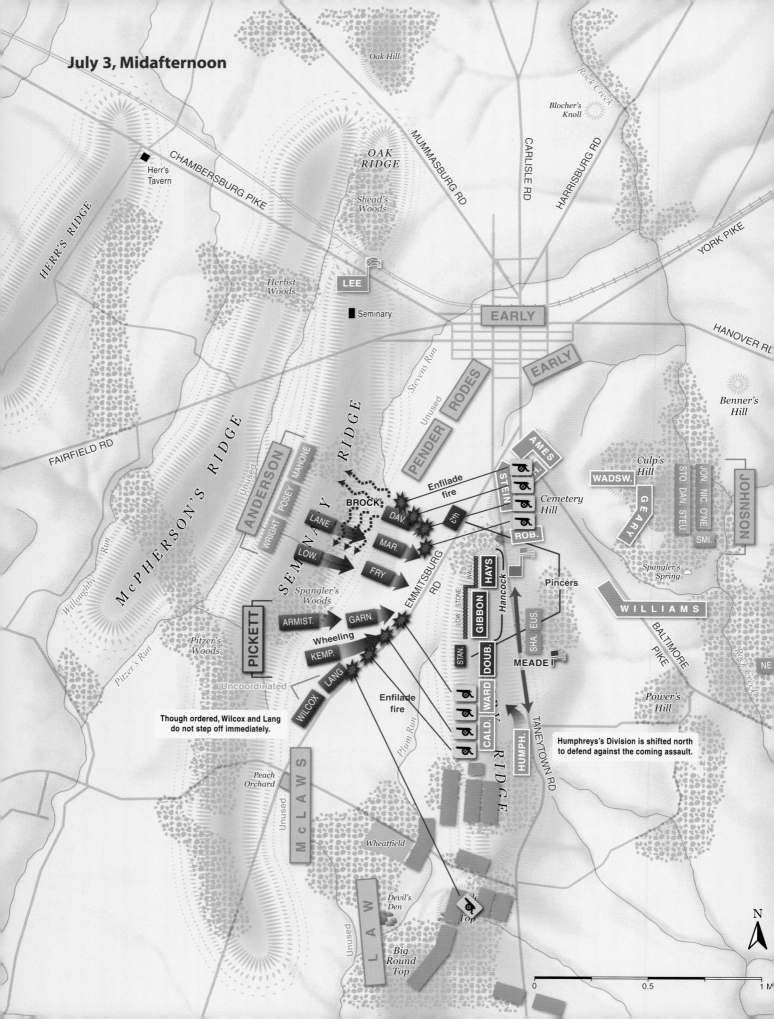

July 3, Midafternoon

Herr's Tavern

CHAMBERSBURG PIKE

Oak Hill

Rock Creek

Blocher's Knoll

MUMMASBURG RD

HERR'S RIDGE

OAK RIDGE

Shead's Woods

CARLISLE RD

HARRISBURG RD

YORK PIKE

HANOVER RD

Herbst Woods

LEE

Seminary

EARLY

EARLY

Benner's Hill

FAIRFIELD RD

M^cPHERSON'S RIDGE

Willoughby Run

Stevens Run

Unused

RODES

PENDER

Culp's Hill

WADSW.

GEARY

STO. DAN. STEU.
JON. NIC. ONE.
SMI.

JOHNSON

SEMINARY RIDGE

Unused

ANDERSON

WRIGHT POSEY MAHONE

BROCK

Enfilade fire

Cemetery Hill

AMES

STEIN

DAV.

143

ROB.

LANE

LOW.

MAR.

FRY

EMMITSBURG RD

Spangler's Woods

PICKETT

ARMIST. GARN.

Wheeling

KEMP.

LANG

WILCOX

HAYS

Pincers

GIBBON

STONE WALL

LOW STONE

HANCOCK

STAN. **DOUB.**

SHA. EUS.

MEADE

Enfilade fire

Though ordered, Wilcox and Lang do not step off immediately.

Uncoordinated

Spangler's Spring

Power's Hill

WILLIAMS

BALTIMORE PIKE

Rock Creek

NE

Pitzer's Woods

Pitzer's Run

McLAWS

Unused

Peach Orchard

Wheatfield

CALD. **WARD**

CEM. RIDGE

HUMPH.

TANEYTOWN RD

Humphreys's Division is shifted north to defend against the coming assault.

LAW

Unused

Devil's Den

Round Top

Big Round Top

Plum Run

0   0.5   1 M

N

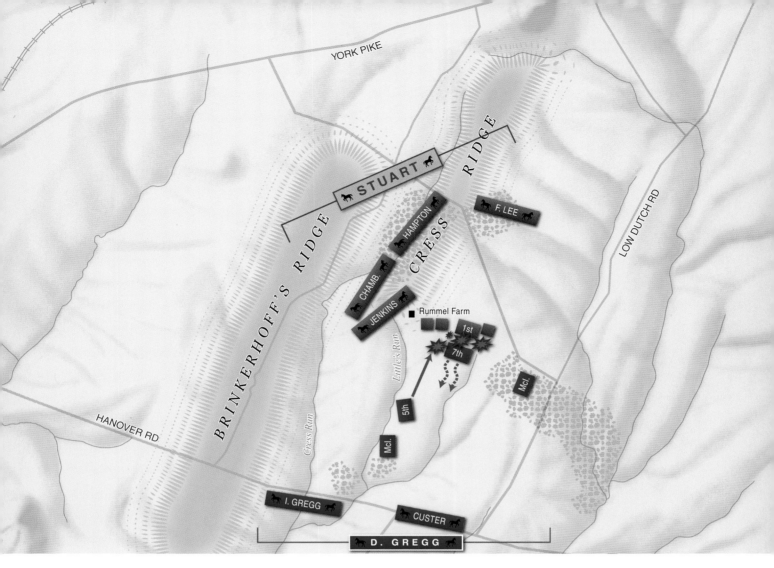

July 3, Midafternoon

Left: Pickett's Charge masses forward, Garnett's Brigade straining toward Fry to close the gap, forcing Kemper's men, on Garnett's other side, to wheel centrifugally like a merry-go-round rim. This will expose Kemper to lethal enfilading fire. More troops crumple, shot, lips sunstroke-frothed, or simply quit. The dead drop in step, the wounded sprawled groaning behind the morphing advance. Lowrance/Lane, coming on behind Pettigrew, are hampered by fleeing men of Brockenbrough/Davis.

Pickett, made aware of the rout over on the far left (Brockenbrough/Davis), messages a lethargic *Longstreet* for help, upon which, grudgingly, Wilcox and Lang are authorized to go forward.

Under extensive Yankee fire (including skirmish parties ducking about no-man's-land between the two great lines), the Charge is delayed. Delay means increased casualties. Increased casualties mean more time for second thoughts to enter your beating breast.

Note LEE's left: disarray, unsupport, brigades unused. LEE's right: twistingly wheeling, unsupported, brigades unused. Note MEADE: the 8th Ohio a pincer, Stannard ditto. Enfilade fire from Little Round Top, Cemetery Hill.

Above: Part of the 5th Michigan strikes the right of Stuart's assault, which stalls. A calm takes hold. An end to the spirited joust?

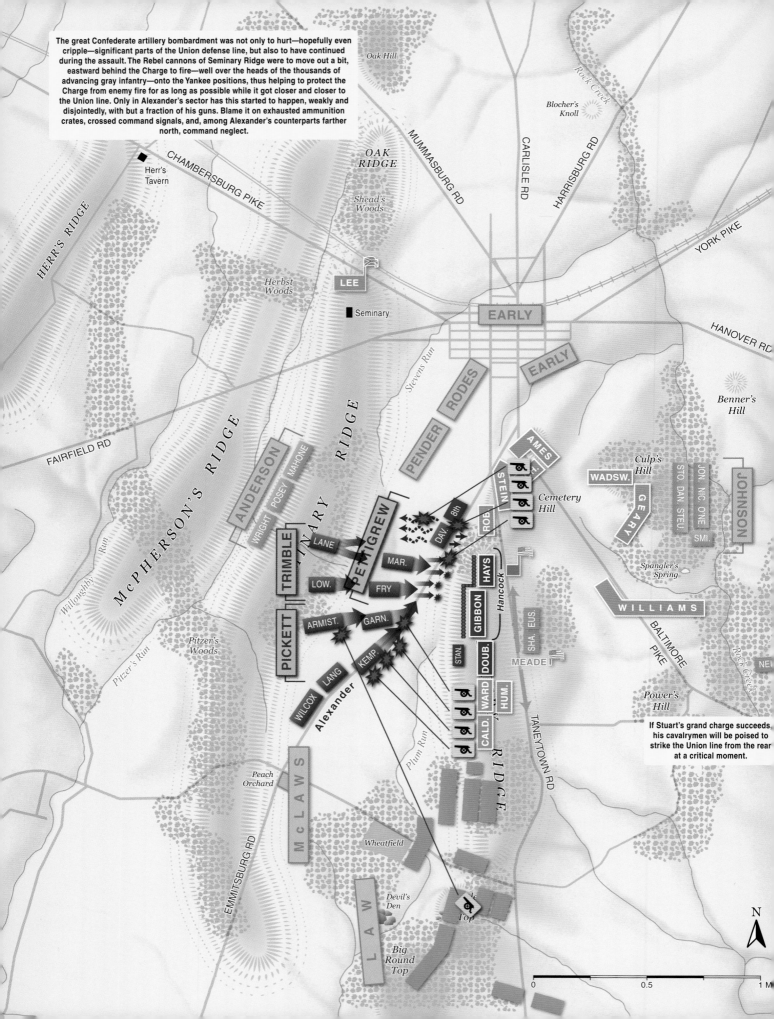

The great Confederate artillery bombardment was not only to hurt—hopefully even cripple—significant parts of the Union defense line, but also to have continued during the assault. The Rebel cannons of Seminary Ridge were to move out a bit, eastward behind the Charge to fire—well over the heads of the thousands of advancing gray infantry—onto the Yankee positions, thus helping to protect the Charge from enemy fire for as long as possible while it got closer and closer to the Union line. Only in Alexander's sector has this started to happen, weakly and disjointedly, with but a fraction of his guns. Blame it on exhausted ammunition crates, crossed command signals, and, among Alexander's counterparts farther north, command neglect.

Oak Hill

Blocher's Knoll

Rock Creek

CHAMBERSBURG PIKE

Herr's Tavern

HERR'S RIDGE

OAK RIDGE

MUMMASBURG RD

CARLISLE RD

HARRISBURG RD

YORK PIKE

Shead's Woods

Herbst Woods

LEE

Seminary

McPHERSON'S RIDGE

FAIRFIELD RD

Willoughby Run

SEMINARY RIDGE

Stevens Run

EARLY

EARLY

RODES

PENDER

HANOVER RD

Benner's Hill

Culp's Hill

WADSW.

STO. DAN. STEU.

JON. NIC. O'NE.

SMI.

GEARY

JOHNSON

AMES

STEIN.

ROB.

Cemetery Hill

Spangler's Spring

ANDERSON

WRIGHT POSEY MAHONE

TRIMBLE

LANE

LOW.

PEMIGREW

MAR.

FRY

DAV.

8th

HAYS

Hancock

GIBBON

DOUB.

STAN.

WILLIAMS

BALTIMORE PIKE

Rock Creek

PICKETT

ARMIST.

GARN.

KEMP.

WILCOX LANG

Alexander

Pitzer's Woods

Pitzer's Run

SHA. EUS.

WARD

CALD.

HUM.

MEADE

RIDGE

TANEYTOWN RD

Power's Hill

If Stuart's grand charge succeeds his cavalrymen will be poised to strike the Union line from the rear at a critical moment.

McLAWS

Peach Orchard

EMMITSBURG RD

Plum Run

Wheatfield

LAW

Devil's Den

Top

Big Round Top

N

0   0.5   1 M

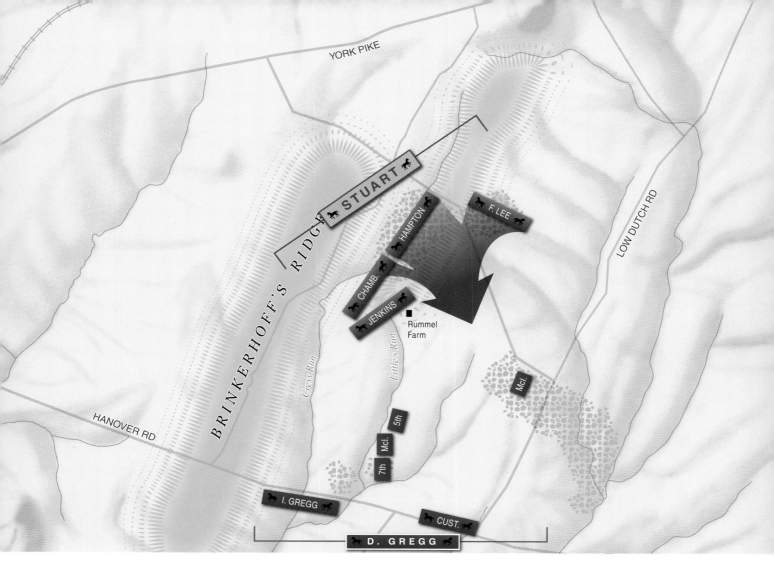

July 3, Midafternoon

Left: At the Emmitsburg Road, midway to their goal still more Confederate infantrymen are wounded or killed clambering over, or attempting to vault, the road-fences: shooting-gallery targets for an eternity of seconds. Or they simply refuse to go farther. A tiny contingent of Davis's Brigade will thrust ahead, getting almost to the Union line, where, solitary, they will surrender. The remainder of Davis, halted at the road (if not already in retreat), attacked on their naked left by Union flankers including the 8th Ohio, break, bolting.

Marshall's and Fry's ranks have marched straight, organized, gallant, the living not missing a beat filling in where the dead fell. A number of Marshall's and Fry's foot troops cross the road. They start up the open grassy incline, the deathly final 200 yards to the Union line where impatient trigger fingers have been twitching and clicking. As many of even Marshall's and Fry's seasoned fighters do not proceed as advance, however, beyond the road.

Garnett and Kemper—Armistead bunching behind them—cross the road together, after their awkward swerve north to get beside Fry.

Above: East Cavalry Field. Most of Stuart's remaining cavalrymen—broad-chested horses shoulder-to-shoulder with a swordsman in each saddle—crest the horizon. At a stately walk, they advance. Their riders' gleaming sabers ring from the scabbard. Ranks of steeds break into a trot. In the distance the watching Unionists murmur with admiration.

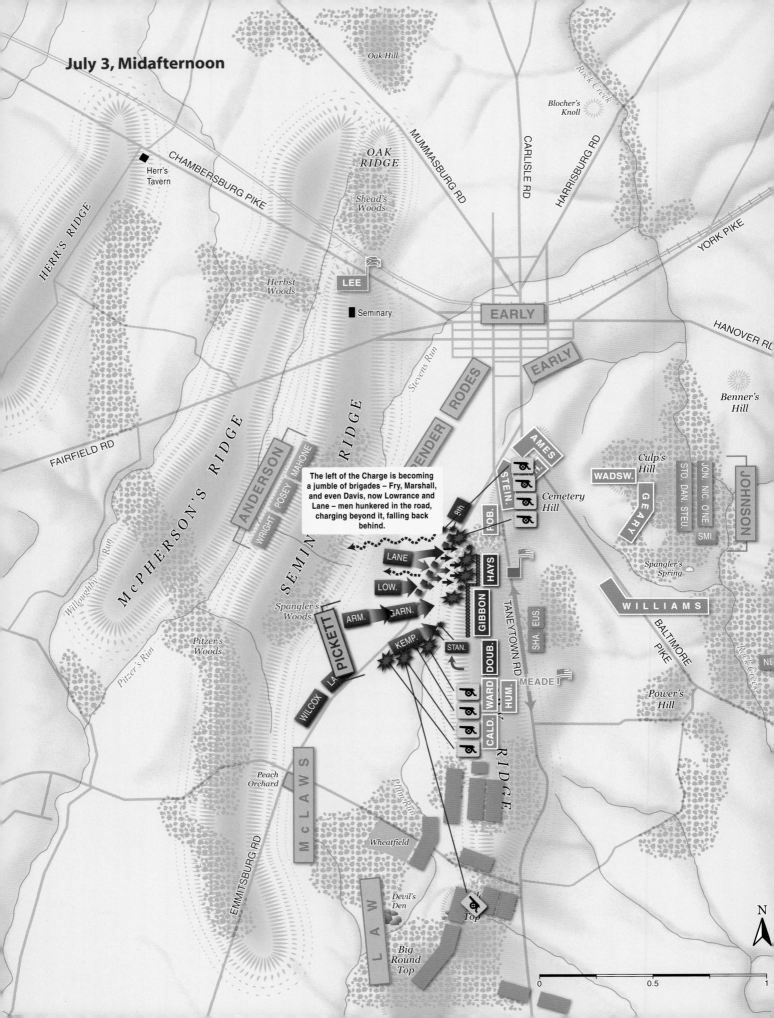

July 3, Midafternoon

Herr's Tavern

CHAMBERSBURG PIKE

HERR'S RIDGE

Oak Hill

OAK RIDGE

MUMMASBURG RD

Shead's Woods

Rock Creek

Blocher's Knoll

CARLISLE RD

HARRISBURG RD

YORK PIKE

LEE

Herbst Woods

Seminary

McPHERSON'S RIDGE

FAIRFIELD RD

Willoughby Run

SEMINARY RIDGE

ANDERSON

WRIGHT   POSEY   MAHONE

EARLY

EARLY

HANOVER RD

Stevens Run

RODES

PENDER

Benner's Hill

Culp's Hill

AMES

STEIN.

FOB.

Cemetery Hill

WADSW.

STO. DAN. ONE.

JON. NIC. ONE.

SMI.

JOHNSON

The left of the Charge is becoming a jumble of brigades – Fry, Marshall, and even Davis, now Lowrance and Lane – men hunkered in the road, charging beyond it, falling back behind.

9th

LANE

LOW.

Spangler's Woods

ARM.   GARN.

HAYS

GIBBON

GEARY

Spangler's Spring

Rock Creek

WILLIAMS

Pitzer's Woods

PICKETT

LA.

WILCOX

Peach Orchard

EMMITSBURG RD

McLAWS

LAW

Pitzer's Run

KEMP.

STAN.

DOUB.

TANEYTOWN RD

SHA. EUS.

MEADE

WARD

CALD.

HUM.

RIDGE

Power's Hill

BALTIMORE PIKE

Wheatfield

Plum Run

Devil's Den

Top

Big Round Top

N

0   0.5   1

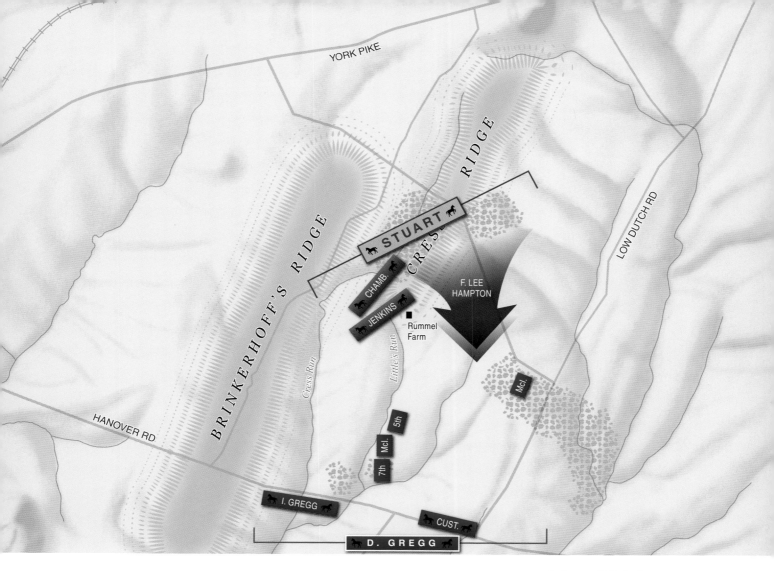

July 3, Midafternoon

Left: Trimble's brigades—Lowrance and Lane—have caught up to and are getting mixed up with Marshall and Fry, past the road. Ahead, behind the low stone fence, wait the trained barrels of Hays and Gibbon. The multiple muskets and rifles we earlier saw General Hays directing his men carefully to collect, where discarded ones lay, and clean and load and set within easy reach for rapid fire, open devastatingly.

Stannard's Brigade of Vermonters—out forward of the Union line at an angle to Pickett—observing Kemper's torquing turn northward to keep up with Garnett think their threatening presence caused it. Not so. But Stannard's riflemen—many firing too early in their excitement—swing out to pour lead  at Kemper: the uncovered right of Pickett's Charge. Soon, closing, the range will become deadly. Pickett's right is damaged also by artillery from Little Round Top. On the great charge's left, Lowrance/Lane/Marshall/Fry continue to get it not merely from their front—Gibbon/Hays—but on their unprotected left: sheets of flame from the brave 8th Ohio and other Union flankers.

The left half of the Charge can't succeed.

Above: East Cavalry Field. As one, Stuart's waves of horsemen—Hampton's and Fitzhugh Lee's Brigades—break into a pounding gallop.

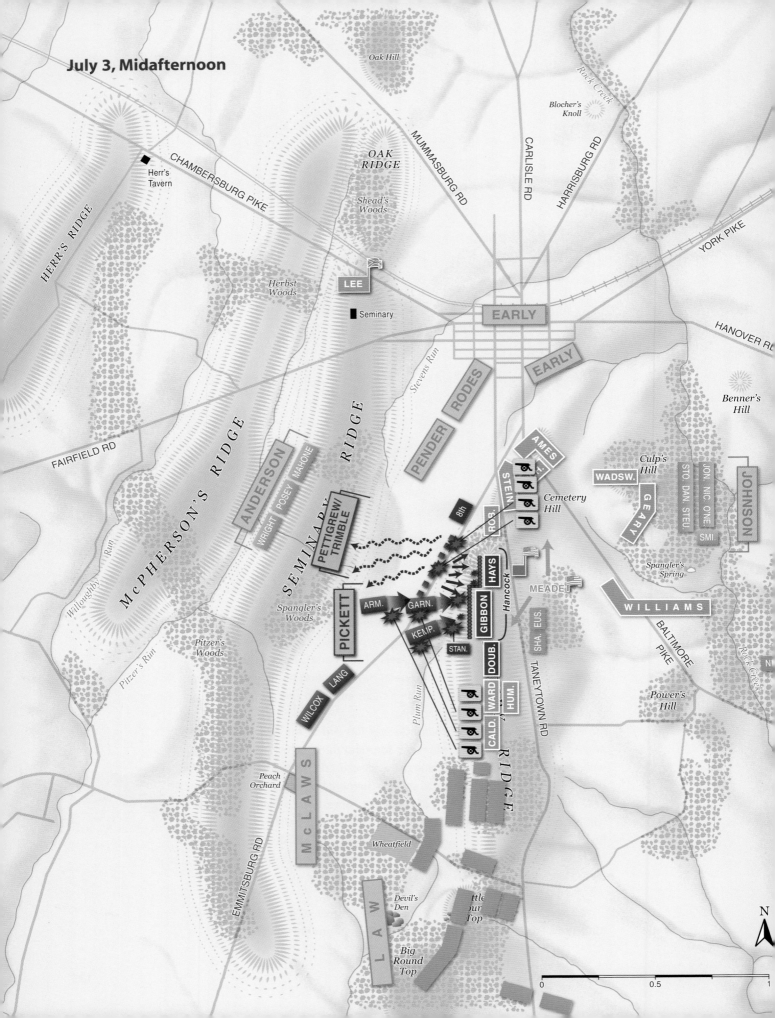

July 3, Midafternoon

HERR'S RIDGE

CHAMBERSBURG PIKE

Herr's Tavern

MUMMASBURG RD

CARLISLE RD

HARRISBURG RD

Oak Hill

OAK RIDGE

Blocher's Knoll

Shead's Woods

YORK PIKE

Herbst Woods

LEE

Seminary

HANOVER RD

McPHERSON'S RIDGE

SEMINARY RIDGE

FAIRFIELD RD

Stevens Run

RODES

PENDER

EARLY

EARLY

Benner's Hill

ANDERSON

WRIGHT   POSEY   MAHONE

PETTIGREW/ TRIMBLE

AMES

STEIN

Cemetery Hill

WADSW.

Culp's Hill

GEARY

STO. DAN. STEU

JON. NIC. O'NE

SMI.

JOHNSON

8th

ROB.

Spangler's Woods

PICKETT

ARM.   GARN.

KEMP.

HAYS

GIBBON

Hancock

MEADE

Spangler's Spring

WILLIAMS

Pitzer's Woods

STAN.

DOUB.

SHA. EUS.

Power's Hill

Rock Creek

LANG

WILCOX

CALD. WARD

HUM.

TANEYTOWN RD

RIDGE

BALTIMORE PIKE

Pitzer's Run

Plum Run

McLAWS

Peach Orchard

Wheatfield

EMMITSBURG RD

LAW

Devil's Den

ttle ur Top

Big Round Top

N

0   0.5   1

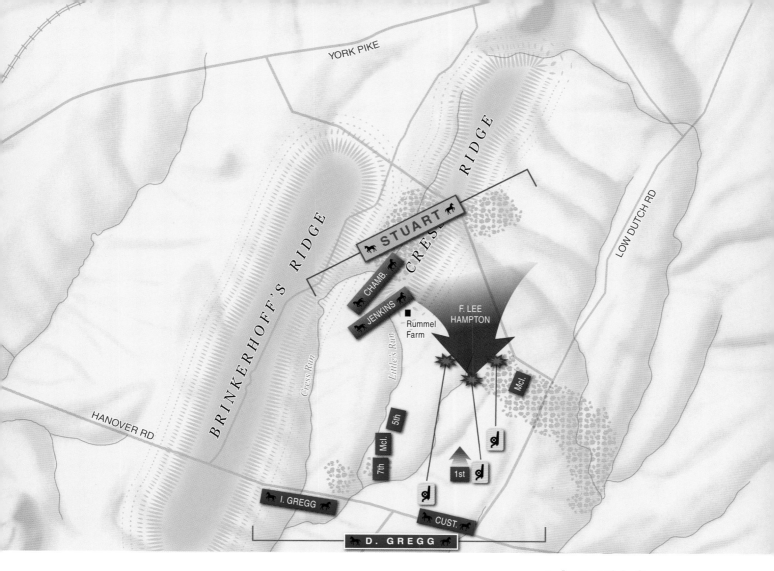

July 3, Midafternoon

Left: Valiantly, pockets and tatters of Marshall/Fry/Lowrance/Lane on the ill-fated Confederate left put up isolated fights, shooting blindly at times in the war fog both literal and figurative, gaps opening by error in the dying charge, Union gunners from front and side methodically aiming and firing. Cheeky Hays in his element puts on the show his men have come to love, heedless under fire, cheering and bellowing encouragement. MEADE is about. Wisely he is leaving moment-to-moment tactics to—among others— the whirlwind *Hancock*, one of Gettysburg's true heroes.

Above: East Cavalry Field. Ululating—the immortal yell—Stuart's thundering cavaliers pound through a squall of Union artillery fire, closing ranks after each killing hit. It's a rip-roaring, classic mounted charge. The Rebs want to end this! Their galloping brandished swords swarm downhill at the Blue. General Gregg rushes a staffer to his forward artillery, ordering withdrawal. A busy Yankee gun officer comments, "Tell the General to go to Hell," and continues with his work.

The 1st Michigan—a lone regiment facing *eight* charging gray ones—is ordered to hit the center of the thundering Rebs. The Yank commander, Town (dying slowly of tuberculosis), tries to make an inspirational speech, but his wired troopers haven't the time; before he can get started, they spur off to the charge. They are joined hastily by Custer, for whom there cannot be enough charges in this world.

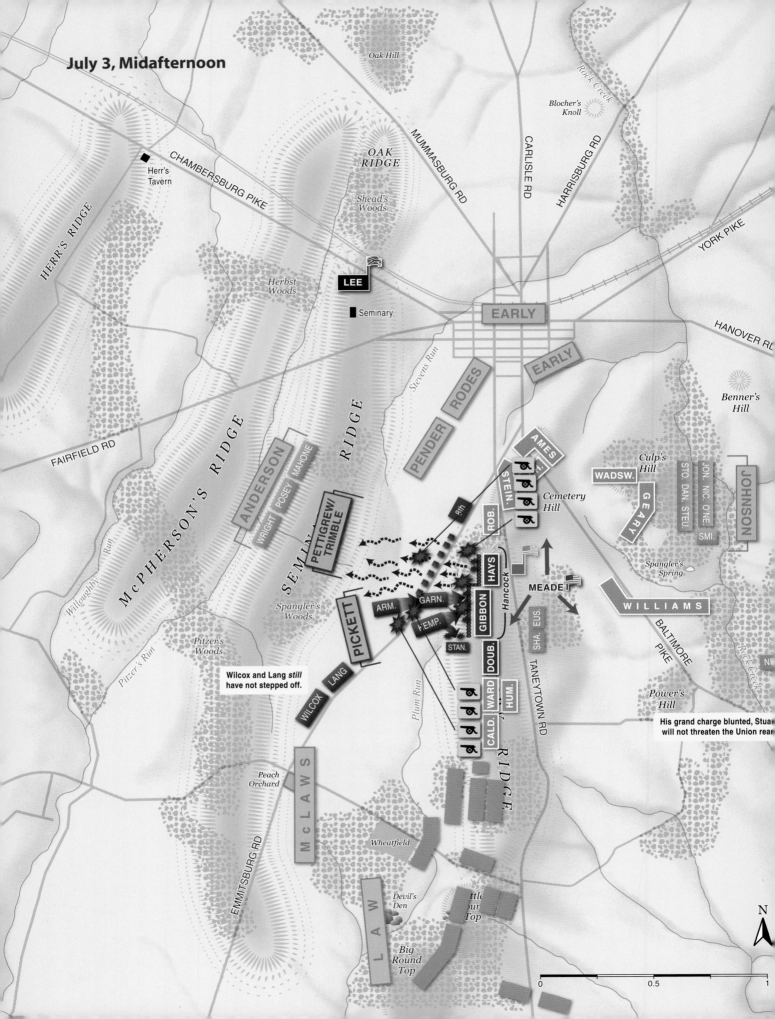

July 3, Midafternoon

Herr's Tavern

CHAMBERSBURG PIKE

HERR'S RIDGE

MUMMASBURG RD

CARLISLE RD

HARRISBURG RD

Rock Creek

Blocher's Knoll

OAK RIDGE

Oak Hill

Shead's Woods

YORK PIKE

Herbst Woods

LEE

Seminary

McPHERSON'S RIDGE

FAIRFIELD RD

Stevens Run

EARLY

EARLY

HANOVER RD

SEMINARY RIDGE

ANDERSON

WRIGHT POSEY MAHONE

PENDER

RODES

Benner's Hill

AMES

Cemetery Hill

STEIN.

Culp's Hill

WADSW.

GEARY

STO. DAN. STEU.

JON. NIC. O'NE.

SMI.

JOHNSON

PETTIGREW/ TRIMBLE

8th

ROB.

HAYS

Hancock

MEADE

Spangler's Spring

GIBBON

PICKETT

Spangler's Woods

ARM.

GARN.

KEMP.

SHA. EUS.

WILLIAMS

Pitzer's Woods

Pitzer's Run

STAN.

DOUB.

TANEYTOWN RD

BALTIMORE PIKE

Rock Creek

Willoughby Run

Wilcox and Lang *still* have not stepped off.

LANG

WILCOX

CALD. WARD HUM.

Plum Run

Power's Hill

His grand charge blunted, Stuar[t] will not threaten the Union rear[.]

RIDGE

McLAWS

Peach Orchard

EMMITSBURG RD

Wheatfield

LAW

Devil's Den

[Li]ttle [R]ou[nd] Top

Big Round Top

N

0   0.5   1

July 3, Midafternoon

Left: On the great charge's left, it's over. In front of Hays and the northern edge of Gibbon, Pettigrew's and Trimble's brigades—Fry, Marshall, Lane, Lowrance—in dribs and drabs—tatters of units—walk back over the smoking fields of dead and moaning injured. Some Rebs, at the road, wait: they'll be prisoners. A breeze clears part of the soiled sky where they smartly marched forward not long ago—shining roofs of shouldered steel and tall red flags aloft (now dropped on the grass).

Pickett hits the wall.

Above: East Cavalry Field. Accelerating, the blue and gray lines gallop with a crash into each other, horses upending, riders airborne, gun blasts at a range of inches, sabers ringing like bells. The 1st Michigan is overwhelmed, but alert Unionists bite hard at the Rebel mass, left and, without orders, right. Minutes of the most savage, hacking, toppling, crushing Medal-of-Honor fighting end. Quick as it began, the fury drains. Cavalry fights were like that. This one, for its duration, however, was as savage as any of the participants could remember.

Call it a draw. Both sides retire, gentlemanly . . . but the Yankees *win* a draw. Stuart will get nowhere near MEADE's rear, let alone the main fight.

Riddled by Stannard's Vermonters with heavy flanking fire, Kemper and Pickett's other Virginia brigades of Garnett and Armistead, heroically preserving the momentum they've generated since stepping nattily from the Seminary Ridge trees some thirty minutes ago, arrive at the flashing Yankee barrels at the wall.

(A low stone fence of rocks solidly piled two to three feet high, the wall runs north-south, but for a ninety-degree jut between Hays and Gibbon: the [Bloody] Angle.)

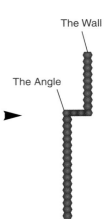

The 71st Pennsylvania retreats (with vague permission), leaving a pocket of unmanned space at the Angle's crux. They'll not get back in the fight.

The clotting, determined troops of Pickett face cannons that can fire, now, needing only short-range canister, devastating clouds of death.

Hunt, right around the artillery shown, is so excited by the drama and how well his gunners have done that, blasting away with his pistol into the swarming, shooting Rebs looming at the wall, he yells, "See 'em? See 'em?"

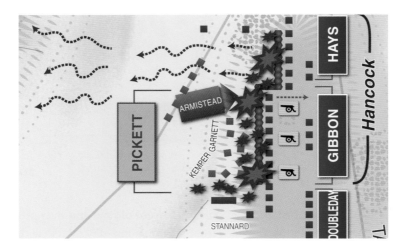

Hancock is everywhere, MEADE never far.

Gibbon, cool and collected, rides his blazing line, reminding his rifles to aim low (to compensate for bullet trajectories but also to target a larger, easier-to-hit area—the chest and stomach compared to the head).

Longstreet, on a fence across the way, watches intently, from time to time sending a messenger forward with advice to one of his generals.

At a distance, LEE watches.

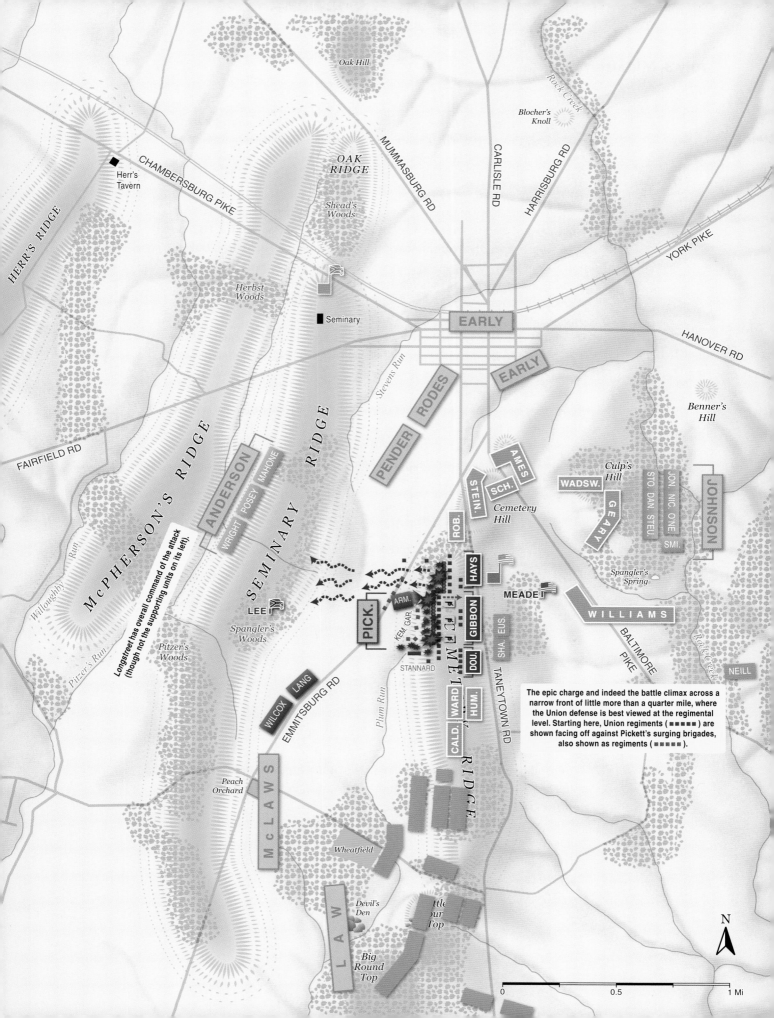

CHAMBERSBURG PIKE

Herr's Tavern

HERR'S RIDGE

OAK RIDGE

Shead's Woods

MUMMASBURG RD

Oak Hill

Blocher's Knoll

Rock Creek

CARLISLE RD

HARRISBURG RD

YORK PIKE

Herbst Woods

Seminary

EARLY

HANOVER RD

McPHERSON'S RIDGE

SEMINARY RIDGE

FAIRFIELD RD

Willoughby Run

Pitzer's Run

ANDERSON

WRIGHT POSEY MAHONE

PENDER RODES

EARLY

Benner's Hill

AMES

STEIN. SCH.

Cemetery Hill

WADSW.

Culp's Hill

GEARY

STO. DAN. STEU
JON. NIC. ONE
SMI.

JOHNSON

Longstreet has overall command of the attack (though not the supporting units on its left).

LEE

Spangler's Woods

ROB.

HAYS

GIBBON

MEADE

Spangler's Spring

PICK.

ARM.

KEM. GAR.

DOU.

SHA. EUS.

WILLIAMS

BALTIMORE PIKE

Rock Creek

NEILL

Pitzer's Woods

STANNARD

CEMETERY RIDGE

WILCOX LANG

EMMITSBURG RD

Plum Run

TANEYTOWN RD

CALD. WARD HUM.

The epic charge and indeed the battle climax across a narrow front of little more than a quarter mile, where the Union defense is best viewed at the regimental level. Starting here, Union regiments (■■■■■) are shown facing off against Pickett's surging brigades, also shown as regiments (■■■■■).

McLAWS

Peach Orchard

Wheatfield

LAW

Devil's Den

Little Round Top

Big Round Top

N

0   0.5   1 Mi

The dense mass of Rebel infantry, a determined few hundred forward-pushing in the skyless din, shooting and pressing at the wall around the Angle, stops. It's natural. They're fatigued. They're under flaming ragged fire. The wall affords cover, respite. They can fire back from it. Their surge has, logically, paused.

The Yank artillery of Cushing, Cowan, and Rorty belches pointblank. Scattered lines of Union rifle and musket crack like firecracker strings. Finding cover as they may, the Rebs fire back. Both sides press the issue with bullets, not, now at the end, maneuver or in any particular order or much of a command structure where the dark noise, the lightning-veined cloud of the finale, is anxiously observed from every direction out across the otherwise quiet square miles, the rolling green farmland ridges and dips.

"empty space"

Where the 71st Pennsylvania was, there's empty space—a lacuna. The Yanks are firing but jumbled, and they have shrunk back. The appearance of swarming Reb rifles out of the smoke right in front of them is daunting.

Hancock's on the way.

In front of Cowan's guns, some Confederates start over the low stacked stones. Cowan has his barrels aimed as low as they'll go. He bids his eager gunners wait. The gray foot infantry is stepping over the low wall . . . fire. Killing winds of scrap metal slaughter them.

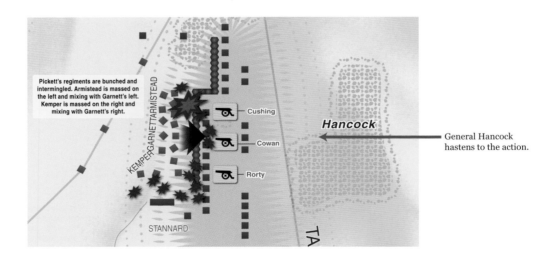

Pickett's regiments are bunched and intermingled. Armistead is massed on the left and mixing with Garnett's left. Kemper is massed on the right and mixing with Garnett's right.

General Hancock hastens to the action.

Cushing takes one in the shoulder. One in the groin. He refuses help. A third, in his mouth, ends life. His guns cut swathes in the Rebel horde, but soon they will have to be abandoned.

Cowan's guns have done savage damage, halting the Rebel wall crossing, but with the gray foot infantry that close Cowan has not even waited to look to see the result of his gunnery: he orders his guns wheeled back, against possible capture.

Cowan

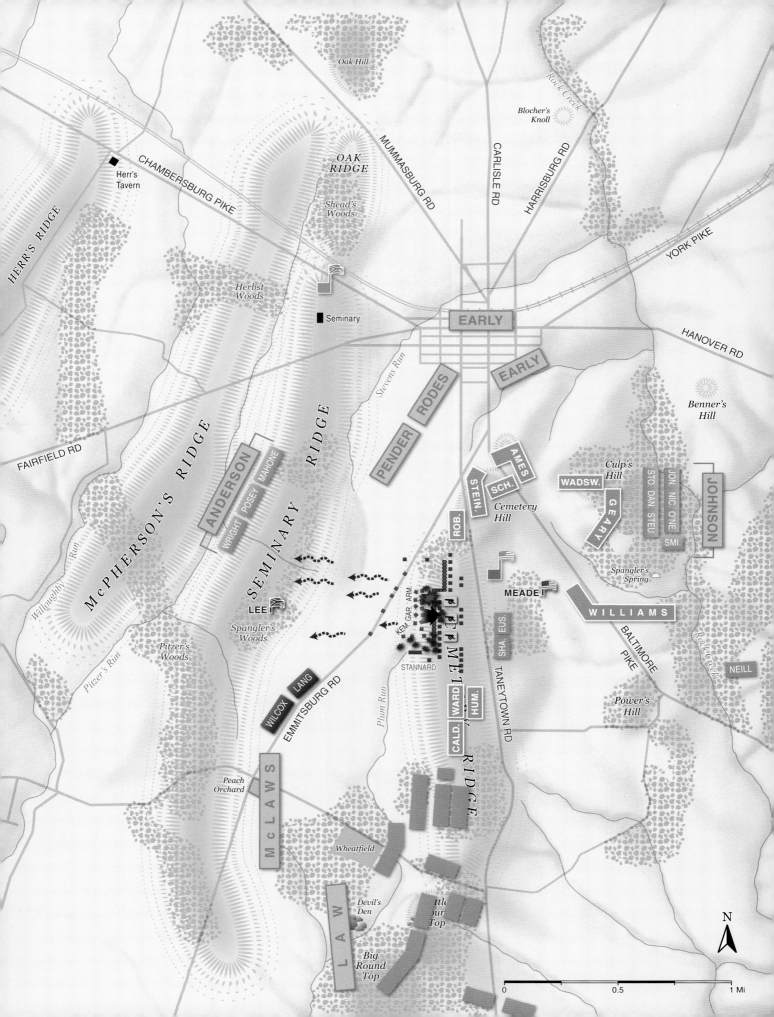

Herr's Tavern

CHAMBERSBURG PIKE

HERR'S RIDGE

Oak Hill

OAK RIDGE

MUMMASBURG RD

Blocher's Knoll

Rock Creek

CARLISLE RD

HARRISBURG RD

Shead's Woods

YORK PIKE

Herbst Woods

Seminary

EARLY

HANOVER RD

FAIRFIELD RD

McPHERSON'S RIDGE

Stevens Run

PENDER   RODES

EARLY

Benner's Hill

ANDERSON

WRIGHT POSEY MAHONE

SEMINARY RIDGE

AMES

STEIN

SCH.

Culp's Hill

WADSW.

STO. DAN. STEU

JON. NIC. O'NE

JOHNSON

Cemetery Hill

GEARY

Willoughby Run

LEE

ROB.

SMI

Spangler's Woods

MEADE

Spangler's Spring

Pitzer's Woods

KEM. GAR. ARM.

WILLIAMS

Pitzer's Run

WILCOX LANG

SHA EUS

Rock Creek

STANNARD

BALTIMORE PIKE

EMMITSBURG RD

Plum Run

TANEYTOWN RD

CEMETERY RIDGE

CALD. WARD HUM.

NEILL

Power's Hill

Peach Orchard

McLAWS

Wheatfield

LAW

Devil's Den

ttle ur Top

Big Round Top

N

0   0.5   1 Mi

Plenty of Union troops and firepower are minutes away. But they're not here. The balance is hanging, and General Armistead sees it. He sees the Confederate "fighting pause" at the wall. He knows the mortal sin hesitation can be in such a charge as this. You go—pour ahead, overrun.

In the opaque curtains of flaming smoke, Cushing's guns are no longer manned. Cowan's guns have rolled rearward.

"Come forward, Virginians!" Armistead cries out. Hat immortally atop his lifted sword's point, on foot he trots forward. It galvanizes the Rebel fighters around him. Hundreds go at the wall. (Hundreds out of the 13,000 who started!) They start over it, in the area of the Angle—the day's all-important pressure point. The Charge resurgent. Churning Dixie flags, soot-faced gray infantry jostling, oncoming. Armistead's hat tilts and hovers above them. They swarm the wall, teeming over it, breaking the plane between MEADE and LEE. It's clang, blast, clatter, ululating, smoke, the dull whack and thud of hand-to-hand.

The Yankees backpedal.

Webb, whose brigade these faltering blue regiments constitute, in anxiety and pride runs back to where the 72nd Pennsylvania, in reserve a hundred yards to the rear, needs to be told twice. Confusedly ordering, yelling, desperate to get them forward, Webb—a new man, not known to all—fails to make himself entirely understood (putting it mildly). He tries to grab a 72nd flag. At last the men of the 72nd advance a bit, toward Armistead's surging scrum of attackers. The 72nd fires. They keep firing, at a bit of a distance. They refuse to advance farther.

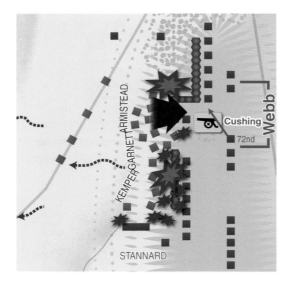

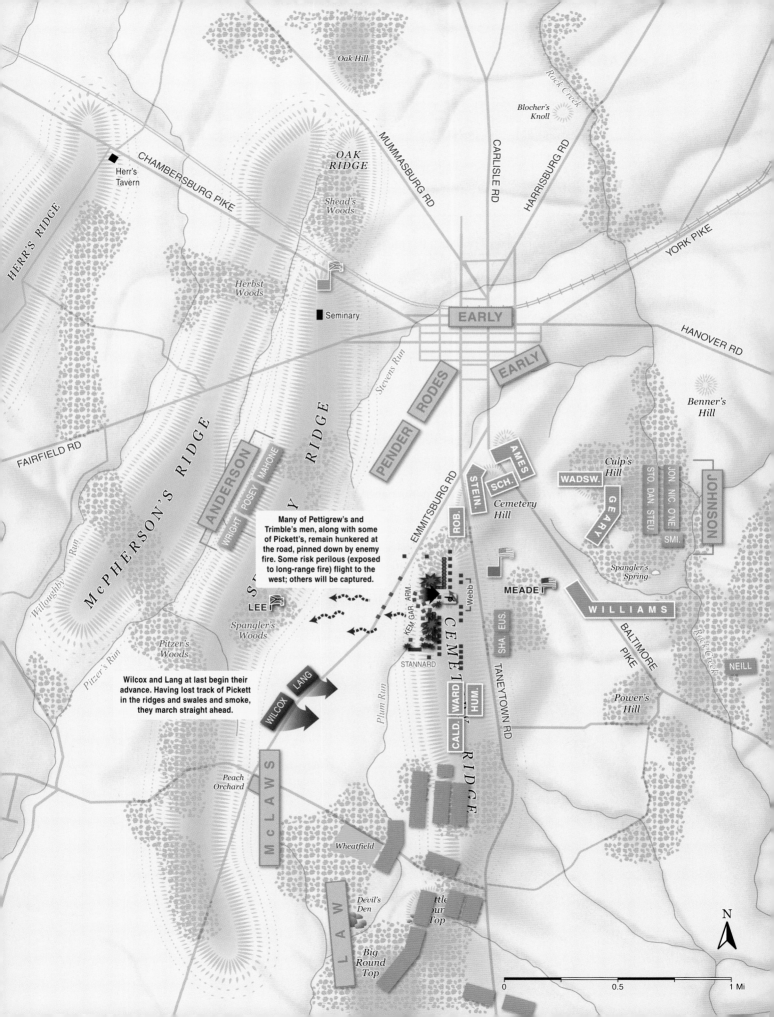

CHAMBERSBURG PIKE

Herr's Tavern

HERR'S RIDGE

OAK RIDGE

Oak Hill

MUMMASBURG RD

CARLISLE RD

HARRISBURG RD

Rock Creek

Blocher's Knoll

YORK PIKE

Shead's Woods

Herbst Woods

Seminary

Stevens Run

EARLY

EARLY

HANOVER RD

FAIRFIELD RD

McPHERSON'S RIDGE

Willoughby Run

Pitzer's Run

SEMINARY RIDGE

ANDERSON

MAHONE
POSEY
WRIGHT

PENDER

RODES

Benner's Hill

AMES

STEIN.

SCH.

ROB.

WADSW.

Culp's Hill

GEARY

Cemetery Hill

STO. DAN STEU

JON. NIC. ONE

SMI.

JOHNSON

Many of Pettigrew's and Trimble's men, along with some of Pickett's, remain hunkered at the road, pinned down by enemy fire. Some risk perilous (exposed to long-range fire) flight to the west; others will be captured.

LEE

Spangler's Woods

EMMITSBURG RD

KEM. GAR. ARM.

Webb

Spangler's Spring

MEADE

WILLIAMS

Pitzer's Woods

SHA EUS

STANNARD

HUM.

WARD

CALD.

CEMETERY RIDGE

TANEYTOWN RD

BALTIMORE PIKE

Rock Creek

NEILL

Wilcox and Lang at last begin their advance. Having lost track of Pickett in the ridges and swales and smoke, they march straight ahead.

LANG

WILCOX

Plum Run

Power's Hill

Peach Orchard

McLAWS

Wheatfield

Devil's Den

LAW

ittle
ur Top

Big Round Top

N

0   0.5   1 Mi

The last cannon is out of it here at the crux where progress and failure measure off by the second. The quarters are far too close for artillery. It's all infantry now.

Hancock, on a new horse, his trusted old one having succumbed to nerves, rides about getting regiments moving.

In the mix of commands—brigades, regiments, and battalions indistinct from each other—fighting blind often, unrecognizable visages in droves shift to collide, blading, firing into the grimed faces firing at them. Some load for others, trying to keep the firing as unremitting as possible. Clubbing, thrusting, crowding, shooting, bludgeoning in the thick chaos . . . use a rock if it's all you have. Faces explode red. The clotted smoke cloud of noise, death's racket, seems eerily small to the idle divisions and corps holding their breath to the west, north, and south.

Webb in a craze of worry hurries past Armistead. Not ten feet from one another amid the flame and grappling, one general may pass near his sworn enemy. Striding Webb does, in the smoke swirls a pebble toss from Armistead. Neither knows it.

Webb races over to the 69th Pennsylvania. They're just south of the Angle. Yelling and waving, he directs them. They move, position, pour fire northward into the living bruise Armistead has opened under MEADE's sleek defense skin.

Armistead stands exultant. His hand rests on the hot iron of a Cushing rifled cannon.

Back in the reserve line, the 42nd New York and 19th Massachusetts have watched Armistead breach the wall and then the 72nd Pennsylvania advance toward the gray flood bursting into the Angle. *Hancock* rides by. The young colonel leading the two regiments asks, practically begs, his corps commander to "let me go in there." "Go in there pretty God damned quick!" barks *Hancock*—and the 42nd and 19th add their shouldered long arms to the speaking Yankee barrels. Armistead's boys are raked with bullets from their right.

If . . .

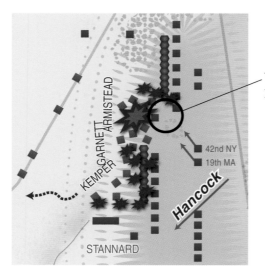

Webb and Armistead pass each other in this vicinity.

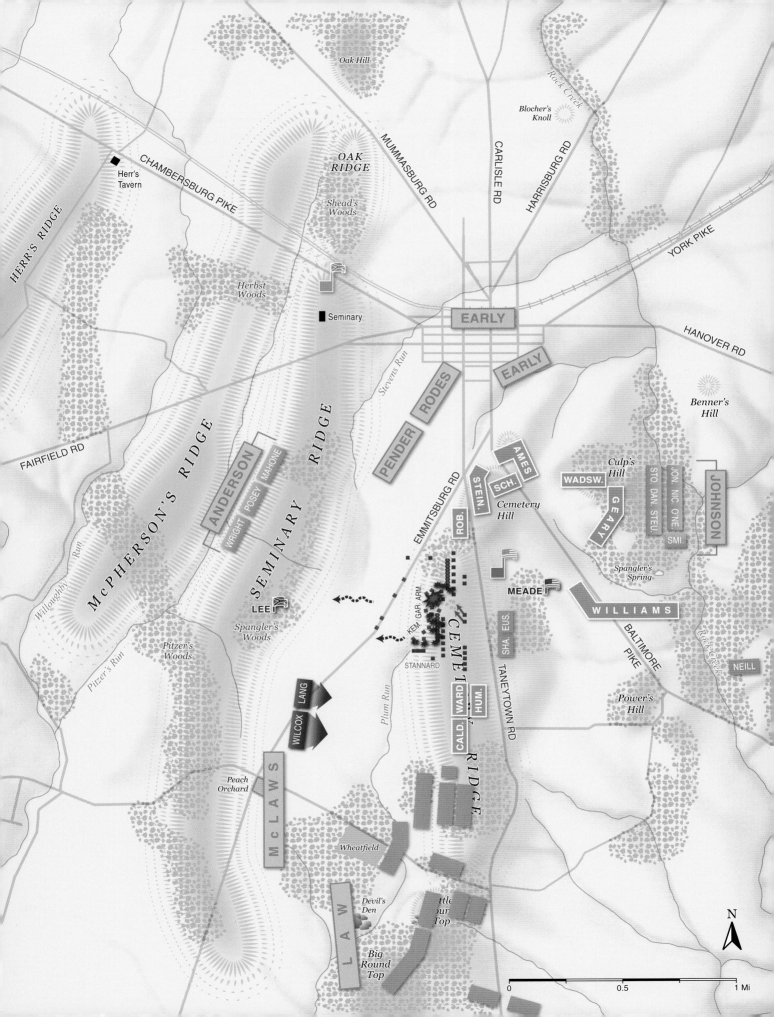

HERR'S RIDGE

Herr's Tavern

CHAMBERSBURG PIKE

OAK RIDGE

Oak Hill

MUMMASBURG RD

CARLISLE RD

HARRISBURG RD

Rock Creek

Blocher's Knoll

YORK PIKE

FAIRFIELD RD

Shead's Woods

Herbst Woods

Seminary

Stevens Run

EARLY

EARLY

HANOVER RD

Benner's Hill

McPHERSON'S RIDGE

SEMINARY RIDGE

ANDERSON

WRIGHT POSEY MAHONE

PENDER

RODES

EMMITSBURG RD

ROB.

AMES

STEIN.

SCH.

Cemetery Hill

WADSW.

GEARY

STO DAN STEU

JON NIC O'NE

SMI.

JOHNSON

Culp's Hill

LEE

Willoughby Run

Spangler's Woods

MEADE

WILLIAMS

Spangler's Spring

Pitzer's Woods

Pitzer's Run

KEM. GAR. ARM.

CEMETERY RIDGE

SHA EUS

Power's Hill

BALTIMORE PIKE

Rock Creek

NEILL

LANG

STANNARD

CALD. WARD HUM.

WILCOX

TANEYTOWN RD

Peach Orchard

McLAWS

Plum Run

Wheatfield

LAW

Devil's Den

ttle
ur
Top

Big Round Top

N

0   0.5   1 Mi

—if more Gray fighters could pour in. Now. If Posey, Mahone, Wright had been used, and/or other of LEE's brigades north, west, and south. Or Wilcox and Lang properly used (whom we see inching vainly eastward below the action).

If . . . History's numbest word.

Armistead still believes. *We can turn it.* He gets some of his men to trundle Cushing's captured cannons around in the blazing confusion. They manage, aim them at their owners.

Union regiments all around are turning toward the fight. They begin to move toward it. There are a lot of them. White blood cells to the wound.

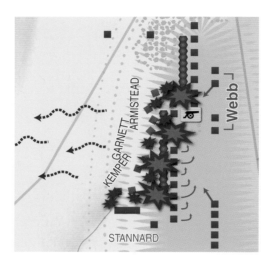

Webb has earned the Medal of Honor.

Armistead frowns. His sword falls. He reaches out—to steady himself—for a cannon barrel . . . his hand never reaches it.

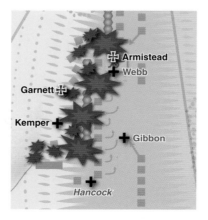

Hancock's down: wounded. Likewise Gibbon, Kemper . . . Garnett's dead. Armistead is wounded mortally. Webb is wounded, still in action. Trimble—on the Charge's left earlier—wounded, and Fry, Pettigrew, Lowrance. Marshall's dead.

Armistead's men can't figure out how to get Cushing's pieces to fire.

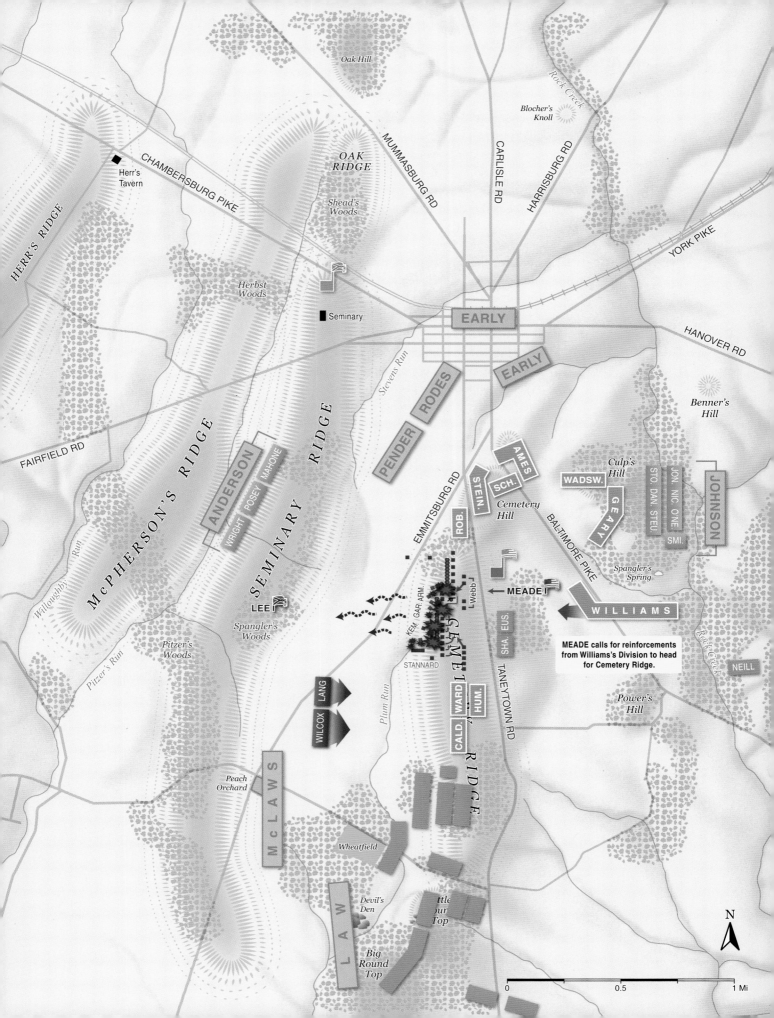

HERR'S RIDGE

Herr's Tavern

CHAMBERSBURG PIKE

OAK RIDGE

MUMMASBURG RD

Oak Hill

Blocher's Knoll

Rock Creek

CARLISLE RD

HARRISBURG RD

YORK PIKE

Shead's Woods

FAIRFIELD RD

McPHERSON'S RIDGE

Herbst Woods

■ Seminary

SEMINARY RIDGE

Willoughby Run

Stevens Run

EARLY

EARLY

HANOVER RD

PENDER

RODES

Benner's Hill

ANDERSON

WRIGHT POSEY MAHONE

AMES

STEIN.

SCH.

WADSW.

Culp's Hill

STO DAN STEU

JON NIC O'NE

JOHNSON

Cemetery Hill

GEARY

SMI.

ROB.

LEE

Spangler's Woods

BALTIMORE PIKE

Spangler's Spring

Pitzer's Woods

Plum Run

Pitzer's Run

KEM. GAR. ARM.

L. Webb J.

← MEADE

WILLIAMS

MEADE calls for reinforcements from Williams's Division to head for Cemetery Ridge.

SHA. EUS.

NEILL

WILCOX LANG

STANNARD

CEMETERY RIDGE

CALD. WARD HUM.

Power's Hill

Rock Creek

TANEYTOWN RD

McLAWS

Peach Orchard

Wheatfield

LAW

Devil's Den

ttle ur Top

Big Round Top

N

0   0.5   1 Mi

The Rebs fight on.

Their backs to their backs. Looking surreally around for a weapon. A dwindling group of them stands weeping, loading, firing, upchucking.

Inertia of bravery.

Memory of pride.

Around them the dead heap. Wounded dance on their backs on the charred earth.

The Yanks need not charge.

Back out over the strewn fields, the expanse of destruction where the Charge unfolded, no one is coming. Not a unit, not a message.

Wilcox/Lang will clash with Stannard to no effect. A post-Charge Union attack will retake the Wheatfield. At the map's bottom a late, exciting cavalry charge will have no effect.

The last of the lost ebb forlornly back, over the fields and across the road.

Others, loitering, await an opportunity to be taken prisoner.

Along Cemetery Ridge the cheering has begun.

Back the survivors trudge, toward the Seminary Ridge tree line where, solitary in his saddle, hat off, a graying gentleman awaits them.

An apology on his lips.

The battle is over.

MEADE has won.

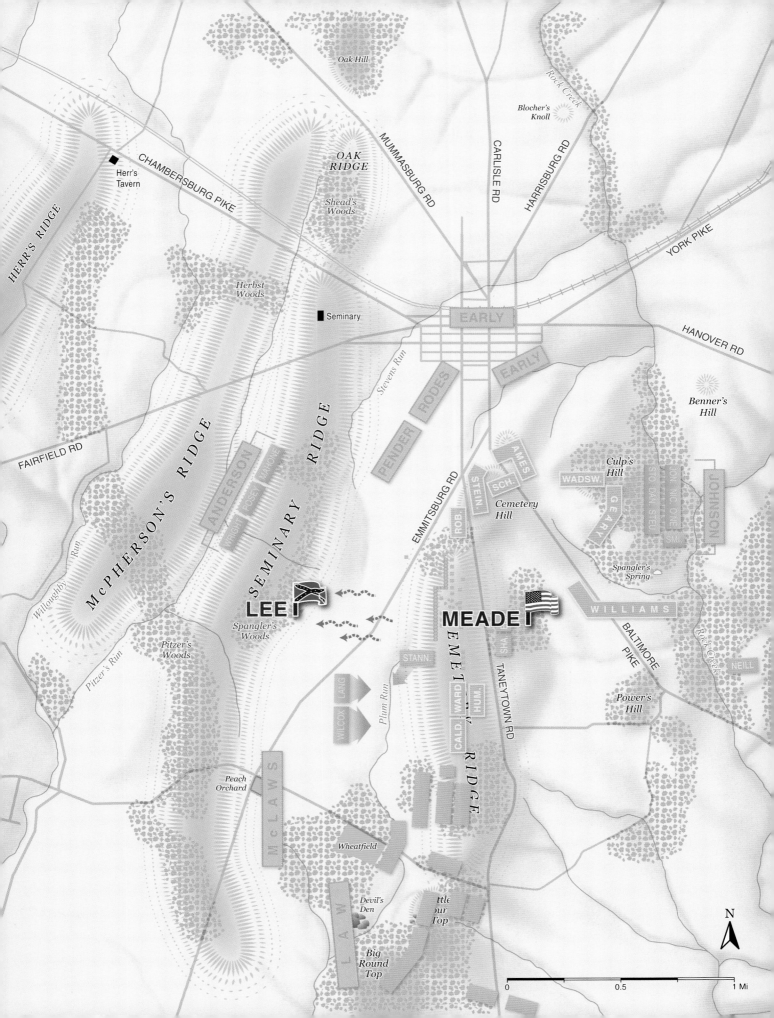

Oak Hill

Blocher's Knoll

Rock Creek

OAK RIDGE

MUMMASBURG RD

CARLISLE RD

HARRISBURG RD

Herr's Tavern

CHAMBERSBURG PIKE

Shead's Woods

YORK PIKE

HERR'S RIDGE

Herbst Woods

■ Seminary

EARLY

HANOVER RD

Benner's Hill

M c PHERSON'S RIDGE

SEMINARY RIDGE

Stevens Run

PENDER

RODES

EARLY

Culp's Hill

AMES

WADSW.

FAIRFIELD RD

ANDERSON

STEIN.

SCH.

Emmitsburg RD

GEARY

JOHNSON

Cemetery Hill

ROB.

Willoughby Run

Pitzer's Woods

LEE ⚔

Spangler's Woods

MEADE ⚑

Spangler's Spring

WILLIAMS

Pitzer's Run

Plum Run

STANN.

BALTIMORE PIKE

Rock Creek

NEILL

WILCOX LANG

WARD

CALD.

HUM.

TANEYTOWN RD

Power's Hill

Peach Orchard

McLAWS

EMMET___Y RIDGE

Wheatfield

Devil's Den

___ttle ___ur Top

⬥ W

Big Round Top

N

0   0.5   1 Mi

Bibliography

Adelman, Garry E., and Timothy H. Smith. *Devil's Den: A History and Guide*. Gettysburg, PA: Thomas Publications, 1997.

Adkin, Mark. *The Gettysburg Companion: The Complete Guide to America's Most Famous Battle*. Mechanicsburg, PA: Stackpole Books, 2008.

Alexander, Edward Porter. *Fighting for the Confederacy: The Personal Recollections of General Edward Porter Alexander*. Edited by Gary W. Gallagher. Chapel Hill, NC: University of North Carolina Press, 1989.

———. "The Great Charge and Artillery Fighting at Gettysburg." In *Battles and Leaders of the Civil War*, vol. 3, edited by Robert Underwood Johnson and Clarence Clough Buel. New York: The Century Co., 1888.

———. "Letter from General E. P. Alexander." *Southern Historical Society Papers* 4 (1877).

———. *Military Memoirs of a Confederate: A Critical Narrative*. New York: Charles Scribner's Sons, 1907.

Archer, John M. "Fury at Bliss Farm." *America's Civil War* 8, no. 3 (July 1995).

Atkinson, Matt. "'More May Have Been Expected of Them Than They Were Able to Perform': Seminary Ridge on July 3." In *The Third Day: The Fate of a Nation, July 3, 1863*. Papers of the 2008 Gettysburg Seminar. Gettysburg, PA: National Park Service, 2010.

———. "'We Were Now Complete Masters of the Field': Ambrose Wright's Attack on July 2." In *The Most Shocking Battle I Have Ever Witnessed: The Second Day at Gettysburg*. Papers of the 2006 National Park Service Seminar. Gettysburg, PA: National Park Service, 2008.

Bachelder, John B. *Map of the Battlefield of Gettysburg: First Day's Battle*. Washington, DC: Office of the Chief of Engineers, U.S. Army, 1876.

———. *Map of the Battlefield of Gettysburg: Second Day's Battle*. Washington, DC: Office of the Chief of Engineers, U.S. Army, 1876.

———. *Map of the Battlefield of Gettysburg: Third Day's Battle*. Washington, DC: Office of the Chief of Engineers, U.S. Army, 1876.

Barnett, Bert H. "'For an Hour and a Half We Had a Grand Fourth of July Performance': Robert E. Lee and the Cannonade of July 3." In *The Third Day: The Fate of a Nation, July 3, 1863*. Papers of the 2008 Gettysburg Seminar. Gettysburg, PA: National Park Service, 2010.

———. "Union Artillery on July 3." In *Mr. Lincoln's Army: The Army of the Potomac in the Gettysburg Campaign*. Programs of the Sixth Annual Gettysburg Seminar. Gettysburg, PA: National Park Service, 2007.

Bigelow, John. *The Peach Orchard: Gettysburg, July 2, 1863*. Minneapolis: Kimball-Storer Co., 1910.

Brooke-Rawle, William. *The Right Flank at Gettysburg: An Account of the Operations of General Gregg's Cavalry Command*. Philadelphia: Allen, Lane & Scott's, 1878.

Campbell, Eric A. "A Brief History and Analysis of the Hunt-Hancock Controversy." In *The Third Day: The Fate of a Nation, July 3, 1863*. Papers of the 2008 Gettysburg Seminar. Gettysburg, PA: National Park Service, 2010.

———. "The Key to the Entire Situation: The Peach Orchard, July 2, 1863." In *The Most Shocking Battle I Have Ever Witnessed: The Second Day at Gettysburg*. Papers of the 2006 National Park Service Seminar. Gettysburg, PA: National Park Service, 2008.

———. "'Sacrificed to the bad management . . . of others': Richard H. Anderson's Division at the Battle of Gettysburg. In *High Water Mark: The Army of Northern Virginia in the Gettysburg Campaign*. Programs of the Seventh Annual Gettysburg Seminar. Gettysburg, PA: National Park Service, 1999.

———. "'We Saved the Line from Being Broken': Freeman McGilvery, John Bigelow, Charles Reed, and the Battle of Gettysburg." In *Unsung Heroes of Gettysburg*. Programs of the Fifth Annual Gettysburg Seminar. Gettysburg, PA: National Park Service, 1996.

Carmichael, Peter S. "'Every Map of the Field Cries Out about It': The Failure of Confederate Artillery at Pickett's Charge." In *Three Days at Gettysburg: Essays on Confederate and Union Leadership*, edited by Gary W. Gallagher. Kent, OH: Kent State University Press, 1999.

Cleaves, Freeman. *Meade of Gettysburg*. Norman, OK: University of Oklahoma Press, 1960.

Coddington, Edwin B. *The Gettysburg Campaign: A Study in Command*. New York: Scribner's, 1968.

Coffin, Howard. *Nine Months to Gettysburg: Stannard's Vermonters and the Repulse of Pickett's Charge*. Woodstock, VT: The Countryman Press, 1997.

Coughenour, Kevin. "Andrew Atkinson Humphreys: Divisional Command in the Army of the Potomac." In *Mr. Lincoln's Army: The Army of the Potomac in the Gettysburg Campaign*. Programs of the Sixth Annual Gettysburg Seminar. Gettysburg, PA: National Park Service, 2007.

Dawes, Rufus R. *Service with the Sixth Wisconsin Volunteers*. Marietta, OH: E. R. Alderman & Sons, 1890.

Desjardin, Thomas A. *Stand Firm Ye Boys from Maine: The 20th Maine and the Gettysburg Campaign*. Gettysburg, PA: Thomas Publications, 1995.

De Trobriand, Regis. *Four Years with the Army of the Potomac*. Translated by George K. Dauchy. Boston: Ticknor and Company, 1889.

Discorfano, Ken. *They Saved the Union at Little Round Top: Gettysburg, July 2, 1863*. Gettysburg, PA: Thomas Publications, 2002.

Doubleday, Abner. *Chancellorsville and Gettysburg*. New York: Charles Scribner's Sons, 1882.

Dougherty, James J. *Stone's Brigade and the Fight for the McPherson Farm*. Conshohocken, PA: Combined Publishing, 2001.

Downey, Fairfax. *The Guns at Gettysburg*. New York: David McKay, 1958.

Early, Jubal. "Leading Confederates on the Battle of Gettysburg: A Review by General Early." *Southern Historical Society Papers* 4 (1877).

Frassanito, William A. *Gettysburg: A Journey in Time*. New York: Charles Scribner's Sons, 1975.

Freeman, Douglas Southall. *Lee's Lieutenants: A Study in Command*. Vol. 3, *Gettysburg to Appomattox*. New York: Charles Scribner's Sons, 1944.

———. *R. E. Lee: A Biography*. Vol. 3. New York: Charles Scribner's Sons, 1934.

Fremantle, Arthur. *Three Months in the Southern States, April–June 1863*. Edinburgh, Scotland: William Blackwood and Sons, 1863.

Gallagher, Gary W. "Confederate Corps Leadership on the First Day at Gettysburg: A. P. Hill and Richard S. Ewell in a Difficult Debut." In *The First Day at Gettysburg: Essays on Confederate and Union Leadership*, edited by Gary W. Gallagher. Kent, OH: Kent State University Press, 1992.

———. "'If the Enemy Is There, We Must Attack Him': R. E. Lee and the Second Day at Gettysburg." In *The Second Day at Gettysburg: Essays on Confederate and Union Leadership*, edited by Gary W. Gallagher. Kent, OH: Kent State University Press, 1993.

———, ed. *Lee the Soldier*. Lincoln, NE: University of Nebraska Press, 1996.

Glatthaar, Joseph T. *General Lee's Army: From Victory to Collapse*. New York: Free Press, 2008.

Gottfried, Bradley M. *The Artillery of Gettysburg*. Nashville, TN: Cumberland House, 2008.

———. *The Brigades of Gettysburg: The Union and Confederate Brigades at the Battle of Gettysburg*. New York: Skyhorse Publishing, 2012.

———. "Mahone's Brigade: Insubordination or Miscommunication?" *Gettysburg Magazine* 18 (January 1998).

———. *The Maps of Gettysburg: An Atlas of the Gettysburg Campaign, June 3–July 13, 1863*. New York: Savas Beatie, 2010.

———. *Stopping Pickett: The History of the Philadelphia Brigade*. Shippensburg, PA: White Mane Books, 1999.

Gramm, Kent. "The Chances of War: Lee, Longstreet, Sickles, and the First Minnesota Volunteers." In *The Gettysburg Nobody Knows*, edited by Gabor S. Boritt. New York: Oxford University Press, 1997.

Greene, A. Wilson. "From Chancellorsville to Cemetery Hill: O. O. Howard and Eleventh Corps Leadership." In *The First Day at Gettysburg: Essays on Confederate and Union Leadership*, edited by Gary W. Gallagher. Kent, OH: Kent State University Press, 1992.

———. "'A Step All-Important and Essential to Victory': Henry W. Slocum and the Twelfth Corps on July 1–2, 1863." In *The Second Day at Gettysburg: Essays on Confederate and Union Leadership*, edited by Gary W. Gallagher. Kent, OH: Kent State University Press, 1993.

Grimsley, Mark, and Brooks D. Simpson. *Gettysburg: A Battlefield Guide*. Lincoln, NE: University of Nebraska Press, 1999.

Guelzo, Allen C. "The Unturned Corners of the Battle of Gettysburg: Tactics, Geography, and Politics." *Gettysburg Magazine* 45 (July 2011).

Hall, Jeffrey C. *The Stand of the U.S. Army at Gettysburg*. Bloomington, IN: Indiana University Press, 2003.

Harman, Troy D. "Entangled Intentionally: The 11th Army Corps and the Battle North of Town." In *This Has Been a Terrible Ordeal: The Gettysburg Campaign and First Day of Battle*. Papers of the Tenth Gettysburg National Military Park Seminar. Gettysburg, PA: National Park Service, 2005.

———. *Lee's Real Plan at Gettysburg*. Mechanicsburg, PA: Stackpole Books, 2003.

Harrison, Kathy Georg. *Nothing But Glory: Pickett's Division at Gettysburg*. Gettysburg, PA: Thomas Publications, 2001.

———. "'Our Principal Loss Was in This Place': Action at the Slaughter Pen and at the South End of Houck's Ridge, Gettysburg, Pennsylvania, July 2, 1863." *Gettysburg Magazine* 1 (July 1, 1989).

Harrison, Walter. *Pickett's Men: A Fragment of War History*. New York: D. Van Nostrand, 1870.

Hartwig, D. Scott. "The 11th Army Corps on July 1, 1863." *Gettysburg Magazine* 2 (January 1990).

———. "The Campaign and Battle of Gettysburg." In *Damn Dutch: Pennsylvania Germans at Gettysburg*, edited by David L. Valuska and Christian B. Keller. Mechanicsburg, PA: Stackpole Books, 2004.

———. "The Fate of a Country: The Repulse of Longstreet's Assault by the Army of the Potomac." In *Mr. Lincoln's Army: The Army of the Potomac in the Gettysburg Campaign*. Programs of the Sixth Annual Gettysburg Seminar. Gettysburg, PA: National Park Service, 2007.

———. "High Water Mark: Heroes, Myth, and Memory." In *The Third Day: The Fate of a Nation, July 3, 1863*. Papers of the 2008 Gettysburg Seminar. Gettysburg, PA: National Park Service, 2010.

———. "'I Ordered No Man to Go Where I Would Not Go Myself': Norman Hall, Alexander Webb, Alonzo Cushing, and the Art of Leading Men in Battle." In *I Ordered No Man to Go Where I Would Not Go Myself: Leadership in the Campaign and Battle of Gettysburg*. Papers of the Ninth National Park Service Seminar. Gettysburg, PA: National Park Service, 2002.

———. "'No Troops on the Field Had Done Better': John C. Caldwell's Division in the Wheatfield, July 2, 1863." In *The Second Day at Gettysburg: Essays on Confederate and Union Leadership*, edited by Gary W. Gallagher. Kent, OH: Kent State University Press, 1993.

Haskell, Frank Aretas. *The Battle of Gettysburg*. Edited by Bruce Catton. Boston: Houghton Mifflin, 1958.

Hassler, Warren W. *Crisis at the Crossroads: The First Day at Gettysburg*. Tuscaloosa, AL: University of Alabama Press, 1970.

Herdegen, Lance J., and William J. K. Beaudot. *In the Bloody Railroad Cut at Gettysburg*. Dayton, OH: Morningside, 1990.

Hess, Earl. *Pickett's Charge: The Last Attack at Gettysburg*. Chapel Hill, NC: University of North Carolina Press, 2001.

Bibliography

Hessler, James A. *Sickles at Gettysburg: The Controversial Civil War General Who Committed Murder, Abandoned Little Round Top, and Declared Himself the Hero of Gettysburg*. New York: Savas Beatie, 2010.

Hood, John Bell. *Advance and Retreat: Personal Experiences in the United States and Confederate States Armies*. New Orleans: Hood Orphan Memorial Fund, 1880.

Howard, Oliver Otis. *Autobiography of Oliver Otis Howard*. New York: The Baker & Taylor Company, 1907.

Hunt, Henry J. "The First Day at Gettysburg." In *Battles and Leaders of the Civil War*, vol. 3, edited by Robert Underwood Johnson and Clarence Clough Buel. New York: The Century Co., 1888.

———. "The Second Day at Gettysburg." In *Battles and Leaders of the Civil War*, vol. 3, edited by Robert Underwood Johnson and Clarence Clough Buel. New York: The Century Co., 1888.

———. "The Third Day at Gettysburg." In *Battles and Leaders of the Civil War*, vol. 3, edited by Robert Underwood Johnson and Clarence Clough Buel. New York: The Century Co., 1888.

Huntington, Tom. *Searching for George Gordon Meade: The Forgotten Victor of Gettysburg*. Mechanicsburg, PA: Stackpole Books, 2013.

Jordan, David M. *Winfield Scott Hancock: A Soldier's Life*. Bloomington, IN: Indiana University Press, 1988.

Jorgensen, Jay. *Gettysburg's Bloody Wheatfield*. Shippensburg, PA: White Mane Books, 2002.

Kershaw, Joseph B. "Kershaw's Brigade at Gettysburg." In *Battles and Leaders of the Civil War*, vol. 3, edited by Robert Underwood Johnson and Clarence Clough Buel. New York: The Century Co., 1888.

Krick, Robert K. "'If Longstreet . . . Says So, It Is Most Likely Not True': James Longstreet and the Second Day at Gettysburg." In *The Second Day at Gettysburg: Essays on Confederate and Union Leadership*, edited by Gary W. Gallagher. Kent, OH: Kent State University Press, 1993.

———. "Three Confederate Disasters on Oak Ridge: Failures of Brigade Leadership on the First Day at Gettysburg." In *The First Day at Gettysburg: Essays on Confederate and Union Leadership*, edited by Gary W. Gallagher. Kent, OH: Kent State University Press, 1992.

Kross, Gary M. "'I Do Not Believe That Pickett's Division Would Have Reached Our Line': Henry J. Hunt and the Union Artillery on July 3, 1863." In *Three Days at Gettysburg: Essays on Confederate and Union Leadership*, edited by Gary W. Gallagher. Kent, OH: Kent State University Press, 1999.

LaFantasie, Glenn W. *Twilight at Little Round Top: July 2, 1863—The Tide Turns at Gettysburg*. Hoboken, NJ: John Wiley & Sons, 2005.

Latschar, Terry. "'My brave Texans, forward and take those heights!': Jerome Bonaparte Robertson and the Texas Brigade." In *I Ordered No Man to Go Where I Would Not Go Myself: Leadership in the Campaign and Battle of Gettysburg*. Papers of the Ninth National Park Service Seminar. Gettysburg, PA: National Park Service, 2002.

Law, Evander M. "The Struggle for 'Round Top.'" In *Battles and Leaders of the Civil War*, vol. 3, edited by Robert Underwood Johnson and Clarence Clough Buel. New York: The Century Co., 1888.

Longacre, Edward G. *The Cavalry at Gettysburg: A Tactical Study of Mounted Operations during the Civil War's Pivotal Campaign, 9 June–14 July 1863*. Lincoln, NE: University of Nebraska Press, 1986.

———. *Lee's Cavalrymen: A History of the Mounted Forces of the Army of Northern Virginia*. Mechanicsburg, PA: Stackpole Books, 2002.

———. *Lincoln's Cavalrymen: A History of the Mounted Forces of the Army of the Potomac*. Mechanicsburg, PA: Stackpole Books, 2000.

Long, Armistead. *Memoirs of Robert E. Lee: His Military and Personal History*. London: Sampson Low, Marston, Searle, and Rivington, 1886.

Longstreet, James. "The Campaign of Gettysburg." *Philadelphia Weekly Times*, 3 November 1877.

———. *From Manassas to Appomattox: Memoirs of the Civil War in America*. 2nd edition. Philadelphia: J. B. Lippincott Company, 1908.

———. "Lee in Pennsylvania." In *Annals of the War*, edited by A. K. McClure. Philadelphia: The Times Publishing Company, 1879.

———. "Lee's Right Wing at Gettysburg." In *Battles and Leaders of the Civil War*, vol. 3, edited by Robert Underwood Johnson and Clarence Clough Buel. New York: The Century Co., 1888.

Luvaas, Jay. "Lee and the Operational Art: The Right Place, The Right Time." *Parameters* 22 (Autumn 1992).

Luvaas, Jay, and Harold W. Nelson, ed. *The U.S. Army War College Guide to the Battle of Gettysburg*. Carlisle, PA: South Mountain Press, 1986.

Martin, David G. *Gettysburg July 1*. Cambridge, MA: Da Capo Press, 1996.

McLaws, Lafayette. "Gettysburg." *Southern Historical Society Papers* 7 (1879).

McPherson, James M. *Hallowed Ground: A Walk at Gettysburg*. New York: Crown, 2003.

Meade, George Gordon, ed. *The Life and Letters of George Gordon Meade*. Vol. 2. New York: Charles Scribner's Sons, 1913.

Miller, William E. "The Cavalry Battle near Gettysburg." In *Battles and Leaders of the Civil War*, vol. 3, edited by Robert Underwood Johnson and Clarence Clough Buel. New York: The Century Co., 1888.

Moe, Richard. *The Last Full Measure: The Life and Death of the First Minnesota Volunteers*. New York: Henry Holt, 1993.

Naisawald, L. VanLoan. *Grape and Canister: The Story of the Field Artillery of the Army of the Potomac, 1861 to 1865*. 2nd ed. Mechanicsburg, PA: Stackpole Books, 1999.

Nesbitt, Mark. *Saber and Scapegoat: J. E. B. Stuart and the Gettysburg Controversy*. Mechanicsburg, PA: Stackpole Books, 1994.

Nolan, Alan T. *The Iron Brigade: A Military History*. New York: Macmillan, 1961.

———. "R. E. Lee and July 1 at Gettysburg." In *The First Day at Gettysburg: Essays on Confederate and Union Leadership*, edited by Gary W. Gallagher. Kent, OH: Kent State University Press, 1992.

Norton, Oliver Willcox. *The Attack and Defense of Little Round Top, Gettysburg, July 2, 1863*. New York: The Neale Publishing Company, 1913.

Oates, William C. *The War between the Union and the Confederacy*. New York: The Neale Publishing Company, 1905.

Owen, William Miller. *In Camp and Battle with the Washington Artillery of New Orleans*. Boston: Ticknor and Company, 1885.

Pfanz, Donald C. *Richard S. Ewell: A Soldier's Life*. Chapel Hill, NC: University of North Carolina Press, 1998.

Pfanz, Harry W. *Gettysburg: Culp's Hill & Cemetery Hill*. Chapel Hill, NC: University of North Carolina Press, 1993.

———. *Gettysburg: The First Day*. Chapel Hill, NC: University of North Carolina Press, 2001.

———. *Gettysburg: The Second Day*. Chapel Hill, NC: University of North Carolina Press, 1987.

Piston, William Garrett. "Cross Purposes: Longstreet, Lee, and Confederate Attack Plans for July 3 at Gettysburg." In *The Third Day at Gettysburg and Beyond*, edited by Gary W. Gallagher. Chapel Hill, NC: University of North Carolina Press, 1994.

———. *Lee's Tarnished Lieutenant: James Longstreet and His Place in Southern History*. Athens, GA: University of Georgia Press, 1987.

Priest, John Michael. *Into the Fight: Pickett's Charge at Gettysburg*. Shippensburg, PA: White Mane Books, 1998.

Pullen, John J. *Joshua Chamberlain: A Hero's Life*. Mechanicsburg, PA: Stackpole Books, 1999.

———. *The Twentieth Maine: A Volunteer Regiment in the Civil War*. Philadelphia: Lippincott, 1957.

Rafuse, Ethan S. *Robert E. Lee and the Fall of the Confederacy, 1863–1865*. Lanham, MD: Rowman & Littlefield Publishers, 2008.

Reardon, Carol. *Pickett's Charge in History and Memory*. Chapel Hill, NC: University of North Carolina Press, 1997.

Robertson, James I. *General A. P. Hill: The Story of a Confederate Warrior*. New York: Random House, 1987.

Robertson, William Glenn. "The Peach Orchard Revisited: Daniel E. Sickles and the Third Corps on July 2, 1863." In *The Second Day at Gettysburg: Essays on Confederate and Union Leadership*, edited by Gary W. Gallagher. Kent, OH: Kent State University Press, 1993.

Ryan, Thomas J. "The Intelligence Battle, July 2: Longstreet's Assault." *Gettysburg Magazine* 43 (July 2010).

Sauers, Richard A. *Meade: Victor of Gettysburg*. Washington, DC: Brassey's, 2003.

———. "'Rarely Has More Skill, Vigor, or Wisdom Been Shown': George G. Meade on July 3 at Gettysburg." In *Three Days at Gettysburg: Essays on Confederate and Union Leadership*, edited by Gary W. Gallagher. Kent, OH: Kent State University Press, 1999.

Schurz, Carl. *The Reminiscences of Carl Schurz*. Vol. 3, *1863–1869*. New York: The McClure Company, 1908.

Sears, Stephen W. *Controversies and Commanders: Dispatches from the Army of the Potomac*. New York: Houghton Mifflin, 1999.

———. *Gettysburg*. New York: Houghton Mifflin, 2003.

Simpson, Brooks D. "'If Properly Led': Command Relationships at Gettysburg." In *Civil War Generals in Defeat*, edited by Steven E. Woodworth. Lawrence, KS: University Press of Kansas, 1999.

Smith, James E. *A Famous Battery and Its Campaigns, 1861–64*. Washington, DC: W. H. Lowdermilk & Co., 1892.

Smith, Karlton D. "Alexander Hays and the 'Blue Birds': Brig. Gen. Alexander Hays and the Third Division, Second Corps, during Longstreet's Assault." In *The Third Day: The Fate of a Nation, July 3, 1863*. Papers of the 2008 Gettysburg Seminar. Gettysburg, PA: National Park Service, 2010.

———. "Honor-Duty-Courage: The 5th Army Corps during the Gettysburg Campaign." In *Mr. Lincoln's Army: The Army of the Potomac in the Gettysburg Campaign*. Programs of the Sixth Annual Gettysburg Seminar. Gettysburg, PA: National Park Service, 2007.

———. "'Never Was I So Depressed': James Longstreet and Pickett's Charge." In *High Water Mark: The Army of Northern Virginia in the Gettysburg Campaign*. Programs of the Seventh Annual Gettysburg Seminar. Gettysburg, PA: National Park Service, 1999.

———. "Pettigrew and Trimble: The Rest of the Story." In *Unsung Heroes of Gettysburg*. Programs of the Fifth Annual Gettysburg Seminar. Gettysburg, PA: National Park Service, 1996.

———. "'To Consider Every Contingency': Lt. Gen. James Longstreet, Capt. Samuel R. Johnston, and the Factors That Affected the Reconnaissance and Countermarch." In *The Most Shocking Battle I Have Ever Witnessed: The Second Day at Gettysburg*. Papers of the 2006 National Park Service Seminar. Gettysburg, PA: National Park Service, 2008.

Sorrel, G. Moxley. *Recollections of a Confederate Staff Officer*. New York: The Neale Publishing Company, 1905.

Stackpole, Edward J. *They Met at Gettysburg*. Harrisburg, PA: Stackpole Books, 1956.

Stackpole, Edward J., and Wilbur S. Nye. *The Battle of Gettysburg: A Guided Tour*. Harrisburg, PA: The Stackpole Company, 1960.

Stewart, George R. *Pickett's Charge: A Microhistory of the Final Attack at Gettysburg, July 3, 1863*. Boston: Houghton Mifflin, 1959.

Swanberg, W. A. *Sickles the Incredible*. New York: Charles Scribner's Sons, 1956.

Symonds, Craig L. *The American Heritage History of the Battle of Gettysburg*. New York: Harper Collins, 2001.

———. *Gettysburg: A Battlefield Atlas*. Baltimore, MD: The Nautical & Aviation Publishing Company of America, 1992.

Tagg, Larry. *The Generals of Gettysburg*. New York: Savas Publishing, 1998.

Taylor, Walter H. *Four Years with General Lee*. New York: D. Appleton and Company, 1877.

Teague, Charles. "Right Gone Awry." In *The Third Day: The Fate of a Nation, July 3, 1863*. Papers of the 2008 Gettysburg Seminar. Gettysburg, PA: National Park Service, 2010.

Thomas, Emory M. *Bold Dragoon: The Life of J. E. B. Stuart*. New York: Harper & Row, 1986.

———. *Robert E. Lee: A Biography*. New York: W. W. Norton, 1995.

Tremain, Henry Edwin. *Two Days of War: A Gettysburg Narrative and Other Excursions*. New York: Bonnell, Silver, and Bowers, 1905.

Troiani, Don, and Brian C. Pohanka. *Don Troiani's Civil War*. Mechanicsburg, PA: Stackpole Books, 1995.

Trudeau, Noah Andre. *Gettysburg: A Testing of Courage*. New York: HarperCollins, 2002.

Trulock, Alice Rains. *In the Hands of Providence: Joshua L. Chamberlain and the American Civil War.* Chapel Hill, NC: University of North Carolina Press, 1992.

Tucker, Glenn. *Hancock the Superb.* New York: Bobbs-Merrill, 1960.

———. *High Tide at Gettysburg.* New York: Bobbs-Merrill, 1958.

U.S. War Department. *The War of the Rebellion: A Compilation of the Official Records of the Union and Confederate Armies.* 128 vols. Washington, DC: Government Printing Office, 1880–1901.

Valuska, David L. "The Pennsylvania Dutch Fight for 'Old Dutch Pennsylvania.'" In *Damn Dutch: Pennsylvania Germans at Gettysburg,* edited by David L. Valuska and Christian B. Keller. Mechanicsburg, PA: Stackpole Books, 2004.

Vanderslice, John M. *Gettysburg Then and Now: The Field of American Valor.* New York: G. W. Dillingham Co., 1899.

Walker, Francis A. "Meade at Gettysburg." In *Battles and Leaders of the Civil War,* vol. 3, edited by Robert Underwood Johnson and Clarence Clough Buel. New York: The Century Co., 1888.

Ward, Eric, ed. *Army Life in Virginia: The Civil War Letters of George G. Benedict.* Mechanicsburg, PA: Stackpole Books, 2002.

Wert, Jeffry D. *Cavalryman of the Lost Cause: A Biography of J. E. B. Stuart.* New York: Simon & Schuster, 2008.

———. *Custer: The Controversial Life of George Armstrong Custer.* New York: Simon and Schuster, 1996.

———. *General James Longstreet: The Confederacy's Most Controversial Soldier.* New York: Simon & Schuster, 1993.

———. *Gettysburg: Day Three.* New York: Simon and Schuster, 2001.

Wilcox, Cadmus M. "General C. M. Wilcox on the Battle of Gettysburg." *Southern Historical Society Papers* 6 (1878).

Wise, Jennings C. *The Long Arm of Lee; or, The History of the Artillery of the Army of Northern Virginia.* Lynchburg, VA: J. P. Bell and Company, 1915.

Wittenberg, Eric J. "John Buford and the Gettysburg Campaign." *Gettysburg Magazine* 11 (July 1994).

———. *Protecting the Flank: The Battles for Brinkerhoff's Ridge and East Cavalry Field, Battle of Gettysburg, July 2–3, 1863.* Celina, OH: Ironclad Publishing, 2002.

Wynstra, Robert J. *The Rashness of That Hour: Politics, Gettysburg, and the Downfall of Confederate Brigadier General Alfred Iverson.* New York: Savas Beatie, 2010.

Young, Jesse Bowman. *The Battle of Gettysburg: A Comprehensive Narrative.* New York: Harper & Brothers, 1913.

Acknowledgments

This team effort included the cartographic savvy and remarkable creativity of Kumiko Yamazaki, Caroline Stover's steady graphic artistry, understanding, and general-manager firmness, and Wendy Reynolds at the helm of pagination. Tom Huntington and Kyle Weaver helped. Judith Schnell acted with tenacious perspicacity as "average reader," while Mark Allison lent his canny eye and ear. I had the idea and launched the maps, sketchily. I wrote the text.

Best for last: David Reisch, historian, research wizard, and no mean cartographer himself as it turns out, is heroically responsible for the maps. David helped edit the text, researched virtually everything, contributed numerous from-scratch corrective and color-enhancing paragraphs, and, generally, toiling with unbelievable efficacy, wove a spell of excellence over every page.

M. David Detweiler
President, Chairman
STACKPOLE INC.